Andre

Cambridge 1991

Cambridge Studies in Speech Science and Communication

Advisory Editorial Board J. Laver (Executive editor) A. J. Fourcin J. Gilbert
M. Haggard P. Ladefoged B. Lindblom J. C. Marshall

The phonetic bases of speaker recognition

The phonetic bases of speaker recognition

Francis Nolan

Department of Linguistics,
Cambridge University

Cambridge University Press

Cambridge
London   New York   New Rochelle
Melbourne   Sydney

Published by the Press Syndicate of the University of Cambridge
The Pitt Building, Trumpington Street, Cambridge CB2 1RP
32 East 57th Street, New York, NY 10022, USA
296 Beaconsfield Parade, Middle Park, Melbourne 3206, Australia

© Cambridge University Press 1983

First published 1983

Printed in Great Britain at the University Printing House

Library of Congress catalogue card number: 83-1828

British Library Cataloguing in Publication Data
Nolan, Francis
The phonetic bases of speaker recognition.—
(Cambridge studies in speech science and
communication)
1. Phonetics
I. Title
414   P221

ISBN 0 521 24486 2

WT

For my parents

Contents

List of tables	viii
List of figures	ix
Acknowledgments	x
Introduction	1
1 **Perspectives on speaker recognition**	5
1.1 Speaker recognition	5
2 **The bases of between-speaker differences**	26
2.1 The received model	26
2.2 The inadequacies of the organic–learned dichotomy	27
2.3 Model of the sources of between-speaker differences	29
2.4 Summary and discussion	71
3 **Short term parameters: segments and coarticulation**	74
3.1 Introduction and survey	74
3.2 The experiments: aims and structure	77
3.3 Spectrograph analysis	85
3.4 Computer analysis	102
3.5 Conclusions	115
4 **Long term quality**	121
4.1 Introduction	121
4.2 The long term suprasegmental strand	122
4.3 The long term segmental strand	130
4.4 Acoustic correlates of supralaryngeal qualities	155
4.5 Long term properties: conclusions	192
5 **Conclusions**	197
5.1 Summary	197
5.2 Criticism of principle and practice in speaker recognition	198
5.3 Directions for speaker recognition	206
References	210
Index	219

Tables

3.1	Frequency of occurrence of English consonant phonemes	81
3.2	Word inventory	83
3.3	Overall means (all speakers) of formants of initial /l/ and /r/, and their vowel environments	90
3.4	Means of consonant formant frequencies for each speaker over 30 items	91
3.5	Spearman coefficients of correlation between formants of /l/ or /r/ and of the following vowel	98
3.6	Formant correlations as a measure of coarticulation for individual speakers	99
3.7	F ratio values of formant parameters	102
3.8	Percentage correct identification using LP spectra	105
3.9	Percentage correct identification with test LP spectra computed from 1, 2, 5 or 10 test items	107
3.10	Values of the DISTANCE measure of coarticulation	110
3.11	Rank ordering of speakers by coarticulation as assessed by formant correlations and by the DISTANCE measure	111
3.12	Spearman correlations of different measures of /l/ coarticulation	112
3.13	Spearman correlations of different measures of /r/ coarticulation	112
3.14	Percentage correct identification using coarticulation	113
4.1	Measures of characteristics of long term spectra of voice qualities	153
4.2	Means of F_1, F_2, F_3 for long term qualities: mp 1–16	160
4.3	Means of F_1, F_2, F_3 for long term qualities – speaker JL	169
4.4	Means of F_1, F_2, F_3 for long term qualities – speaker FN	178
4.5	Pole frequencies of vowels produced with a change in larynx height	186
4.6	Identification of voice qualities across speakers: six-value descriptor	189
4.7	Mean F_2 and F_1, and the ratio between them, for pairs of vowels representing three vowel categories, according to speaker type	190
4.8	Mean F_2:F_1 ratios for vowels of three categories, for nine voice qualities realised by two speakers	190
4.9	Identification of voice qualities across speakers: three-value descriptor	191

Figures

1.1	'Voiceprint' of *The Phonetic Bases of Speaker Recognition*	19
2.1	Overview of model of sources of between-speaker differences	30
2.2	The segmental strand	39
2.3	The suprasegmental strand	47
2.4	Integration rules, phonetic representation, implementation rules and physical constraints	52
2.5	Schematic impression of part of a phonetic representation	57
2.6	Schematic representation of the use of a prestige value of a socio-linguistic variable according to class and style	64
3.1	Means (over 15 speakers) of formant frequencies of /l/ and the vowel environments	88
3.2	Means (over 13 speakers) for formant frequencies of /r/ and the vowel environments	89
3.3	Mean formant frequencies of /l/ for each speaker	92
3.4	Mean formant frequencies of /r/ for each speaker	93
3.5	Means for speaker GRP of formant frequencies of /l/ and the following vowel environment	94
3.6	Means for speaker TL of formant frequencies of /l/ and the following vowel environment	94
3.7	Means for speaker JB of formant frequencies of /l/ and the following vowel environment	95
3.8	Means for speaker NL of formant frequencies of /l/ and the following vowel environment	95
3.9	Means for speaker JRC of formant frequencies of /r/ and the following vowel environment	97
3.10	Means for speaker PVE of formant frequencies of /r/ and the following vowel environment	97
3.11	Rank ordered coefficients of correlation (r_s) for 13 speakers	100
3.12	Identification rates averaging items to form test sample	108
3.13	Rank ordering of speakers by /l/ coarticulation	109
3.14	Rank orderings of speakers by /r/ coarticulation	112
3.15	Coarticulatory implementation strategies	119
4.1	Summary of Laver's descriptive framework for long term qualities	137
4.2	Sagittal section showing stylised radial displacements of the notional centre of mass of the tongue body in settings	138
4.3a-c	Long term spectra of voice qualities (speaker JL)	144–6
4.4a-c	Long term spectra of voice qualities (speaker FN)	148–50
4.5	Long term spectra of voice qualities: amplitude ratios	152
4.6	Long term spectra of voice qualities: slope approximation	154
4.7	Means for formant frequencies for long term qualities: mp 1–16	161
4.8	Means of formant frequencies for nine long term qualities: mp 17–67 and (circled) 1–16	170
4.9	Subcategorisation of measurement points (JL)	172
4.10	Subcategorisation of measurement points (FN)	179
4.11	Tracings from x-ray pictures of the larynx and pharynx in neutral, extreme raised larynx, and extreme lowered larynx settings	183

Acknowledgments

This book is based on my 1980 Cambridge University PhD dissertation of the same title. It therefore owes its existence to my supervisor, John Trim, who gave me incisive criticism at crucial stages, support throughout, and, at the appropriate time, the impetus towards completion.

Many others have given me advice and help in discussion at various times, notably Tony Bladon, John Bridle, Andrew Crompton, Niels Davidsen-Nielsen, John Holmes, Melvyn Hunt, Peter Matthews, and Ailbhe Ní Chasaide. Marion Shirt kindly shared with me the preliminary results of her experiment on auditory speaker identification, and James Anthony gave me access to his highly useful file on forensic speaker identification in the UK. During the instrumental work in my own department I received moral as well as technical support from Peter Jones and Dave Hurworth; and Ritva-Liisa Cleary dispatched with characteristic efficiency and good humour the chore of computerising the references.

In carrying out the research reported in Chapter 4 I relied greatly on the facilities and expertise of others; in particular, Frank Fallside of Cambridge University Engineering Department allowed me free access to the analysis facilities of his Speech Group, which also led to me receiving a vast amount of help from members of the group. Steve Brooks, Geoff Bristow, Steve Terepin, and Roger Meli, especially, gave generously of their time to explain, with exemplary clarity and patience, aspects of acoustics and computing. Above all, they helped to make phonetics fun.

The intellectual debt to John Laver, whose pioneering work on voice quality is of profound significance to speaker recognition, will be obvious from the book; but no less important is the close interest he has taken in my work, and the considerable personal encouragement he has given me.

And it was Terry Moore who, 10 years ago, convinced me that linguistics was worthwhile; since then he has helped me in more ways than he realises.

To the many who have played a part, whether mentioned or not, thank you.

Introduction

The recognition of individuals from their speech is an area of speech science which reliably arouses public attention. Interest in scientific controversies is always greatest when the issue concerned has direct practical consequences in everyday life. Thus, interest in speaker recognition peaks when voice recordings seem to offer the hope of identifying the perpetrator of some well-publicised crime. But, however pressing the practical needs, understanding of the bases of speaker recognition has remained primitive; and, because of this, attempts to satisfy those needs are fraught with danger.

The notion that an individual has 'a voice' by which he can be recognised is a natural one, given our day-to-day experiences of successfully recognising people by their speech alone – typically over the telephone. It is so natural that it was adopted by many speech scientists without fundamental scrutiny, with the result that the usual question posed was not whether individuals could be uniquely recognised from their voices, but how this recognition could be most effectively and reliably carried out in an objective way.

This book will explore in detail the relationship between an individual and his 'voice'. Doing this will necessitate developing a model of the processes underlying the phonetic information which appears to give cues to the speaker of a sample of speech.

It might be expected today, 20 years after the start of intensive research into speaker recognition, that such a model must be long in existence – stimulating, defining, and guiding the research – and that in the present book the task might be at most to revise and refine it. In fact, in the welter of work seeking cues to the identity of individuals in their speech, little attempt has been made to elaborate such a model – certainly not one which encompasses the complexity of the speech communication process in its entirety.

Perhaps Hollien (1981:264), reviewing Tosi's (1979) *Voice Identification: Theory and Legal Applications*, is right to suggest that 'It is not surprising. . .that Tosi's book is one of the first published in this area' precisely because of the 'extremely challenging' nature of the area of speaker recognition. However, the situation is disquieting in more ways than one. Firstly, the previous lack of a full-scale theoretical treatment of the subject contrasts with the large number of papers already published detailing empirical work (some of it directed towards practical implementation) with the goal of associating voices with individuals. And secondly, whilst Tosi's book implies in its title that it is to correct the lack of a theory of speaker recognition, it quickly becomes obvious that it goes no further than the previous work towards building up a general model of the ways in which a person's identity is cued in his speech.

In any successful scientific discipline, a reciprocal relationship must exist between the development of a theory and the pursuit of experiments. Clearly, theories which do not yield predictions susceptible to empirical test belong in the realm of metaphysics rather than science as generally understood today; but equally, experiments performed in a theoretical vacuum risk futility. Only a theory, not experiments themselves, can guide interpretation of results, and motivate and delineate further experiments. An absence of theory leads to patent experimental chaos; but, more dangerously, an oversimplified yet received and unquestioned set of theoretical assumptions allows the researcher blithely and unwittingly to draw misleading conclusions from experiments, and leave unthought and untried many of the experiments relevant to the phenomena in the field of investigation.

For instance, the dangers of treating speech as simply the acoustic result of highly trained gymnastic routines performed by the vocal tract – a view quite generally encountered – are enormous, since such a view obscures the range of ways in which a speaker exploits his vocal apparatus for a variety of communicational ends. It thus spuriously circumscribes the search for the variation in the speech of individuals – variation which may in principle increase the similarity between one speaker and another (see especially Chapter 2).

The present book, then, responds to what Bolt *et al.* (1979:15) refer to as

the lack of a mature scientific discipline for analysing speech in terms that characterise the speaker, analogous to the science of phonetics for analysing the speech sounds.

If this quotation implies, however, the growth alongside phonetics of a parallel, but distinct, discipline, then its orientation conflicts with the one adopted here. An emerging discipline of speaker recognition should instead develop as an integral element of phonetics, which itself, being principally though not exclusively the study of language realised in the spoken medium, must constitute part of a broadly delimited linguistics. The benefits of this inclusion will be mutual. On the one side, speaker recognition can only achieve justified acceptance as a discipline if its at present unsound theoretical basis is improved in the light of what is known in the other linguistic disciplines about spoken communication. On the other side, whilst phonetics, as a branch of linguistics, has been concerned traditionally with the realisation of the abstract linguistic code, and has (with a few exceptions) seen differences between the speech of members of the same language community as noise to be abstracted away from in obtaining its true data, interest in differences between speakers is now increasing: that objectively different acoustic signals from two speakers can be normalised by a hearer and perceived as the same, and that individuals may use different articulatory strategies to produce equivalent auditory effects, are just two of the phenomena which are today seen to constitute data for phonetics, and which may necessitate revisions in phonetic theories. Work on the theory and practice of recognising speakers is clearly of relevance to modelling human speech perception, and production (cf. Hollien and McGlone 1976:39).

If a closer relationship between speaker recognition and phonetics brings these advantages, it additionally reduces a danger inherent in their separation – specifically, the misconception that properties of speech fall into two discrete sets, one functioning communicatively, and the other characterising the speaker. That this is not so will become apparent, particularly in Chapter 2.

The book takes the following form. Chapter 1 presents a selective over-view of the field of speaker recognition in order to orientate readers un-familiar with the field, and to question and revise some of the definitions currently popular. An exhaustive survey of existing research seems in-appropriate, since comprehensive reviews are available elsewhere, with emphases on different aspects of speaker recognition – notably Tosi (1975), Bricker and Pruzansky (1976), Atal (1976), Rosenberg (1976), Bolt *et al.* (1979), and Tosi (1979).

Chapter 2 attempts to develop a model which reveals the sources, in the speech communication process, of variation between speakers, and of the variation which occurs in the vocal output of one individual. Bolt *et al.* (1979:61) suggest four principal categories of research which need to be pursued, the first of which is 'the origins and characteristics of variability'. It is hoped that the model worked out in this chapter, whilst clearly not definitive, draws together sufficient of the many strands of speech communication to afford a useful framework for research of this kind.

Following the presentation of the model, an experiment is described in Chapter 3 which exploits variation between speakers of a very specific kind predicted by the model; and Chapter 4 presents the results of an analysis of the acoustic correlates of a number of long term qualities or 'voice qualities' which an individual has the potential to produce, demonstrating among other things the considerable scope for variation there is in the output of one person's vocal tract.

The final chapter summarises the main points made concerning the theory of speaker recognition, and draws together their implications for practical applications of speaker recognition techniques – particularly in forensics. Additionally, some suggestions are made for future research into the classification of voice samples and the association of voice samples with individuals – research more broadly conceived than most in progress today, and which promises to further understanding of the bases of the differences between speakers as well as bearing fruit in practical applications.

The emphases of the book as a whole may be unexpected to some readers familiar with the speaker recognition literature. That this study leans uncharacteristically towards the phonetic and linguistic aspects of the subject reflects the background and interests of the author; but is also fitting since these aspects have been the most neglected. Studies in areas not treated in detail in the text – statistical and signal processing methods for speaker recognition, for instance – are referenced at appropriate points.

1

Perspectives on speaker recognition

1.1 Speaker recognition

1.1.1 *The task of speaker recognition*

The kind of activity covered by the term speaker recognition is conceptually straightforward, and definitions abound. Hecker (1971:138) suggests that speaker recognition is

any decision-making process that uses the speaker-dependent features of the speech signal,

and Atal (1976:460 fn. 1) offers the formulation

any decision-making process that uses some features of the speech signal to determine if a particular person is the speaker of a given utterance.

The latter formulation is preferable, as it can be objected that decision-making processes are required in the decoding of the linguistic content of an utterance which nevertheless use speaker-dependent features of the signal. In recognising a vowel from a previously unfamiliar speaker, for example, a listener interprets its formant frequencies in the light of characteristics of the speaker inferred from the signal (perhaps, for instance, the likely size of the speaker and hence his approximate vocal tract length, on the basis of fundamental frequency – and so on). Such speaker-dependent normalisation is also, of course, a necessary part of any device built to respond appropriately to speech utterances from more than a single speaker (see e.g. Jaschul 1982). The latter task is usually known as speech recognition. Speaker recognition and speech recognition are occasionally confused; they are distinct tasks, but complementary at least in the sense that the data for the former (differences between equivalent utterances from different speakers) is 'noise' which the latter has to contend with.

As pointed out by Brown (1982) different aspects of the identity of an individual may be successfully accessed as a result of the matching process between an input voice stimulus and a stored reference voice – aspects such as the individual's name, physical appearance, or description (e.g. role in society). The everyday process of recognising a speaker from a voice sample involves these aspects to greater or smaller degree – it is possible simply to recognise a voice as familiar, but not recall details of its producer (if these were indeed ever known); to associate the voice with a description (e.g. 'the telephone receptionist'); and so on. Clearly any speaker recognition task (apart from, in human terms, the simple question 'have you heard this voice before?', or in machine terms, 'does this input voice sample match one of a number of stored, but unlabelled, reference patterns?') involves accessing some sort of identity characteristics. But these various processes will be treated here as logically subsequent to, and therefore secondary to, the initial decision process which confirms or denies that two voice samples were the product of the same vocal apparatus; and it is this decision process which is dealt with in this book.

The definitions of speaker recognition above leave unstated the linguistic levels at which speaker recognition may exploit speaker-specific information. Syntactic and lexical clues to identity are undoubtedly frequently present in utterances, and are clearly worthy of exploration for speaker recognition. The present study, however, confines itself to speaker-specific characteristics deriving from the speaker's realisation of language in sound.

1.1.2 *Types of speaker recognition*

Under the overall heading of speaker recognition, it is necessary to distinguish a number of distinct fields of study. Bricker and Pruzansky (1976) recognise three major divisions: speaker recognition by listening, by machine, and by visual inspection of spectrograms (SRL, SRM and SRS). In this categorisation, SRL involves the study of how human listeners achieve the task of associating a particular voice with a particular individual or group, and indeed to what extent such a task can be performed. SRM encompasses the attempts to develop automatic and semi-automatic strategies, standardly computer-based, for associating voices with speakers; SRM is therefore often thought of as 'objective' in comparison with SRL because of its relative freedom from human decision-making. The third category, SRS, comprises efforts to make decisions on the identity or non-identity of voices on the basis of visual examination of speech spectrograms by trained observers. The importance of this type of work stems from its practical application; since the mid 1960s there has been a continuing and heated debate as to whether visual spectrographic evidence should be admitted as legal evidence, and, if so, what its status should be.

There are, however, reasons for preferring a twofold division of a slightly different nature. The characteristic of SRL, as investigated by most studies, which sets it apart from all other types of speaker recognition is not so much the fact that the recognition is performed by listening, but rather that it is performed by untrained observers in real-life (or experimentally simulated real-life) conditions. On the other hand SRM and SRS both involve the application of analytic *techniques* to the problem, whether humanly acquired or automatically programmed. A twofold classification is therefore proposed here, into *technical speaker recognition* and *naive speaker recognition*.

There are two further considerations favouring a twofold categorisation. Firstly, the division between automatic methods and SRS is contingent, resulting from the history of the methods concerned, rather than essential in the way that the distinction between technical and naive speaker recognition is. Given an accurate (probably computer-based) spectrograph, it should be possible for an observer to make reliable measurements on the given spectrograms which he could then use as input to objective decision strategies. This is similar to the kind of semi-automatic recognition strategy developed, for example, by Broderick *et al.* (1975) where a human operator selects specific speech events, by visual observation, as input to statistical decision procedures. A continuum of potential methods exists, therefore, within technical speaker recognition; whereas the division between technical and naive speaker recognition is a fundamental one based on the two recognition situations.

Secondly, the traditional threefold categorisation does not readily provide a place for technical speaker recognition by listening – that is, the application of auditory techniques acquired through phonetic training to making decisions about the identity of speech samples. This approach to recognition is quite different from the recognition processes which are normally studied under the SRL heading. The latter involve decisions made on the basis of largely subconscious general impressions about the similarity or dissimilarity of given speech samples; on the other hand the phonetician engaged in a speaker recognition task (Baldwin 1977:1609) 'is not concerned with general impressions unless they are supported by phonetic description', and is all the time applying a detailed system of analysis. The tendency in discussions of speaker recognition techniques is not to draw any distinctions within speaker recognition relying on aural capabilities. The result of this, even with writers who are aware of the limitations of visual inspection of spectrograms, is an underestimation of the relative value of careful auditory analysis compared with spectrogram observation; for example Tosi (1975:401):

Typically, all types of aural examination of voices and visual examination of speech spectrograms are considered subjective methods, although the latter is closer to the objective part of the spectrum of methods than the former.

A generalisation of this kind is not possible without specifying exactly the degree and kind of analysis implied in the aural and the visual examination. The methods, applications, and status of technical speaker recognition by listening are dealt with in 1.1.7.

In short, a categorisation of speaker recognition tasks is proposed which is based on whether only normal everyday human abilities are exploited or whether specialised techniques – aural, visual, or electronic – are brought to bear. The present study addresses itself primarily to technical speaker recognition. Because of the practical applications of techniques for speaker recognition, especially in the forensic field, questions in this area have a particular urgency. It is notable not only that questions of principle in this area remain to be answered, but even more so that many pertinent ones have simply not been asked. Chapter 2, in particular, will pose some of the questions which from a linguistic perspective would seem to call for consideration.

1.1.3 *Identification and verification*

Within technical speaker recognition a distinction is generally drawn on the basis of the assumptions under which decisions about speakers' identity have to be made. In the real-world task of speaker *verification* (or *authentication*), and its experimental simulations, an identity claim by an individual is accepted or rejected by comparing a sample of his speech against a stored reference sample spoken by the individual whose identity he is claiming, and making a decision on the basis of a predetermined similarity threshold. Speaker verification has applications in security checking, for example, where it may be desired to establish the identity of a person seeking admittance, or in banking, where an automated money dispenser might test the voice of the customer wanting to withdraw money against a sample of the voice of the owner of the account in question. Speaker verification involves the comparison of a test sample of speech with a reference sample from just one speaker, requires a preset similarity threshold, and usually yields one of four kinds of decision: correct acceptance, correct rejection, false acceptance, false rejection (although a 'no decision' response may also be permitted). The relative acceptability of one or other kind of error determines the tolerance at which the similarity threshold will be set – a system which cannot be permitted to accept impostors will almost certainly reject true identity claims from time to time. The assumptions underlying speaker verification tasks are that both test and reference samples will be from cooperative speakers, so that vocal mimicry on the part of an impostor, but not vocal disguise on the part of the 'true' speaker, may be encountered; and that the utterance type(s) on which verification is to be performed may be specified.

In speaker *identification* (and *elimination*) an utterance from an unknown speaker has to be attributed, or not, to one of a population of known speakers for whom reference samples are available. Speaker identification is usually considered to include the kind of recognition which forensic work entails – a sample of speech recorded during the commission of, or constituting, a crime must often be compared with samples of speech from a number of suspects. Here the number of decisions increases with the size of the reference population; and the cost, in practical applications, of errors of identification or elimination is so high as to necessitate a 'no decision' option. It is necessary to assume the possibility of attempted disguise in the test or reference samples; and the same utterance type may not be available in both test and reference samples.

Under speaker identification three types of recognition test can be carried out: closed tests, open tests, and discrimination tests (cf. Tosi 1979:7). In a closed test it is known that the speaker to be identified is among the population of reference speakers, whilst in an open test the speaker to be identified may or may not be included in that population. Thus in the closed test, only an error of false identification may occur, whilst in open tests there is the additional possibility of incorrectly eliminating all the reference population when in reality it included the test speaker. In a discrimination test, the decision procedure has to ascertain whether or not two samples of speech are similar enough to have been spoken by the same speaker; errors of false identification and false elimination are possible.

It is apparent that an open test is simply an iterative discrimination test, in which the test sample undergoes a discrimination test with each of the reference samples in turn; and that in both open and discrimination tests some form of acceptance threshold is required. In the closed test such a threshold is not needed as the 'nearest' reference speaker is automatically selected.

It is also apparent that speaker discrimination most closely resembles speaker verification in the nature of its decision problem – a point which seems to have escaped comment. In both tasks a test sample and a reference have to be evaluated, and designated as produced by the same or different speakers, according to an acceptance threshold. As far as the nature of the decision problem is concerned, the usual forensic situation should be classed as a type of speaker verification – typically an incriminating sample has to be attributed, or not, to a suspect. The fact that it is universally dealt with under the heading of identification (see for instance the titles of Bolt *et al.* (1979), Tosi (1979)) has to do with the circumstantial characteristics associated with the two categories of recognition – the fact that, as mentioned above, lack of cooperation, and disguise attempts, may be expected in the forensic case; in contrast to, for instance, access control, where genuine claimants can be expected to be cooperative, but impostors attempting mimicry must be guarded against.

Experiments assessing the value of particular parameters for speaker recognition have most frequently adopted the closed test design. The reason for this is not that this design best approximates real-life applications – it is in fact the one least likely to occur in forensic cases – but rather that it gives the most straightforward comparison of parameters without the complication of choosing a threshold for identification, as explained by Atal (1976:467):

Both speaker-recognition tasks, identification and verification, have been investigated in past experimental studies. Of the two, the identification task is the more suited for comparing the performance of different parameters. In [closed test] speaker identification, a single error rate can provide a measure of the performance, while in speaker verification, two kinds of errors, namely, the probabilities of false verification and false rejection as functions of a threshold parameter, determine the performance. Also, the identification accuracy is a more sensitive indicator of the ability of a parameter for discriminating speakers.

1.1.4 *Stages in the recognition procedure*

Speaker recognition is essentially a two-stage process. The two stages may be termed *feature extraction* and *feature comparison*. A given recognition task is approached with a set of parameters defined, as, for example, average fundamental frequency or the frequency of a formant in a particular phonetic segment, which it is hoped will be adequate to characterise the speakers; and for each of the speakers values must be measured for these parameters. Each speaker may then be thought of as represented in a feature space, of as many dimensions as there have been parameters used, by his values along those parameters. It is then a matter of employing a distance measure (together with an acceptance threshold in the case of open tests) suitable to the parameters in use to estimate the nearness of the test speaker to each of the reference speakers.

In practice it may be desirable to carry out an intermediate step involving the statistical transformation of the parameters in question, by, for example, discriminant analysis, in order to reduce the dimensionality of the space within which the distance between speakers is to be measured, and in order to reduce the dependence of parameters which may be correlated with one another; such statistical techniques have been dealt with by, for instance, Bricker *et al.* (1971). The output of the feature–comparison stage is a decision about the similarity of the test sample in question to the various reference samples, and, depending on the type of recognition involved, the selection of one (or none) of the reference speakers as the speaker of the test sample.

1.1.5 *Criteria for parameters*

Feature extraction presupposes knowledge of which aspects of the acoustic signal yield parameters whose values are most dependent on the identity of the speaker, and it is towards the discovery of these aspects that much of the research in speaker recognition is oriented. Although in practice the parameters chosen in a particular investigation have tended to be dictated by the analysis techniques available at the time of the study, and assessment to be made on the basis of performance in simulated recognition trials, it is nevertheless possible and useful to set out criteria which a theoretically ideal parameter would meet. Such a parameter would have the following characteristics:

1 High between-speaker variability: the parameter needs to exhibit a high degree of variation from one speaker to another. Whilst clearly there may be no parameter with sufficient different values for each speaker within even a small population to have a value of his own, a set of parameters can be sought which together will uniquely define a coordinate for a given speaker.

2 Low within-speaker variability: as well as yielding good differentiation on one occasion between speakers, a useful parameter will have to show consistency throughout the utterances of an individual; and preferably be insensitive to his state of health, emotional condition, or the communicational context.

3 Resistance to attempted disguise or mimicry: the parameter needs to withstand attempts on the part of the speaker to disguise his voice or mimic that of another, either by virtue of being the acoustic consequence of a physiological characteristic of the speaker which he is not able to alter at will, or by being in some way a 'less obvious' attribute of speech which will escape his attention during attempts at disguise or mimicry.

4 Availability: it is of little use basing speaker recognition on a parameter which occurs only seldom in speech and therefore necessitates large amounts of data in both test and reference corpora.

5 Robustness in transmission: the usefulness of a parameter will be limited if its information is lost or reduced in telephone transmission or tape recording.

6 Measurability: the extraction of the parameter in question must not be prohibitively difficult.

Criteria *1* and *2* have been of most general concern in studies on speaker

11

recognition. Parameters have, for example, been explicitly evaluated in terms of these two criteria by the use of the F ratio of analysis of variance, which in this context is calculated as the ratio of the variance of speakers' mean values for a parameter to the average within-speaker variance – see, for instance, Pruzansky and Mathews (1964) and Wolf (1972); and the majority of studies would be considered as attempts to define parameters which are 'efficient' in this sense. There has been, however, a tendency to underrate the importance of criterion 2 – many studies (including the two above, and also Glenn and Kleiner (1968), Su *et al.* (1974), etc.) have used data only from a single recording session, thus ignoring the possibility that a parameter which is efficient in the short term may fail in the longer term due to purely physiological variation, let alone as a result of its being susceptible to changes in emotional states, etc., or to manipulation by the speaker for communicative reasons (see Chapter 2), or to the special communicative intents of disguise or mimicry. There is in fact overwhelming evidence that significant reductions in recognition rates occur when trials are performed with noncontemporaneous test and reference samples, instead of test and reference samples coming from the same recording session – for just one example see 3.4.2.

As for state of health, one of the most efficient sets of parameters, those based on nasal sounds (see 3.1), are highly sensitive to distortion by bad health; Sambur (1975:180) presents two spectra from /n/ clearly illustrating 'the variability of the nasal measurements when the speaker is suffering from a mild head cold'; and Doherty and Hollien (1978) found a reduction from 100% to 72% in (closed test) identification on a population of 25 speakers, using long term power spectra, when the test utterances had been produced under conditions of stress induced by randomly administered electric shocks.

In a spectrographic study, Endres *et al.* (1971) found that two professional imitators produced imitations which were sometimes not distinguishable by listening from the voice being imitated, and in which the fundamental frequency contour matched that of the voice being imitated fairly realistically; but that the formant structure of the imitator and the person to be imitated did not in general agree closely, particularly in the higher frequency bands. In disguise, they found that individual formants were shifted to higher or lower frequencies with respect to the normal voice, only the first formant remaining relatively stable. Doherty and Hollien (1978) found that their identification rate quoted above dropped drastically to 24% when the speakers were allowed freedom to disguise their voices as they chose (barring whisper or foreign accents) in production of the test samples. This suggests that the present parameters used in speaker identification must be examined carefully in the context of disguise if their true effectiveness is to be known; it may be that speaker recognition systems will have to include parameters which by normal standards are inefficient. Doherty and Hollien's (1978) results showed that although a parameter based on two duration measurements (the proportion of time that voicing was present in the 32 second section of speech, and rate in terms of the number of phonemes articulated) yielded a poor identification rate (20%) in optimum conditions, its performance sank proportionately little (to 16%) in disguise.

One class of speaker recognition parameters, those based on long term measurements of speech, are superior in terms of criterion 4; for instance, whatever the content of a speech sample, it is possible to calculate statistics relating to its fundamental frequency, or obtain its long term spectrum. In contrast, information from the /ʒ/ phoneme in English would be available on average only once every 1000 phonemes (see the table of frequency of occurrence of consonants quoted from Fry (1947) by Gimson (1980:217–18)), and so necessitate large samples of speech. Criterion 4 is nevertheless relevant for assessing long term parameters in so far as meaningful values can only be obtained from a sample of speech which is of sufficient duration – see, for example, 4.2.2, 4.3.4. From the work cited in these sections it appears that as little as 10 seconds of speech may provide a viable long term spectral characterisation of a speaker, whereas at least 30 seconds are required for fundamental frequency parameters. If these figures are reliable, criterion 4 would motivate a preference for long term spectra over fundamental frequency parameters, other factors being equal.

The opposite preference would be motivated by criterion 5. In what Tosi (1975:399) disarmingly terms 'this era of widespread usage of voice communication' the significant facts are that people talk through telephones and get recorded by bad tape recorders, sometimes committing crimes or discussing them in the process. A forensic speaker-identification system in particular has to be designed with awareness that some acoustic features may be lost, and, perhaps worse, distorted, by the transmission system through which a given sample of speech has passed, and the characteristics of which may not be recoverable. In general the most robust parameters will be those dependent on temporal aspects of speech, including the fundamental frequency; Atal (1976:471):

Pitch has an important advantage over the spectral information since it is not affected by frequency characteristics of the recording or the transmission system.

A study by McGonegal *et al.* (1979), in which verification tasks were performed by an automatic system using test and reference samples subjected to different telephone transmission coding systems – ADPCM (adaptive differential pulse code modulation) and LPC (linear predictive coding) – confirmed the robustness of (time-normalised) fundamental frequency, and also gain (intensity) contours.

The interpretation of criterion 6, measurability, is dependent on the kind of recognition system which is envisaged. The difficulties inherent in the automatic location of particular phonetic events make features derived from specific segments difficult to measure in a fully automatic system to a degree which they would not be in a semi-automatic system (e.g. that of Broderick *et al.* 1975) where a human operator locates the segments of interest. Das and Mohn (1971) provide a rare example of a system incorporating automatic segmentation of speech; in general fully automatic recognition systems have relied on parameters such as long term spectra or long term fundamental frequency statistics which do not require the isolation of specific events. An evident problem of measurability in the case of a verification scheme where recognition could be based on a predetermined utterance token, namely that of the potential difference in time alignment between test and reference tokens which would cause an artificially large disparity between the values for test and reference utterances on the parameters in question at a given time, is successfully approached by Doddington (1971). He introduced a technique called 'time-warping', which, unlike ordinary time normalisation which squashes or stretches two utterances so that they have the same overall duration but disregards the relative timing of specific events within the two utterances, nonlinearly warps the time dimension of the test utterance so as to obtain the best correspondence, at all points, of a given parameter in the test token and the reference token. In Doddington's version the time registration is performed on the basis of the second formant contour, which has fairly large and well-defined excursions; Lummis (1973) uses the computationally more economic gain (intensity) contour. The time axis of the other parameters then undergoes identical time-warping; in this way comparison of the parameters involves comparison of corresponding events in the utterances – assuming of course that the parameters are time-locked in equivalent ways in the two tokens to the contour matched in the warping procedure. A comparable method employing time-warping is implemented by Furui (1981).

1.1.6 *Motivation for research*

It is necessary for an understanding of existing research on speaker recognition to appreciate the motivations behind it. These have been largely of a practical nature, which explains the present strong empirical bias in research and the comparative lack of interest in a theoretical basis.

Speaker verification has been seen as an answer to the problem of regulating access either to areas of high security, or to money or credit facilities, or of authenticating military reports. An automatic voice check may become as routine a way of checking identity as a signature or a secret code number. In these applications speaker recognition is relatively uncontroversial and is already usable; Beek *et al.* (1977:311):

ASV technology has proved highly successful for fixed context speaker verification when using cooperative speakers in a good S/N environment. . .[and] has successfully coped with the problems of mimicry, day-to-day speaker variability, colds, sinus congestion, and respiratory ailments.

The first work on speaker identification (see Bricker and Pruzansky 1976:296) started in the USA during World War II and was aimed at identifying monitored radio voices. It is, however, the forensic applications of speaker identification which have been most controversial since the 1960s, and which have stimulated most research. Particularly controversial has been the acceptance by certain courts in the USA of identification evidence based on visual examination of speech spectrograms.

Before examining this technique and the controversy surrounding it, it is worth looking briefly at the legal applications of what was termed above technical speaker recognition by listening.

1.1.7 *Auditory identification by phoneticians*

In the United Kingdom evidence produced in courts of law to establish speaker identity has been almost exclusively auditory. Widespread press coverage was given to a case in Winchester Magistrates' Court (24 November 1967) where a man was convicted of making fire hoax calls. The coverage implied that spectrographic evidence, 'voice pictures' (*The Times*, 25 November 1967), had constituted crucial evidence. However it appears that in fact the phonetician called as an expert witness by the prosecution based his opinion on auditory judgments, and produced spectrograms in court only in response to a request from the prosecution to present relevant speech samples in visual form; and so the case was not fully comparable to those in the USA where spectrograms had been used as the primary means of identification.

Considerable alarm was felt among phoneticians in the UK lest, despite a lack of theoretical justification and empirical validation of the technique, a precedent be set for the use of evidence based on spectrograms, and this alarm was voiced in, for example, a letter drafted by J. L. M. Trim and signed by the majority of phoneticians in the UK. A copy was sent to the Home Secretary; and in Scotland contact was made by J. K. F. Anthony with the Lord Advocate, explaining with supporting evidence phoneticians' disquiet at speaker identification based on spectrograms. Subsequently, to the author's knowledge, no use has been made in courts in the UK of spectrographic speaker identification evidence.

For a number of years, however, there has been a practice of calling on phoneticians and others considered to be competent in auditory analysis of speech to assist the police in investigations, and to appear in court in the role of expert witness to give opinions on speech samples.

Little explicit discussion, with the exception of Baldwin (1977), and certainly nothing detailed or comprehensive, has been published on the methods employed by those phoneticians who have undertaken such work. They have worked largely as individuals, without coordination, furthermore presenting their evidence with varying assessments of the general reliability of the technique. It seems, however, that the methods used are essentially those of the traditional dialectologist: noting detailed realisational differences of elements (both segmental and suprasegmental) of the phonological system, and differences in the system itself (see 2.3.4, 2.3.5), by repeated listening, and analysis according to the established auditory/ articulatory phonetic framework of classification.

Whilst it seems reasonable to assume that trained listeners with an analytic framework for speech at their disposal should be able to offer more reliable auditory judgments in speaker recognition than untrained listeners, a number of factors have caused such applications to be gravely questioned in the phonetic community, and the issue is currently highly controversial. Among these factors are the following.

In the absence of an integrated theory of the origins and nature of speaker-dependent characteristics used by phoneticians, and the extent to which they may vary in the speech of an individual, opinions on the reliability of the technique are prone to be based on incomplete information. Secondly, phonetic training does not train the listener to set aside the default human ability to normalise across speakers – the ability which enables him to hear as the same sounds from different speakers which are objectively acoustically distinct; it might be, therefore, that a decision made by the phonetician principally on the basis of phonological factors would be altered, or at least given different weight, if supplemented by objective acoustic information. Associated with this is the problem that whilst the ideal of phonetic training is to free the phonetician's perception totally from the habits and biases ingrained by experience of his native language(s) and accent(s), it is unlikely that this ideal state is ever achieved;

consequently a phonetician's sensitivity to fine distinctions between speakers is in practice likely to be highly correlated with his familiarity with the accent of the speakers. Thirdly, there are no commonly agreed methods of listening and analysis, allowing potentially great inconsistency across cases; further, no specified professional qualification or standard of proficiency is required before a person may offer an expert opinion. Above all, there has been a lack of empirical research directed to demonstrating the reliability or otherwise of this method of speaker identification.

In 1978 the Colloquium of British Academic Phoneticians, prompted by concern at instances of its members and others being called upon to give opinions in court on speaker identity, set up a committee to report on forensic applications of phonetics. A survey of phoneticians conducted by the committee elicited a variety of views on auditory speaker identification by phoneticians in legal cases, most replies stressing that at the very least the limitations of the technique need to be made clear before opinions are given. At the 1980 Colloquium a special session on the topic revealed considerable disagreement over the weight that should be attached to evidence given by phoneticians – disagreement understandable, but less than fruitful, in the absence of empirical research. The motion that 'phoneticians should not consider themselves expert in speaker identification until they have demonstrated themselves to be so' was carried by 30 votes to 12 with eight abstentions (including absent members later balloted). This motion clearly expressed the need for scientific evaluation of phoneticians' auditory judgments in speaker identification, and prompted the setting up of a project in the area.

This project is being carried out by Marion Shirt at Leeds University, and is directed specifically to the question of whether phoneticians do in fact perform better than untrained listeners in a number of speaker recognition tasks.

The first experiment took the following form. Studio-quality recordings were made of pairs of male speakers discussing similar pictures out of sight of each other, their task being to decide whether the pictures were identical. Voice samples of approximately five seconds' duration were excerpted and grouped, the different groups containing voices of various degrees of accent homogeneity. The tasks comprised six closed identification tests, in which a test sample had to be matched to one of six references; a closed test where 10 samples from a total of five speakers had to be matched; a closed test, where a match known to exist among 10 samples had to be found; and two open tests, in which the listeners had to decide if any matches existed among 10 samples. Additionally, three discrimination tests were included using samples of around 20 seconds' duration.

Phoneticians and phonetically naive subjects took part in the experiment. Preliminary indications are that whilst the phoneticians did on average achieve better accuracy than the non-phoneticians (53% compared with 46%), even the best performance of the phoneticians (76%) fell well short of 100% accuracy; and the group of phoneticians as a whole exhibited a wide range of performance (down to 38%), as did the non-phoneticians.

Two kinds of limitation in the experiment should be noted. Firstly, relating to the conditions of the experiment, although both groups of listeners were allowed unlimited time to make their decisions, the naive subjects had in practice to complete the task in an afternoon, whilst the phoneticians could spread their listening over a longer period, in some cases totalling many hours of listening; and also the naive subjects were provided with twin cassette players, whereas the phoneticans were allowed to use listening facilities of their choice (e.g. tape loop repeaters). Secondly, relating to the task, the five-second samples were too short to permit systematic phonetic and phonological comparisons to be made between samples, and thus precluded the phoneticians bringing to bear many of the strategies they would standardly employ when assessing the similarity of speech samples.

These limitations notwithstanding, the results of the study will be of use in evaluating auditory identification by phoneticians, and will serve as a starting point for further much needed research into the reliability of the technique.

1.1.8 *'Voiceprint' identification*

The term 'voiceprint' was promoted by Kersta (1962a) who argued the parallelism of spectrograms and fingerprints. Fig. 1.1 is an example of a wideband (300 Hz analysing filter) spectrogram, a 'voiceprint', of an utterance of the title of this book spoken by the author. A fairly broad phonetic transcription has been added along the time base to indicate the position, as far as is possible in the speech continuum, of the succession of phonetic events. (Notice the voiceless velar fricative, instead of stop, in *recognition* – this is not unexpected especially in fairly rapid speech.) For an introduction to interpreting spectrograms see e.g. Ladefoged (1975:Ch. 8) and Fry (1979:Chs. 9 and 10).

Kersta cited, in support of his claim that spectrograms could be used for speaker identification, an experiment in which high-school girls were trained in spectrogram reading and then presented with spectrograms of 10 frequently occurring monosyllables. Tests, in which these 'examiners' were given a matrix of four voiceprints for each speaker and then had to sort test

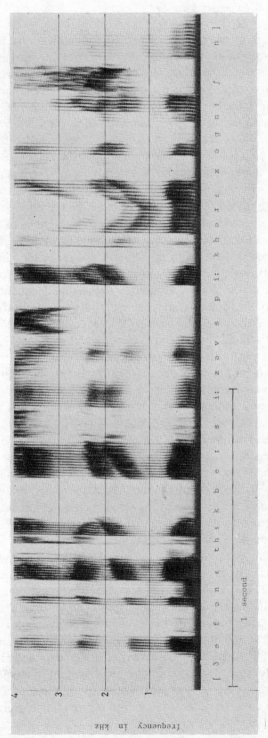

frequency in kHz

[ðə fənɛ θɪk bɛɪs iː z ə v s pɪː k hɔə x əgnɪ ʃ nl]

1 second

1.1 'Voiceprint' of *The Phonetic Bases of Speaker Recognition*

utterances into piles for each speaker (closed identification), were carried out for populations of five, nine, and 12 males, yielding promising 99.6%, 99.2%, and 99.0% identification rates respectively. When words excerpted from the context of a cue sentence instead of spoken in isolation were used, the deterioration in the lumped error rate was merely from 0.8% to 1.0%. It might be inferred that the very high identification rates indicate optimum conditions for speaker recognition; Kersta's account lacks details of the procedure, and so it is not clear that the margin by which his results exceed those of other experimenters did not result from, for example, a less rigorous choice of speakers from the point of view of dialect variation.

Young and Campbell (1967) set out to examine the effect of taking the words on which visual spectrographic identification might be based from the context of a sentence. They used some of the same words as Kersta, and had five speakers record them, both in isolation and embedded in sentences. They trained 10 observers, all familiar with spectrograms, pointing out possible 'unique clues' to speaker identity such as the frequency, intensity and bandwidth of the formants, and the regularity of the vertical striations as an indication of the 'melodiousness' of the voice. It was Young and Campbell's thesis that if 'unique clues' to speaker identity did exist, the level of identification performance for words in differing contexts should be similar to the level for words spoken in isolation. In fact the results show that observers had much greater difficulty identifying speakers by means of words taken from a sentence context than from words spoken in isolation, the respective rates being 37.3% and 78.4%. This is in considerable contrast to Kersta's (1962a) difference of 0.2% for the two contexts. There is also an appreciable discrepancy between error rates in the comparable task with a five-speaker population and words spoken in isolation, where Kersta obtained 99.6% to Young and Campbell's 78.4%. This discrepancy may well be accountable for in terms of the speakers used in the two studies, as Young and Campbell chose speakers who were 'quite homogeneous with respect to sex, dialect, age and education'.

In an attempt to assess the artificiality of using data from read sentences, Hazen (1973) used as his data words extracted from spontaneous speech obtained in interviews with 60 males, and then used spectrograms of these words in open and closed identification trials. The observers were given a 'file-card' for each speaker in the population which consisted in two examples of the word in question, chosen as the visually least similar of the examples available. Identification was carried out in two stages: reduction of the population to 'suspects', and positive identification or elimination. The test word came from the same context as one of the file-card examples, or from a different context; these two conditions providing correct identification rates of 57.4% and 16.8% respectively. Hazen concludes that (p. 658)

given the conditions of this study, accurate identification of speakers by visual comparison of spectrograms is not possible

– a conclusion which has serious implications for the forensic application of the technique, where spontaneous speech is usually involved.

The most extensive of the investigations carried out with the intent of checking Kersta's claims and estimating the validity of such procedures in forensics was that of Tosi *et al.* (1972). The experiments extended over a two-year period, used recordings from 250 speakers randomly selected from a population of approximately 25 000 male students at Michigan University, and involved 34 996 trials of identification performed by 29 examiners with a month's training. They were asked to grade their degree of confidence in each decision on a four point scale.

Although the large numbers involved in the investigation appear to lend it an impressive scale, and lead to it being frequently cited as if it gave definitive evidence on 'voiceprinting', caution is needed in its interpretation. Hollien (1977:12) gives a reminder that identification trials were carried out on subsets of between only 10 and 40 speakers drawn from the 250 for whom recordings were available; and Thomas (1975:293) points out that if the 250 speakers were chosen by a successfully random selection procedure, they would constitute a 'heterogeneous group representative of all elements comprising the population', whereas it would be more relevant to establishing the reliability of speaker identification if the speakers were as homogeneous as possible with respect to accent. He also draws attention (1975:294) to the fact that the 'continuous speech' in the experiment consisted of readings of 'nonsensical' sentences containing the nine key words *it, is, on, me, and, the, I, to, you*; it is far from obvious that read nonsense bears a close relationship to meaningful spontaneous speech.

The experiments included investigation of the effect of using noncontemporaneous reference and test samples, as well as the open/closed nature of the test and the context from which samples were taken. Overall, the tests which best replicated the forensic situation (open tests with noncontemporaneous samples taken from 'continuous speech') yielded 6.4% false identification and 12.7% false elimination. It was argued that as 60% of wrong answers (though also 20% of correct answers) were graded 'uncertain', had the examiners had the option of expressing no opinion when in doubt, false identification errors would have been cut to 2.4% and false elimination to 4.8%. These results, together with those of a field study conducted for Michigan State Police to discover the relation between laboratory experiments and 'the actual situation a professional examiner

21

encounters when handling forensic situations' (Tosi 1975:418) led Tosi to the opinion that, if certain conditions are fulfilled, identification by visual examination of spectrograms can offer 'reasonable reliability' (Tosi 1975:418). These conditions specify that visual examination should be combined with listening; examiners should be qualified, including a training in phonetics and a two-year apprenticeship in field work; they should avoid positive conclusions if the slightest doubt exists; and they should be entitled to ask for as many samples of speech, and as much time, as is needed.

Tosi's at least qualified approval of 'voiceprinting' as a means of establishing a speaker's identity contrasts with the unqualified championing of the technique by Kersta:

Voiceprint identification is a method by which people can be identified from a spectrographic examination of their voice. Closely analogous to fingerprint identification, which uses the unique features found in people's fingerprints, voiceprint identification uses the unique features found in their utterances (1962a:1253)

. . .experiments showed that professional ventriloquists and mimics cannot create voices or imitate others without revealing their own identities (1962b:1978)

. . .we know of no way a person can change his speech such that it is impossible to identify him. . . (Kersta in a 1967 television broadcast, quoted by Vanderslice (1969:391)),

and with its forthright application by Lt Ernest Nash of Michigan State Police:

It is my opinion that the voice of. . .and the voice of the unknown caller are one and the same and could not possibly be the voice of any other human being (quoted by Hollien (1974a:211) from the transcript of a trial in California).

The fragility of the specific evidence associated with such claims is well illustrated by Ladefoged and Vanderslice (1967), who include a critical re-presentation of the voiceprints on which Kersta based a positive identification in a case in California (People vs. King). Not only are the claimed points of similarity between pairs of spectrograms often highly dubious, but, as Ladefoged and Vanderslice point out, the evidence even includes a blatant and basic error of missegmentation (or mislabelling) in the case of one of the spectrograms used.

Nevertheless, faced with an increasing need to identify speakers from recordings, a number of states in the USA, including Michigan and California, began to accept evidence based on voiceprints, a move which brought forceful protest from phoneticians and speech scientists – see for example Vanderslice (1969), Bolt *et al.* (1970, 1973), Hollien (1974a). The

22

objections to the use of voiceprint techniques may be classified into three kinds concerning the interpretation of laboratory assessment, the procedures of decision-making, and (most fundamentally) the nature of the information on which those decisions have to be based.

The interpretation of results from laboratory trials is confounded by the conflicting identification rates found by different experimenters (see above). It is clear, however, that none of the experimenters who have sought to replicate Kersta's original experiments have achieved such high rates. Secondly, few of the investigations have included the kind of trial which most closely approximates the common forensic situation, namely the discrimination test (see 1.1.3). A significant way in which forensic conditions differ from those of the laboratory investigations is the quality of the recordings which may be available. In practical applications it is likely that low quality equipment will have been used to record a speech signal transmitted through the telephone network from an unknown and perhaps noisy place. The characteristics of the total transmission system are most unlikely to be recoverable in detail, and so its distorting effects and the effects of the various noise sources are irretrievably confused with the speech signal itself. Nevertheless, attempts have been made to use voiceprint methods on a recording which was 'of such poor quality as to be virtually useless' and in which 'the speech during several parts of the conversation was unintelligible' (Hollien 1974a:211).

The first question to be asked about the procedures entailed in voiceprint identification is whether the visual examination of speech samples gives more accurate results than aural examination. *A priori*, it might be expected that the human ear, inherently suited to the communication mode which its capacities have helped to shape, and which has been practised in speech skills throughout the observer's life, should be more acute than the eye, trained at most for a few years at an unnatural task. On the other hand perhaps the ear is most adept at achieving the converse of speaker identification – ignoring speaker-dependent information which can be regarded as noise with respect to the linguistic message, and allowing conscious appreciation primarily of that message. The experimental evidence, however, points strongly to the conclusion that aural identification is more successful than visual. Young and Campbell (1967:1253) point out that the results they obtained for visual identification were worse than comparable results in Bricker and Pruzansky (1966), who investigated the ability of untrained listeners to identify the speakers of utterances having various content and duration:

We conclude, then, that humans can extract more relevant information from the unprocessed acoustic signal than they do from a visual representation.

23

This indirect conclusion is supported by the work of Stevens *et al.* (1968) who compared aural and visual strategies directly. Their judges had to perform a series of open and closed tasks, identifying speakers from samples of their speech presented either aurally through headphones, or visually as spectrograms. The error rates were found to be about 6% for aural presentation, and about 21% for visual. Only within the verification task, as opposed to the identification task, has the ear's capacity for speaker recognition been surpassed, as demonstrated by Rosenberg (1973); and there, significantly, by an automatic verification scheme not human inspection of voiceprints. (Even so, some listeners performed better than the machine.) It seems clear, then, that the voiceprint procedure can at best complement aural identification, perhaps by highlighting acoustic features to which the ear is insensitive; and at worst it is an artifice to give a spurious aura of 'scientific' authority to judgments which the layman is better able to make.

The other major cause for concern relating to the procedures of voiceprinting stems from their subjective nature. Tosi (1975:419) concedes that

The crucial problem with subjective methods is testing the honesty and reliability of the examiner,

and it is easy to suspect that a voiceprint examiner who is employed for his ability to identify and eliminate speakers would be tempted to make a positive decision on inadequate evidence if faced with a whole series of cases where a 'no decision' response was appropriate. The concern is the more acute for attempts, in the face of strong opposition from phoneticians, by a self-appointed set of voiceprinters to gain a monopoly (in the USA) over court testimony; Hollien (1974a:211):

it would appear that, if the proponents of 'voiceprints' are successful, a subculture would develop expressly for the judicial system, where only certified 'professional examiners' could testify in courts of law. Further, since presumably they would be the only individuals empowered to certify new examiners, an uncertified scientist, no matter how distinguished and well regarded by his peers, simply could not qualify to testify without their approval.

Successful contesting of voiceprint evidence in the 1970s by prominent phoneticians and speech scientists such as Ladefoged and Hollien to some extent checked such a development and led to reversals in a few states, including Michigan and Pennsylvania, of earlier rulings which had admitted voiceprint evidence (Tosi 1979:143ff). Nevertheless, despite the fact that voiceprinting is very vulnerable to criticisms that it is a subjective and unvalidated technique, and its practitioners do not undergo objective, independent, controlled testing in realistic conditions, precedents have been set for its use in courts in 23 states of the USA, and in Canada, Italy, and Israel (Tosi 1979:143). Perhaps emboldened by this success (irrelevant as it is to proving the effectiveness of the technique) voiceprinters have shown little sign of taking up the challenge of Hollien (1977:17) that the ' "voiceprint" enthusiasts' should follow the example of those working on automatic and semi-automatic speaker identification systems and resist premature application of their technique in court and in forensic investigation; specifically that they should apply a 'moratorium' to their activities until they can unequivocally demonstrate that their system provides acceptable identification levels at least under favourable forensic conditions – that is, where the speech samples are not contemporary, where there are a number of suspects (including some sounding similar), where some stress and disguise are possible, and where mild system distortions may be present; that examiners can be expected to make acceptable (correct) identifications and eliminations under these conditions; and that examiners can be expected to perform 'in an ethical and professional manner' in forensic conditions. Hollien also challenges them to provide information about the conditions under which their approach can be expected to fail; and a method of calculating the probabilities of examiners being wrong when they make positive identifications or eliminations.

Automatic and semi-automatic speaker recognition techniques are likely in future to be applied in forensics. Presumably they will offer much greater objectivity than aural or spectrographic identification. But the most fundamental of the objections to voiceprint identification, based on the nature of the information in the speech signal, will still be damaging as long as the observation of Bolt *et al.* (1973:532) holds true:

The present level of knowledge about personal voice characteristics, their recognition, and how they change under different conditions, is still rudimentary.

It is appropriate therefore to turn to a detailed examination of how the speech signal may be differentially determined by individuals.

2

The bases of between-speaker differences

2.1 The received model

Familiarity with what has been written on speaker recognition would, by itself, give the impression that no problems exist in understanding the origin of between-speaker differences in the speech signal – the task being merely how to extract information from such differences so as to be able reliably to identify speakers. It will, however, become clear in this chapter that a lack of concern for the complexity of the bases of between-speaker differences, whether through ignorance of this complexity, or through over-reliance on ever-greater technological and statistical sophistication, leaves those who advocate the practical application of speaker recognition schemes open to serious theoretical criticism.

The widely accepted model of between-speaker differences divides them into categories according to whether the aspect of speech production underlying them is a structural one or a functional one; that is, whether the difference derives from the shape, size, and inherent dynamic limitations of the speaker's vocal apparatus or rather the manner in which he manipulates it. Glenn and Kleiner (1968:368) commence by stating:

Acoustic parameters of speech reflecting speaker identity must be derived either from the unique physiological characteristics of the speaker's vocal apparatus or from idiosyncrasies in his manner of speaking,

and this is echoed by, among others, Wolf (1972:2045)

Differences in voices stem from two broad bases: organic and learned differences,

Atal (1976:461)

Speaker-related variations in speech are caused in part by anatomical differences in the vocal tract and in part by the differences in the speaking habits of different individuals,

and Bricker and Pruzansky (1976:297)

Specifically, speaker information is latent in the speaker in the form of anatomical features and neurally stored habit patterns.

26

The latter three quotations are all followed by a reference to Garvin and Ladefoged (1963:194), who write

We can tentatively categorise speaker-diagnostic variables in terms of two basic distinctions: organic versus acquired or learned, and individual versus group.

It appears that writers subsequent to Garvin and Ladefoged have not felt the need to modify or extend this tentative categorisation; and indeed it continues as the theoretical mainstay of the most recent discussions of speaker recognition. Tosi (1979:55) comprehensively summarises his discussion of between-speaker differences as follows:

Organic and learned differences are the sources of intertalker variability,

having implied that the problem is trivial (1979:44):

Actually there is no controversy concerning intertalker variability other than possible confusion arising when two people's speech is very similar.

For him a 'more important problem' is within-speaker variability; but it is not made clear in what sense this can be treated as a problem distinct from that of the sources of between-speaker differences.

2.2 The inadequacies of the organic–learned dichotomy

The model of between-speaker differences outlined above is rejected in the present work not because it is incorrect, but because in its gross oversimplification it conceals the complexity of the bases of speaker-specific information in speech, and in doing so undercuts any attempt to predict what may or may not be reliable cues to speaker identity. This claim may at first seem paradoxical, since it might reasonably be expected that the cues for speaker recognition which would be reliable should be precisely those which depend on the invariant organic characteristics of speakers, rather than on their learned and presumably re-learnable habit patterns. But two major factors militate against this simple account.

Firstly, the plasticity of the vocal tract means that in few, if any, cases, does a given organic feature leave an invariant imprint on the acoustic signal. Whilst it is true to say, for example, that there is considerable between-speaker variation in the size and mass of the vocal folds, and that this has a determining influence on the fundamental frequencies used by a speaker, the determination is by no means absolute. There may be a physiologically determined maximum and minimum to a given speaker's fundamental frequency range; and his preferred range may in some sense be the optimal one given his particular larynx; but he nevertheless has at his disposal a variety of other fundamental frequency ranges within the absolute physiological limits (the upper physiological limit, in particular, is most unlikely to be attained in normal speech). The case nearest to an invariant organic characteristic may be that of the nasal cavities, which (alterations in physiological state, e.g. head colds, apart) would appear to be invariant and perhaps bestow invariant cues on nasal sounds; but even here, although nasal sounds have been used successfully in speaker recognition experiments (see 3.1), the spectral properties of nasals are affected by coupling through the velic orifice to the variable oral and pharyngeal vocal tract. And in the extreme, of course, a speaker can choose not to reveal any information about his nasal cavities by speaking with fully denasalised voice – that is, with the velum raised all the time.

The second complication is that whilst organic characteristics of a speaker set the limits to variation in a particular dimension such as fundamental frequency, or height of the second formant, information about these limits is conflated with linguistic information which exploits exactly the same dimensions. Much more needs to be known about a sample of speech than just its fundamental frequency statistics before reliable inferences can be drawn about the laryngeal properties of the speaker and thence his identity.

On the other side of the dichotomy, it will become clear below that what is 'learned' by a speaker of a language is of far greater complexity than is apparent from the discussion of 'habit patterns' found in work on speaker recognition. According to Wolf (1972:2045), features of 'learned' origin are

the result of differences in the patterns of coordinated neural commands to the separate articulators learned by each individual. Such differences give rise to variations in the dynamics of the vocal tract such as the rate of formant transitions and coarticulation effects.

Whilst variations of this kind are of considerable theoretical interest and will form the focal point of the research presented in Chapter 3, to limit the domain of what the speaker has learned to such low-level phonetic performance strategies (the 'implementational' strategies of 2.3.8 below) is to ignore the vast core of knowledge the speaker has about the phonetics and the phonology of his language, and about how these may be modulated according to the situation in which he is speaking. The variety of this knowledge will become apparent in 2.3.10.

To be fair, in existing work on speaker recognition there are occasional insights into the complexity of the problem of the sources of speaker-dependent information. Atal (1976:461) writes that

Speech is produced as a result of a complex sequence of transformations occurring at several different levels: semantic, linguistic, articulatory and acoustic. In general, differences in these transformations are likely to show up as differences in the acoustic properties of the speech signal.

The following sections will implicitly stress the importance, for an understanding of the speaker-dependent information in the speech wave, of recognising the various levels of abstraction underlying the production of an utterance, and of identifying the choices available to an individual at each of these levels; though it seems unlikely that a simple linear sequence of transformations, as suggested by Atal, will provide an adequate model. Bolt *et al.* (1979:17–18), in discussing the 'submessages' which may be transmitted in an act of speaking over and above the literal meaning of the concatenated words composing it, correctly hint at the kind of factor which must be considered when examining these choices:

Regardless of the speaker, some aspects of the sound are non-essential in that they are not always used to identify words, so speakers are free to produce them in various ways. Different speakers will develop characteristically different habits in using these nonessential aspects, or a single speaker will show considerable variation in their use from one utterance to another. This freedom allows a speaker substantial latitude in fitting speech to a situation, to a mood, to the interpersonal relationship of the speaker and the listener, and even to a temporary emotional state and to health.

In neither Atal (1976) nor Bolt *et al.* (1979), however, is the recognition of the complexity underlying speaker-dependent features of speech followed up with an attempt to formulate an overall model of speaker-specific information; such an attempt is made in the following sections.

2.3 Model of the sources of between-speaker differences

2.3.1 *Introduction*

Section 2.3 will build up a model which will enable discussion of the levels underlying the acoustic realisation of a speech signal token at which freedom of choice permits one speaker to vary from another. To a first approximation it may be thought of as a model of a speaker producing speech, that is as a 'performance' model in the sense of Chomsky (e.g. 1965:4), which attempts to describe the processes involved in 'the actual use of language in concrete situations'.

However, the higher one removes in the speech production process from the physically observable acoustic end product and the vocal tract gestures immediately preceding it, the more inaccessible become the actual processes involved, and the greater must be the reliance placed on the type of abstract linguistic description normally thought of in Generative Linguistics as a 'competence' model – that is, a description of the knowledge of a native speaker/hearer concerning his language, but which does not necessarily map isomorphically onto structures and processes in the speaker/hearer using language. The psychological reality, and its role in speech production, of a higher level element such as the phoneme in the present model is open to question (though there appears to be good evidence of such a role in that many speech production errors of the 'Spoonerism' type can be described in terms of phoneme switching – albeit constrained by syllable structure and stress pattern), but these linguistic constructs may be viewed heuristically as constituting a hypothesis about how speech production might take place, and which more importantly for present purposes allows for discussion of speaker-specific information.

2.3.2 *Overview of the model*

Viewed from a distance, the model which will be developed has the form diagrammed in Fig. 2.1. At the top of the model is the *communicative intent* of the speaker. It is important to recognise that this is complex and

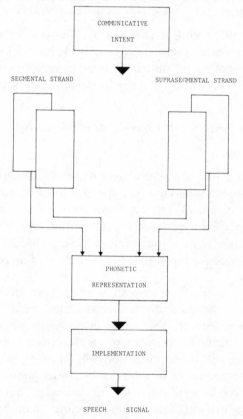

2.1 Overview of model of sources of between-speaker differences

many-sided; it is partly for this reason that the term 'meaning' has been avoided, since this is often associated with simplistic views of speech communication as a process whereby a speaker conveys a single 'meaning' or 'message' to a listener – for example Tosi (1979:12):

This speech wave, modulated according to a phonetic code or language, conveys a message to the listener.

Such a concept of 'meaning' or 'message' ignores the fact that at the same time as communicating the bald cognitive content of an utterance, the speaker is communicating information about many aspects of his attitude – towards himself (self-image), towards the status relationship between himself and others present, towards the situation in which the utterance is spoken, and so on. Of course not all that a listener can infer from speech is intended by the speaker; here a distinction drawn by Lyons (1977:33) between 'communicative' and 'informative' signals is apt. This distinction depends on the intention of the speaker:

a signal is informative if (regardless of the intentions of the sender) it makes the receiver aware of something of which he was not previously aware,

whereas a signal is communicative

if it is intended by the sender to make the receiver aware of something of which he was not previously aware. Whether the signal is communicative or not rests, then, upon the possibility of choice, or selection, on the part of the sender.

(Lyons' initial restriction of 'communicative' to 'factual, or propositional information' will not be adopted here.) It is, of course, not possible to determine merely by inspection of some aspect of the signal whether it is functionally communicative or merely informative.

The phonetic resources onto which the speaker maps his communicative intent have traditionally been regarded as structured into two *strands* – to use the term of Abercrombie (1967:89ff); both the dividing line between them and their labels are not unproblematical, but here they are termed *segmental* and *suprasegmental*. Other terms for the latter include 'prosodic' (e.g. Crystal (1969)) and the rather confusing 'voice dynamics' – the term in fact adopted in Abercrombie (1967).

There are intuitively unproblematical clear cases where the distinction between the two strands would give rise to general agreement; 'phonemes' of a language such as /i/, /p/, /n/ belong to the segmental strand, and intonation contours to the suprasegmental strand. The distinction may be approached from a number of viewpoints. From that of function, Crystal (1969:5) suggests

we may define prosodic systems as sets of mutually defining phonological features which have an essentially variable relationship to the words selected, as opposed to those features (for example the (segmental) phonemes, the lexical meanings) which have a direct and identifying relationship to such words.

This has the undesirable consequence of excluding lexical tone (in those languages such as Chinese, Igbo, etc., where a change in tonal pattern over identical segments may change the lexical identity) from the suprasegmental strand, with which they have most in common realisationally, including an independence from segmental occurrence (see the mention below of 'autosegmental' phonology). In terms of realisation, either auditorily or articulatorily, Crystal (1969:128) claims that

prosodic features may be defined as vocal effects constituted by variations along the parameters of pitch, loudness, duration and silence. . . This then excludes vocal effects which are primarily the result of physiological mechanisms other than the vocal cords.

But a list is arguably not a definition (Lehiste 1970:1), and it would in any case have to be extended to cover, for example, phonation type, which plays a part in tone and intonation; and then it is fairly opaque how duration is primarily dependent on the vocal cords. Lehiste (1970:2) remarks that

suprasegmental features are established by a comparison of items in a sequence (i.e. syntagmatic comparison), whereas segmental features can be defined without reference to the sequence of segments in which the segment appears, and their presence can be established either by inspection or by paradigmatic comparison. . .

This ignores on the one hand the paradigmatic identifiability of certain tone patterns (e.g. the fall–rise English intonation nucleus), and on the other the role of, for example, formant transitions in adjacent vowels in the identification of consonantal place of articulation.

The definition favoured here (which follows closely that tentatively offered by Lehiste (1970:3)) is that the suprasegmental strand comprises phonetic systems whose contrastive patterns occupy a linear domain greater than the extent of a segment; the norm is for suprasegmental contrasts to be realised over units of the extent of a syllable up to the tone unit (or greater – cf. the work of Lehiste (1975, 1979) on 'paragraph intonation').

Despite these problems of definition, the two strands represent a fundamental division of the spoken medium. The traditionally recognised independence of representations in segmental and suprasegmental strands has had its most recent formal recognition in 'autosegmental' phonology. Here, suprasegmentals receive a representation quite autonomous of the segmental phoneme string; this accounts, for example, for the perseverance of lexical tone patterns despite deletion of segments by phonological rule (e.g. Goldsmith 1976); or the underlying unity of an intonation pattern which may be realised over a variety of segmental strings.

The two strands are not kept separate in the speech signal, nor can they form independent production targets for the speaker, since the temporal overlaying of the two strands is not arbitrary (there are an unlimited number of incorrect time alignments of a string of segments and an intonation contour, for example). The integration of the two strands yields the *phonetic representation*. This contains all details of an utterance which are of potential linguistic relevance. It may be thought of as specifying all the aspects of an utterance about which there is public agreement by virtue of a culturally shared language. Such aspects will include those determined in any way by the communicative intent, and also those which are purely informative in that they characterise a particular language or language subdivision.

Finally, the specifications of the phonetic representation are acted upon by the *implementation rules*, of which the output is neuromuscular commands, yielding movements of the vocal organs and their acoustic transform.

Omitted from mention so far have been the other two inputs to the phonetic representation in Fig. 2.1. Abercrombie (1967:91) writes of three, rather than two strands composing the phonic medium; the third comprises 'features of voice quality':

The term voice quality refers to those characteristics which are present more or less all the time that a person is talking: it is a quasi-permanent quality running through all the sound that issues from his mouth.

For Abercrombie, such features can be divided into those which are outside the speaker's control (by virtue of being determined by some aspect of his vocal structure, or his transient condition) versus those which are within the speaker's voluntary control – corresponding to Laver's distinction of *intrinsic* versus *extrinsic* features; for example Laver (1976:57):

Intrinsic features. . .derive solely from the invariant absolutely uncontrollable physical foundation of the speaker's vocal apparatus. They contribute only to voice quality. . .extrinsic features are made up of all aspects of vocal activity which are under the volitional control of the speaker, whether 'consciously' or not.

('Voice quality' is unfortunately used with many different meanings; for a discussion of some of these see Crystal (1969:99ff) who himself seems to favour restricting its use to intrinsic voice quality in the above sense (1969:100):

Causing much more of a problem is the second kind of physiologically controlled communication, namely the phenomenon of *voice quality* or *voice set*.

It is also frequently used, without any implication of 'quasi-permanency', to refer specifically to the mode of vibration of the larynx, for which the term 'phonation type' will be employed here.) It follows from Laver's definition that extrinsic voice quality is susceptible to exploitation by the speaker in conveying (part of) his communicative intent – as, for example, when the speaker indicates the secrecy of what he is saying by using a whispery voice – and so a third 'strand' parallel to the segmental and suprasegmental might be expected in the upper part of the model.

But on closer examination it appears that the 'voice quality' strand, or as it will be called here the *long term* strand, is of a rather different status from the other two. Long term characteristics are derivative of the two main strands; so a long term component such as 'palatalised voice' exists not in isolation, but by virtue of a tendency towards palatalisation recurring through a substantial proportion of elements in the segmental strand. Similarly an impression of a speaker as having a 'high pitched' voice, or a 'monotonous' voice, stems not from an isolated suprasegmental element, but from a 'cumulative abstraction' (Laver 1980:1) from an appreciable proportion of the suprasegmental strand. Thus a component of long term quality can be thought of as resulting from a configurational trend (or possibly a dynamic trend – a particular quality might derive for instance from characteristic rates of pitch change, or transition between segments) in the action of the vocal apparatus; this trend is referred to as a 'setting' of the vocal apparatus. Laver's (1980) framework for the description of these settings is explained in some detail in 4.3.3.

As Laver (1980:3) puts it

It is not proposed that the settings and segments are complementary divisions of phonetic quality. . . The analysis of phonetic quality into settings is a second-order analysis, abstracting data from a prior segmental analysis.

Since it is clear that such abstraction is equally possible from the suprasegmental strand, the present model incorporates two second-order *long term* strands, corresponding to the two primary strands, and each forwarding long term target specifications to the phonetic representation.

As a descriptive device the notion of long term settings is justified firstly behaviourally because it corresponds to the capabilities of listeners to make judgments of this kind; and secondly because it offers the potential of descriptive economy in cases where, for example, in comparing two varieties of a language or two languages, a parallel difference is noted to recur throughout a number of segments which is compatible with the effects of a single long term quality specification (cf. Trudgill 1974a:185ff; Labov 1972:40). (It may well be that phoneticians have always covertly acted in this way, though without explicit recognition of their practice, given the surprisingly large number of languages which from their descriptions appear to have vowels approximating to the extreme qualities of the Cardinal Vowels.) But the hypothesis implicit in the present model is that long term properties have reality for the speaker. As in all questions of the reality of linguistic constructs, the impenetrability of mental activity to direct investigation leaves justification of the constructs dependent on their ability to predict observed behaviour, and on the overall economy of the model of which they form a part. Taking as an example the use of long term effects for paralinguistic communication, such as the reported use of strong nasalisation in (especially American) English to signal irony, or of whispery voice to convey conspiratoriality, a model without a long term mechanism would equally well predict the manifestation of these segmental modfications on every segment, on every second segment, on every second pair of segments, on completely arbitrary segments, and so on. In fact (setting aside the question of blocking by conflicting segmental specifications, such as oral stops (nasalisation) or voiceless segments (creaky voice) – see 4.3.2 for discussion) there is no evidence that any but the first of these actually occurs. This is precisely the result predicted by the present model, where the speaker has the facility to set a target in a particular phonetic dimension which remains in force until cancelled. In the alternative model the value alteration for each successive segment would be a separate operation to be performed, unrelated furthermore to identical operations on preceding and following segments.

In the sections below, details of the model are given, and then discussed in terms of the sources of between-speaker phonetic differences, and then within-speaker variation as a result of the mapping of communicative intent.

2.3.3 *Communicative intent*

In discussing possible analytic subdivisions of what is here called communicative intent, Lyons (1977:54–5) admits that

There is perhaps no single classificatory scheme that can be described as the only one which is correct.

The most clearly definable subpart seems to be what Lyons (1977:50) calls the 'descriptive' function of language – 'the transmission of factual, or propositional information' which will here be termed *cognitive*. The apparent primacy of this aspect of communication may, however, be circumstantial, resulting from a linguistic tradition which has until recently paid rather little attention to other aspects of communicative intent – influenced perhaps by the importance of written language, which transmits optimally the cognitive intent.

Crystal (1975:12) divides 'meaning' into 'cognitive' and 'affective' subparts:

It is not assumed that these are the only two types of meaning which need to be recognised, nor is it assumed that a clear *a priori* distinction can be made between them.

The *affective* part of communicative intent is taken to refer to the attitude of the speaker, as, for instance, when a person speaks using a wide pitch range on specific contours to indicate friendliness, or speaks loudly to convey anger.

In fact, consideration of the next subpart isolated here, *social* intent, at once demonstrates the impossibility of drawing clear-cut dividing lines. Sociolinguistics has recently made considerable progress in describing those features of speech which are informative of a person's group membership (socioeconomic, ethnic, regional etc.), but it has also revealed and quantified the degree to which a person's speech changes with the context in which he is speaking (or more accurately with his interpretation of that context); specifically, as the context becomes more formal, so a speaker will tend (in many urban communities at least) to change values for sociolinguistic variables in the direction of those of people of higher status (see e.g. Labov 1972). One important aspect of context is the addressee (or addressees); depending on his interpretation of the relative status of speaker and addressee, and on their roles defined in a particular interaction, a speaker may 'converge' or 'diverge' to make his speech more or less like that of the other participant(s) (cf. Giles *et al.* 1979). Increasingly it is being observed that sociolinguistic markers are not invariant, but depend on (the participants' interpretations of) social aspects of the interactional context (see e.g. Brown and Levinson 1979). Returning to the question of borderlines between categories of cognitive intent, since context clearly plays an important role in determining features of speech, it is no longer certain that, for example, the loudness of angry speech is isolatably the result of affective communicative intent; it might also be communicating the speaker's understanding of the interactional context – for instance a dispute, or the exercising of authority.

A fourth subdivision of communicative intent is the *self-presentational*. A wide variety of information may be encoded by a speaker in order to project a personality corresponding to his self-image (in a particular context); Argyle (1967: 162):

Certain aspects of behaviour during social encounters can be looked at as consequences of the participants having self-images. They present themselves in a certain way, adopt a particular 'face', and try to get others to accept this picture of themselves.

Personality dimensions such as extroversion–introversion, dominance–dependence, masculinity–femininity, or their perceptual correlates are associated with particular ways of speaking, and these can to some extent be intentionally adopted.

The last subdivision of communicative intent to be considered here concerns the control and structuring of any verbal interaction. In conversations, it is generally found unsatisfactory if both participants speak, and are silent, simultaneously. The participants therefore manage the interaction so that 'speaking turns' are allocated to each; and it is likely that a speaker communicates, perhaps through his overall pitch level, loudness, and rate of utterance whether he is (in his interpretation) approaching the end of a turn, or conversely is 'in full flow' and unwilling to be interrupted; compare Laver and Hutcheson (1972:14–15):

Signals for yielding the role of speaker to the other participant are given by eye-contact behaviour, particular intonation patterns and body movements, for instance.

Quite possibly the work of Lehiste (1975), which showed that listeners were to some extent able to tell whether excerpted read sentences were paragraph-final or not, was exploring cues similar to those used in *interaction management*.

The above categorisation cannot claim to be exhaustive; but it begins to indicate the complexity of communicational functions which are encoded in the speech signal, and which must be considered when an apparently speaker-specific variable is selected for speaker recognition.

2.3.4 *The segmental strand*

2.3.4.1 *Segmentation and the phoneme* The widely accepted view that spoken language consists in a linear succession of discrete segments, reflected in alphabetic writing systems, cannot be induced from the speech signal. There are sharp discontinuities of the speech signal in time, but these are by no means in one-to-one correspondence, in position or number, with segment boundaries. The hypothesis stems rather from speakers' intuitions about where in a word a change in a sound will change the identity of the word. Thus in the word *bid*, there are three and only three such points. At the beginning, a *d* (or *k*, *l* etc.) could be substituted; in the middle, an *e* (or *a*, *u* etc.); and at the end a *b* (or *t*, *n* etc.). In each of these positions of choice, by such a process of commutation, a system of distinct elements is discovered; each of these elements exists merely by being significantly different from, or *in opposition* with, the others. Identity can be established between particular elements occurring in different positions in the word when at each position the particular element enters into a similar relationship (in phonetic terms) with the other elements that can occur in that position; for example, initial *p* can be identified with final *p* by virtue of entering into a similar relationship in terms of phonetic properties with *b*, and the other elements in both positions – in spite of the fact that in absolute phonetic terms the initial *p* and the final *p* are not identical ([pʰ] versus [²p], for example, in certain dialects of English). The abstract oppositional element /p/, realised in different environments as [pʰ], [²p] and other positional variants or *allophones*, is known as a *phoneme*.

There are many theories of the phoneme; and many of the basic tenets of phoneme theory (though not, in practice, segmentation) have been rejected by 'Generative' phonologists; for a good introductory account of the issues see Fischer-Jørgensen (1975). There is not the space here to debate such issues, and it is proposed to adopt a traditional 'classical phonemic' model, as this is likely to be familiar to workers in speaker recognition, and to be used by phoneticians when analysing voice samples from the point of view of speaker identity. The sentiment expressed by Wells (1970:232) dealing with accent differences still seems appropriate:

> The material presented here is formulated in phonemic terms. This would seem to make for easier understanding than a possible alternative presentation in terms of generative rules, particularly when the proper formulation of phonological rules is still a matter of some dispute.

The phonemic symbols used below are those of Gimson (1980).

2.3.4.2 *Structure of the segmental strand* Fig. 2.2 shows the primary and secondary (long term) segmental strands in more detail. An utterance in phonemic representation is input to *realisation rules*, which specify the (segmental) phonetic properties the speaker has to achieve when producing the utterance. As an example from a variety of English, the word *teal*, phonemically /tiːl/, would be subject to rules specifying a *realisation* including, but not exhausted by, the following degree of detail:

$$[t^{shh}ɪ̈ɫ]$$

that is, an aspirated alveolar stop with slightly affricated release; a diphthong gliding from half front half close to just short of close front; and a strongly pharyngalised lateral. In fact such a representation is quite inadequate, as it is still largely bounded by the constraint of a segmental transcription, whereas clearly if the speaker is to produce the utterance

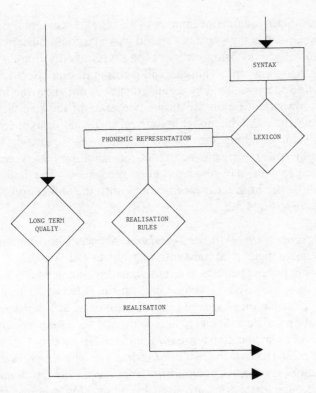

2.2 The segmental strand

correctly a time base is needed. This will be discussed further in relation to the final *phonetic representation* (see 2.3.7).

The phonemic representation is composed of items from the *lexicon* chosen, and appropriately concatenated by the syntactic component, in accord primarily, though not exclusively, with the cognitive intent of the utterance. The lexicon is like an ordinary dictionary in that it stores the words known by the speaker, associating their meanings, connotations, syntactic properties, and (all non-predictable) information about their phonological form; though undoubtedly the retrieval mechanism will be far more complex than the alphabetical ordering used in dictionaries. Associated with the lexicon will be an inventory of the segments – phonemes – which can function to differentiate lexical items, and also rules specifying restrictions on their linear combination (/stnaɪ/ and /tætf/ are not possible words of English, though /splaɪ/ and /tæft/ are, even though they happen not to occur).

The other component in Fig. 2.2 is labelled *long term quality*. It is assumed that the complex structural mechanism of the primary segmental strand does not have a parallel in the long term strand, and that communicative intent is mapped directly onto components of long term quality (nasalised voice, etc.). The phonetic representation will incorporate the effect of the long term quality specifications; but the diagram does not show the input from the long term strand before or during operation of the realisation rules, which entails the claim that no realisation rule depends for its operation on a particular value of a long term dimension; no cases are known, but in the absence hitherto of even this degree of formalisation of a 'voice quality' strand the problem may not have been recognised. The nature of the integration of the long term specifications with the short term segmental ones is discussed in 4.3.2.

2.3.4.3 *Categorisation of between-speaker differences* Notice that in Fig. 2.2 and subsequent figures components relevant to the sources of phonetic differences between speakers are represented by diamonds.

In 2.3.10.4 the division sometimes drawn between 'accentual' and 'personal' information in speech is argued not to be at all sharp, and that demonstration will be anticipated here in the adoption for between-speaker differences of a classification normally used for differences between accents. Wells (1982:22ff), on which the following draws heavily, employs a four-way categorisation: *systemic, phonotactic, incidential* and *realisational* differences; similar categories are used by others, for example O'Connor (1973:176–90). Of these, the realisational category relates, appropriately, to the realisation rules; the other three have more to do with the lexicon. In the following exposition, most examples will be taken from Southern British English, with special attention to Received Pronunciation (RP – for a discussion of this definitionally elusive entity see e.g. Gimson (1980:87ff)), this being a widely known and investigated variety.

2.3.4.4 *Systemic differences* Two speakers may have differing phonemic *systems* – in terms of the total number of phonemes, or phonemes of a particular kind (e.g. front short vowels). A Scottish English speaker may have only /u/, where RP has the opposition /u:/–/ʊ/, so that for the former *good* and *food* rhyme; a South Yorkshire speaker may have three different phonemes /iː/, /ɪə/ and /ɛɪ/ in the words *three, tea* and *teach* which all have /iː/ in RP. Within RP a few speakers still have a phonemic opposition between /ɔə/ and /ɔː/, whereas for most *lore* rhymes with *law*; less likely is a system lacking the opposition /ʊə/–/ɔː/ because although *your* and *yore, sure* and *shore/Shaw* undoubtedly rhyme for many RP speakers, /ʊə/ would be found in a few (mainly rarer?) words (e.g. *sewer* /s(j)ʊə/, *Ruhr* /rʊə/). This means that it will not be possible for the phonetician analysing limited samples for speaker recognition to arrive at firm systemic statements; rather, observations of potentially systemic import will have to be treated as incidental (see below). Among the consonants, a number of RP speakers lack /r/, /w/ being substituted (but see the discussion of /r/ in 2.3.4.9); /h/ on the other hand is a popular social shibboleth, its systemic absence certainly a non-RP feature. Concessions to foreign pronunciation may add phonemes of marginal status to a speaker's system: *Jean* and *salon* as /ʒɔ̃:/ and /sælɔ̃:/ rather than /ʒɔ:n/ and /sælɒn/ add marginal /ɔ̃:/ (if not the two French phonemes involved, /ɑ̃/ and /õ/).

2.3.4.5 *Phonotactic differences* When a speaker has a phoneme which is equivalent to a phoneme of another speaker (in terms of its systemic relationship to the other phonemes), but the range of phonological environments it can occur in differs, the difference is considered to be *phonotactic*. For example /r/ does not occur preconsonantally or prepausally in RP (hence *car* /kɑ:/, *fierce* /fɪəs/, etc.), but is permitted in these environments in many other varieties of English. For some speakers /ʒ/ does not occur word-finally, being replaced by /dʒ/ in words such as *garage* /gærɑ:dʒ/ or /gærɪdʒ/, *beige* /beɪdʒ/. Word-initial stop plus fricative clusters are not normally permitted, but some speakers apparently have /ps-/ in words like *pseudonym* as well as *psi* (Jones 1975:384). However in many cases a phonotactic classification seems no more appropriate than an incidental one; and for practical purposes, since an absolute phonotactic difference cannot be established without examining all a speaker's lexical items, phonotactic differences are more likely to have to be treated as incidental.

2.3.4.6 *Incidental differences* Incidental (or *lexical-incidental*) refers to the incidence of a phoneme with respect to individual lexical items or groups of lexical items. Some incidental differences in particular words are popularly commented on – the variation of /i:/ with /aɪ/ in *either*, *neither*, or /i:/, /ɪ/ and /e/ in *economics*, and presence or absence of /h/ in *hotel* (for a speaker who elsewhere pronounced /h/) being cases in point. In other cases alternatives operate over a morphemic class of words: RP /æ/, or /ɑ:/ in stressed *trans-* (*transport, transfer*. . .), /æ/, /ɑ:/ or /ə/ in unstressed *-graph* (*telegraph, spectrograph*. . .); /ɪ/ or /ə/ in *-less, -ness* (*hopeless, goodness*. . .), in *be-, de-* (*besides, decide*. . .), and in *-age, -es, -ed* (*manage, dances, batted*. . .); and /ʌ/ or /ə/ in unstressed *sub-* (*subservience*). (It is by no means certain, of course, that a speaker will treat all items of a class in the same way.) The following contrived example demonstrates some of the incidental features which might be used by a phonetician asked to assess the similarity of voice samples (cf. Baldwin 1977):

Associated Garages telegraphed on Tuesday – they'd solved the cost
əsəʊsɪeɪtɪd gærɑ:ʒɪz telɪgræft ɒn tju:zdɪ ðeɪd sɒlvd ðə kɒst
ʃ ə ɪdʒ ə ɑ: tʃ eɪ əʊ ɔ:
problem
prɒblɪm
ə

As well as their possible speaker-diagnostic value at the phonemic level, incidential variations must also be taken into account in any scheme which exploits the phonetic quality of a particular phoneme. It would be unfortunate to weight the decision against identification by mistakenly comparing the /u:/ of *Ruth* and *proof* in a recording A, with the '/u:/' of *tooth* and *roof* in a recording B, where the speaker in fact had used /ʊ/, which is occasionally heard in these words.

2.3.4.7 Stress Before leaving the categories of speaker difference dependent on the lexicon a mention must be made of stress. In its realisation – in dimensions such as pitch, amplitude, duration and phonation type (the last under-researched as yet in this context) – it resembles suprasegmental features; but it seems that the presence or absence of stress regularly conditions a number of segmental realisation rules, such as aspiration and vowel quality changes, so it must be represented in the segmental strand.

Stress placement in some languages is highly predictable – in Finnish it always comes on the first syllable of a word, and in Welsh (with certain exceptions) on the penultimate. Even in English, where stress placement is apparently free, Chomsky and Halle (1968) have demonstrated that it is possible to predict it in a large number of cases using appropriate phonosyntactic rules; for discussion here, however, the more traditional position, that free stress is marked on words in the lexicon, is adopted.

In quite a number of words in English speakers may choose from alternative common stress patterns: *(')ex(')quisite, (')for(')midable, (')dis(')pute* (noun), *(')con(')troversy, (')con(')tribute*, and in compound words such as *(')ice-(')cream, (')shop-(')steward*; for further examples see Gimson (1980:230ff). However it is important to recognise that one speaker may change his stressing of a given word according to its rhythmical context, usually so as to avoid two adjacent stressed syllables; thus *she s 'just fif'teen*, but *'fifteen 'years*.

2.3.4.8 Realisation rules, allophones, and coarticulation The realisation rules convert an abstract string of phonemes into a representation which contains specifications for all the culturally shared segmental phonetic properties which are controlled by the speaker and have a potentially informative capacity, including those which inform that the speaker is exploiting a particular variety of a language. Thus two speakers may have phoneme *systems* which are identical in every respect, but in realising the phoneme string /tu:/ one produces [tʰʊu] and the other [tˢʰiʉ]. Gimson (1980) discusses, for each of the phonemes of RP, the variant realisations which a learner of English may expect to encounter.

Realisation rules, then, are triggered by the phonemic representation to supply phonetic detail, a phoneme normally being thought of as comprising the minimum specification of phonetic detail which will distinguish it from any other phoneme. But the phonetic detail supplied is crucially dependent on the position in which the phoneme occurs – its position in relation to higher order structures such as the syllable, word, etc., which will be termed here its *context*; and its relation to the linear sequence of segments of which it is a part, particularly adjacent segments – its *environment*. Phonetic detail of this kind is traditionally termed allophonic; and since Wang and Fillmore (1961) two kinds of allophone have been distinguished termed *extrinsic* and *intrinsic*. For Wang and Fillmore extrinsic allophones reflect speech habits of a particular community, whilst intrinsic allophones reflect (universal) constraints of the vocal apparatus. This use of these terms for allophones seems to be equivalent to that of Laver (see 2.3.2 above) for voice qualities.

Clear cases of extrinsic allophones are those where the phenomenon only occurs in a limited number of languages (therefore is not universally constrained), and which are contextually determined (in the sense above) and so lack an explanation in terms of smoothing between segments. Classic examples are the post syllable-nucleus 'dark' lateral [ɫ] which occurs in some varieties of English regardless of the quality of the preceding vowel (as opposed to the relatively 'clear' [l] allophone before the syllable nucleus); and again for certain varieties of English the (roughly speaking) word-final glottalised allophones of the voiceless stops.

The definition of an intrinsic allophone, and hence the cut-off point between the two, is problematical, however. At first sight the tongue–body accommodation of the initial 'clear' [l] allophone in English to the quality of a following vowel (Bladon and Al-Bamerni 1976) would appear to be ascribable to purely mechanical, 'automatic' smoothing between segments. But the finding that neither is such lateral-vowel accommodation constant across extrinsic allophones in one language (Bladon and Al-Bamerni 1976), nor does it necessarily occur in another language (Ní Chasaide 1977), nor is it constant in degree across speakers of the same language (Chapter 3 below)

43

indicates that the situation is considerably more complex. The problems will be treated more fully in 3.5.2 below; the direction in which solutions will have to be sought is suggested in Tatham (1969), who argues convincingly that between the two categories of 'extrinsic events', which 'do not occur except under direct voluntary control', and 'uncontrollable intrinsic events' which are 'bound to occur when an intrinsic event takes place', there is an intermediate category of events which will take place, due to mechanical smoothing and the like, unless they are specifically inhibited by 'extrinsic resistance'.

In summary, then, the realisation rules will have to specify extrinsic allophones, and (where necessary in a particular language) the limits on the freedom of the speaker to indulge in mechanically natural but resistable assimilation processes. The notions of 'allophone' and 'coarticulation' have been given a perhaps disproportionate amount of attention in this treatment of the segmental strand since they are basic to an understanding of Chapter 3, which investigates between-speaker differences in coarticulation.

2.3.4.9 *Realisational differences* Realisational between-speaker differences are of three types. In the first case, all realisations of a phoneme for one speaker are different from all those of another speaker in a regular way. Clear examples of this are the realisation of RP /r/ (normally a postalveolar sound [ɹ]) by instead a labio-dental frictionless approximant [ʋ] (which is nevertheless still distinct from [w]</w/) or by a velar or uvular sound; or the realisation of RP /s/ as a voiceless lateral fricative [ɬ] (which would be counted a speech defect); less clear cases are the realisations of certain vowels: the realisations of RP /ʌ/ vary from nearly back to nearly front vowels, and though the environmentally determined range of one speaker's realisations may partially overlap with that of another, it is possible in such a case to draw a generalisation that in the same environment one speaker uses, for example, a fronter vowel than the other; similar are the cases of /u:/ (varying across speakers from almost back to front of central), and the diphthong /əʊ/ (varying considerably in frontness from speaker to speaker, but also subject to environmental determination – especially before [ɬ]).

In the second case, the realisation rules determine a speaker-specific allophone in one or more contexts. RP /p/, /t/, /k/ may be aspirated to greater or lesser degree before stressed vowels, or glottalised or not word-finally; /l/ may have an extrinsic allophone in post syllable-nuclear position which is 'darker' than other allophones in greater or lesser degree. Of course, if the number of contexts in which a different realisation occurs is large, and the difference between speakers in each context is in the same direction, there may be ambiguity between this case and the preceding one. Both categories underlie information which may be exploited by an auditory phonetician using a detailed phonetic descriptive framework.

Thirdly, the realisation rules govern the (culturally shared) adjustment of segments according to their environment – their coarticulation with each other. Su *et al.* (1974) were the first to explore the speaker-specificity of coarticulation, in a study of the effect of vowel quality on a preceding nasal; Chapter 3 below reports an investigation of the speaker-specificity of the coarticulation of /l/ and /r/ with following vowels, and further discussion of the control of coarticulation will be found there. In general the between-speaker differences resulting from this category of realisational source are rather fine and amenable only to instrumental investigation. The realisation rules are also responsible for determining the durational relationships of the elements of the segmental sequence, which are sensitive to both context (e.g. Umeda 1977) and environment (English vowels before voiceless obstruents are as little as half as long as when they occur in other environments (e.g. Gimson 1980:98)) – though their final duration will be subject to further modification by suprasegmental factors. According to Lehiste (1970:41)

Under otherwise identical conditions, a speaker produces durations that are normally distributed within a range characteristic of the speaker. Differences between speakers are often quite large,

and Umeda (1977:857) in an appended brief comparison between speakers of durations in /st(r)/ clusters found that

the closure time is fairly well regulated while the aspiration period seems to have a good deal of room for options;

but there does not seem to have been a systematic study of such durations from the point of view of speaker recognition.

2.3.4.10 *The long term segmental strand* The contribution of the *long term segmental* strand to between-speaker differences is in the form of a set of default values for the various segmental phonetic dimensions. These default values normally fall within the ranges defined by what is acceptable in the speech community (if they do not, judgments such as 'his horrible nasal/adenoidal voice' may be made, for values which would pass without comment in another speech community); and they apply unless the requirements of the communicative intent of some utterance map onto the long term strand and select some specific values instead. They determine (the segmental aspect of) what Laver (1976:57) refers to as 'concurrent features':

The concurrent features make up the extrinsic contribution to voice quality. They

45

provide the background, quasi-permanent auditory colouring to a person's voice which together with the intrinsic features give a person his characteristic overall voice quality.

Among the dimensions involved will be nasality and other resonance characteristics such as palatalisation and pharyngalisation; and also phonation types such as breathy, creaky, or falsetto phonation. These latter are regarded here as part of the long term *segmental* strand as they represent long term modulations of what is essentially an inherently segmental property, voicing, rather than of a suprasegmental pattern (which may however itself be 'overlaid' on the voicing, in the case of pitch patterns (cf. Lehiste 1970:2)).

In the case of long term properties phonetics has only recently addressed the problem of their objective description, and so phoneticians have not had quite the same advantage over the lay listener (who may have a wide range of labels for 'voice qualities' which he can often apply confidently, even if their import is not generally agreed on) which they have enjoyed in the short term strand, where they could bring to bear a well established technical framework in which they had been trained; though now such a framework is available for long term quality (see Chapter 4). Chapter 4 is mainly concerned with the segmental long term strand, and discusses speaker recognition schemes which have exploited it; it then investigates acoustic correlates of long term qualities. A distant objective of such work might be an automatic classification of voices according to phonetic categories of long term quality.

2.3.5 *The suprasegmental strand*

2.3.5.1 *Structure of the suprasegmental strand* Fig. 2.3 shows the suprasegmental strand, long and short term aspects, and its relation to syntax and the lexicon. It can be questioned to what extent discreteness of form, parallel to that of phonemes, exists in the suprasegmental strand (for discussion, see Crystal 1969:7.2); however it is assumed here that at least some of the suprasegmental systems do involve discrete contrastive primes, whilst in other cases communicative intent may map into continuous variables (such as the precise height from which the voice might fall in *I was* `*SHOCKED*, according to the degree of shock to be conveyed) by direct input to the realisation rules.

The analysis assumed here for intonation, which is at the most systematic end of the continuum of discreteness in suprasegmental effects, is one which (in the British tradition) takes as its basic unit of analysis the *tone unit*. One of a number of contrastive *tunes* is chosen in each tone unit, the tune being

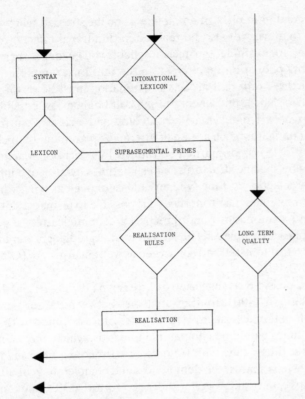

2.3 The suprasegmental strand

comprised of subcomponents which correspond to four divisions of a tone unit: *prehead, head, nucleus* and *tail*. The nucleus occurs on the stressed syllable of a particular word, and makes it the most prominent, usually by virtue of a pitch glide; the other subcomponents are optional and depend on the presence of appropriate syllables for their realisation. (Whether glides should be represented as such, or as sequences of levels – fall–rise as H(igh)-L(ow)-M(id), etc. – will not be discussed here.) For further explanation and definitions, see for example O'Connor and Arnold (1973), Crystal (1969:Ch. 5). As an example:

it	'won t	even	'S T A R T	to·day
PREHEAD	H E A D		NUCLEUS	TAIL

Although the interlinear graph gives an impression of the pitch movement, and by larger dots implies greater loudness on the stressed syllables of lexical items, the pattern will also be realised in durational effects (other things being equal, for example, the nuclear syllable will be longer than the others) and possibly phonation type (creak in the tail, for example).

At least three different aspects of intonation must be distinguished (cf. Crystal 1975:11–15): placement of tone unit boundaries, possible positions being derivable from syntactic structure and actual occurrence being dependent on factors such as rate of utterance; placement of nucleus, which (Crystal 1975:15) 'is primarily determined by lexical or semantic factors, sometimes by specific structures, and sometimes by affective information'; and thirdly selection of tune type, or at least of nucleus type, which may be determined by syntactic properties (it is possible to change a statement into a question by intonation) and directly by communicative (e.g. affective) intent – a particular tune may be 'in statements: grudgingly admitting. . .; in questions: . . .interested and concerned as well as surprised' (O'Connor and Arnold 1973:170).

It may be possible, as suggested by Liberman (1978:88ff) and discussed by Ladd (1980:11ff; 140ff), to draw analogies between the segmental lexicon and an intonational lexicon, where tunes are associated with meanings. Complete tunes would be comparable to words, which may be made up of morphemes; thus a tune with (in present terminology) a rising head and a high fall nucleus shares 'the definiteness and completeness of all the falling tone groups', but 'adds an attitude of protest' (O'Connor and Arnold 1973:73), in the way that words containing same morphemes may thereby share some component of meaning, even though the meanings of the complete words are not totally predictable from the constituent morphemes (e.g. *tele-graph, tele-phone, ideo-graph, ideo-phone*).

The systemic suprasegmental representation derives from the selection made from the intonational lexicon of tunes on the basis of syntactic properties and direct affective information. It will consist in a number of layers, one being the tunes; another being a representation of the structure of the utterance in terms of stressed and unstressed syllables, in which tone unit boundaries, and nucleus placement, might be indicated; and another, in the case of a tone language, being the succession of tonemes. Schematically for English

He ˅didn t ˊwant to ·buy it | but I perˋsuaded him ‖

the representation at the level of suprasegmental primes might be

H-M   H-L-M   H-L
s S s *S s S s | s s s *S s s ‖

Realisation rules will then perform a number of operations. One of these will be the specification of integer pitch values for the tonal and intonational primes, which underlyingly may be specified with only three or four levels – whatever the minimum needed to describe the suprasegmental contrasts. Thus a high fall nucleus may be underlyingly H-L, and a low fall M-L, but the realisation rules will specify (according to communicational requirements) how wide the fall will be. Some such specifications will be context-sensitive, determining for example the step down in pitch which occurs between heads in successive minor tone units (see Trim 1959:27; Crystal 1969:5.10). Similarly in tone languages they will make language-specific adjustments to tones according to their tonal environment (e.g. tone sandhi in Chinese, and 'downstep' in certain African languages). They will also be responsible for associating suprasegmental representations correctly with the syllable string – given the stress pattern indicated above, *He did ˇ nt want ʼto buy it|*, and many others, are not possible associations.

2.3.5.2 *Between-speaker differences* As far as locating the points at which speaker-specific information may be based is concerned, at least some parallels may be drawn with the segmental strand. Again, the differences between speakers are the same in kind as those between accents.

In the intonational lexicon, the system of primes from which the 'words', the tunes, are composed, may be different. It is theoretically possible that a speaker would lack a particular nucleus type used by another speaker, and so his system of elementary contrasting primes would be non-isomorphic. Evidence on this within a speech community seems scant, and from the point of view of speaker recognition, as with phoneme-systemic differences, finite samples do not permit firm conclusions regarding a systemic difference.

Parallel to segmental phonotactic differences are differences between speakers in the cooccurrence restrictions between types of prime (head and nucleus, etc.). Similar reservations about data limitations are in order here, but in the writer's experience teaching intonation analysis such differences do seem to exist. O'Connor and Arnold (1973:288ff) suggest that in RP the combination high head plus low rise nucleus is normal (especially for 'interested' questions); yet some (near) RP-speaking students find such a combination very hard to produce, the natural tendency being to replace it by high head plus fall–rise nucleus.

Incidential differences are not directly parallelled in the suprasegmental lexicon. To establish an incidential difference (recall e.g. /iː/ versus /aɪ/ in *either*), a notion of 'same word', in which the different phonemes occur, is implicit. The knowledge of 'sameness' derives from factors such as semantic equivalence, phonological similarity in other than the crucial respect, spelling, and etymology. In the case of an intonational 'word' the latter two factors are absent, and the first three are considerably more obscure, given the less discrete nature of intonational function, and form. A more feasible approach would be to examine the selectional frequency of particular intonational words, for example, with respect to syntactic types such as questions, non-final and final statement clauses, etc. Clearly work of such a statistical nature would only be possible given rather large data samples.

The discussion which follows of realisational sources of speaker differences is perforce largely hypothetical, as no work in speaker recognition has attempted to isolate suprasegmental primes (as opposed to the frequently used segmental phonemes) and compare their realisations across speakers; it is an approach worth exploring.

The suprasegmental realisation rules provide a phonetic interpretation of the sequences of contrastive primes. A fall–rise nucleus, for example, may be specified underlyingly as H-L-M, but the operation of the realisation rules will determine the detailed pitch movement; Australian English, for example, appears often to have a realisation where the pitch rises back almost to the starting point: ⬤〰, which is unlike a frequent RP realisation with very little rise: ⬤〰; less dramatic differences will exist between speakers of the same accent. There is also scope for idiosyncrasy in syntagmatic pitch relationships – for example the degree of step down between successive high heads mentioned above, or the relationship between the last syllable of a head and the start of a falling nucleus. The realisation rules will specify the cooccurrence of phonation-type correlates of suprasegmental primes; different speakers will vary in their predilection for creaky voice in the lower part of a fall–rise, or their preparedness to adopt falsetto as an adjunct of an 'H' specification. Likewise, syllables will be assigned an amplitude factor and duration factor which will interact with segmental durations and amplitudes. It is possible that individuals exploit freedoms in the associating of tunes with syllables; a rise–fall nucleus (perhaps M-H-L) on a phrase such as ˆ*two in·deed* may, according to O'Connor and Arnold (1973:12) be 'spread over two or three syllables. . .both patterns being commonly heard' thus

50

t is not known whether tone-language realisational operations such as
andhi and downstep leave scope for idiosyncrasy.

Finally, the contribution of the long term suprasegmental strand to
etween-speaker differences consists in a set of default values for
uprasegmental dimensions, including perhaps mean pitch, pitch range,
1ean loudness, and information about normal speaking rate, which apply
hroughout a given speaker's vocal production unless they are manipulated
·y the requirements of communicative intent. They comprise the supra-
egmental aspect of Laver's 'concurrent features' (see above, 2.3.4.10).

.3.6 *Integration rules*

Vhen a speaker produces speech he must achieve a correct integration of
he segmental and suprasegmental specifications; a particular language
nposes limits on variation in this integration, as discussed by Lehiste
1970:84):

,anguages seem to differ with respect to the distribution of the fundamental
requency contour over the voiced portion of the syllable. [A deaf subject] produced
he word *feel* with a fundamental frequency movement that continued into the final
√; the result sounded nonnatural and nonnative. On the other hand, in languages
uch as Lithuanian the fundamental frequency contour clearly includes both a vowel
nd a postvocalic resonant.

t is an empirical question how much tolerance a language permits in this
ntegration for speaker idiosyncrasy.

The integration rules (see Fig. 2.4) will have to perform at least the
ollowing tasks: adjust segmental durations; and align segmental and
uprasegmental specifications in time.

In considering segment duration three aspects have to be taken into
.ccount. A phoneme may be thought of as having firstly an intrinsic duration
.ssociated with it, which is then adjusted by the realisation rules according
o segmental environment (e.g. the shortening of vowels before voiceless
·bstruents in English); and thirdly each syllable in the suprasegmental
trand will have a duration factor associated with it, affected by nucleus
·lacement and type, and other intonational features, which will define the
hythm of the utterance. These factors will interact with the segment
lurations (probably in a complex way – vowels and consonants, syllable
nitials and finals, may not all be lengthened proportionally in, for example,
·uclear position) to produce the durational properties of the segments.

The necessity and nature of temporal integration has already been
xemplified in the quotation above from Lehiste, by a deaf speaker's failure
n this respect. Loudness as well as pitch will have to be correctly aligned:

51

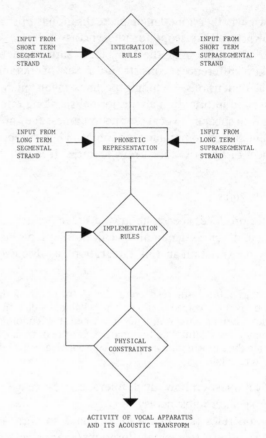

2.4 Integration rules, phonetic representation, implementation rules and physic constraints

Kratochvil (1973:345) shows how Modern Standard Chinese tone 3 befor another tone 3 receives the same fundamental frequency shape, unde sandhi, as tone 2, but retains a difference in amplitude shape.

2.3.7 *Phonetic representation*

So far questions about the nature of the phonetic representation have no been addressed. The whole concept of a phonetic representation i problematical; it is dealt with more extensively in Nolan (1982a). At first might seem that the nature of the speaker/hearer's phonetic representatio is a matter of purely theoretical interest, but in fact it has considerab bearing on the central issues of speaker recognition – the character o between-speaker differences, and within-speaker variation; and so it will be discussed in some detail here.

A first question concerns what information the phonetic representation contains. Andrew Crompton (personal communication) has suggested a formulation which corrects the view implicit in a lot of work, and reinforced by segmental 'narrow phonetic' transcriptions, that a phonetic representation is merely a string of phonemes with some allophonic detail added; rather, according to him, the phonetic representation specifies

all the linguistically relevant features of an utterance, where by linguistically relevant I refer to anything language users can make use of or react to; this therefore includes, for instance, voice quality differences of a dialectal or idiolectal kind.

However there is tension in this formulation between 'linguistically relevant' and 'anything language users can make use of or react to', since listeners can react to aspects of the speech signal which neither derive from any facet of the speaker's communicative intent, nor constitute part of the particular linguistic system (dialect, accent, etc.) used by the speaker, but are purely intrinsic; for instance, it was shown by Lass *et al.* (1978) that listeners can judge a speaker's height and weight from speech samples to within, on average, 1.5 inches and 4 pounds respectively – presumably on the basis of absolute formant frequencies and bandwidths, fundamental frequency, and other such features. These intrinsic properties are not linguistically relevant, given the premise that any individual can potentially control the complete resources of the linguistic system as a vehicle for the transmission of the types of communicative intent discussed in 2.3.3.

Crompton (1981:7) recognises this tension:

Such things are by their nature outside the control of speakers, and the properties of the speech signal to which they give rise are neither universal nor part of any individual language. This suggests that they should not be represented in [the phonetic representation]. On the other hand, it is a fact that listeners are able to identify talkers on the basis of their personal quality, of which these biologically determined characteristics are a part. It would therefore appear that our linguistic knowledge includes details of the personal characteristics of individual talkers, and this must presumably be accounted for in a comprehensive theory of linguistic abilities. . . How these two conflicting arguments are to be reconciled is not clear to me.

However it is argued in Nolan (1982a) that one of the two ways in which a phonetic representation must be *remote* from the physical acoustic signal is that it is the product of a process of *normalisation* (across speakers) – it is the level at which all linguistically relevant information in completely equivalent utterances is identically represented for speaker and listeners. That language users have available the kind of information of intrinsic origin exemplified above is a by-product of this normalisation process, not part of the phonetic representation itself.

If such purely intrinsic information were to be included in the phonetic representation it would mean firstly that the speaker would be redundantly programming himself to do what he can't avoid doing; and, more importantly, there would be no possibility of regarding the phonetic representation as a level of information neutral to different language users – the level at which they can judge two utterances by two physically different speakers as being in all respects linguistically equivalent.

A complicating corollary of this viewpoint, which must be noted, is that for the same physical signal-token, the phonetic representations of speaker and hearer (or those of two hearers) need not be identical – the absence of nasal resonances in the signal might be due to intrinsic adenoidal denasality, and therefore not specified in the phonetic representation of the speaker; but be incorrectly inferred by a listener as specified in it (i.e. intended), leading at a higher level to inferences about its possible informative import (regional–sociolinguistic, for example), or communicative intent (where the speaker intended to transmit regional information). And since the sources of intrinsic features (e.g. a long vocal tract) are usually imitable within limits (e.g. by larynx-lowering), listeners will never *know* that two utterances are equivalent in phonetic representation – they can only hypothesise that they are.

The second question concerns the domain in which the phonetic representation exists. It may be that as part of a model of the knowledge that a speaker has about his language the phonetic representation's dimensions are purely abstract, and of the same theoretical status as syntactic constructs such as *sentence, noun*, and so on, and would have equally specifiable mappings into perceptual, acoustic, and articulatory domains (Crompton 1981). However, this merely sidesteps the issue of whether speakers' behaviour indicates that the knowledge they have of phonetic properties is, perhaps, in one domain rather than another. If mapping between the three domains were absolutely isomorphic, the issue would not be resolvable; but the mapping is not one-to-one, in so far that each successive transformation in the direction articulation-acoustics-audition involves information loss – compare Jakobson *et al.* (1952:12–13):

Each of the consecutive stages, from articulation to perception, may be predicted from the preceding stage. Since with each subsequent stage the selectivity increases, this predictability is irreversible and some variables of any antecedent stage are irrelevant for the subsequent stage. The exact measurement of the vocal tract permits the calculation of the sound wave, but the same acoustical phenomenon may be obtained by altogether different means

– and therefore it seems legitimate to ask, when speakers believe themselves to be producing utterances with the same phonetic properties, in which domain(s) the sameness exists. If evidence could be found that speakers producing phonetically same effects exploit different articulatory strategies, this would argue in favour of the phonetic representation being an auditory 'goal' which the speaker is free to implement as best he can. (Note that 'auditory' here implies some linguistic-specific transformation of primary auditory space abstracted away from intrinsic speaker differences – modelling such a space is a considerable challenge for phonetics.)

In fact such evidence does exist. Care must be taken in interpreting likely evidence, as some of it ambiguously indicates either sameness of auditory target or of vocal tract configuration, as indicated by MacNeilage (1979:18–20). This is probably the case with several experiments: with Lindblom *et al.*'s (1979) demonstration that speakers achieve accurate vowel formant frequencies even immediately at voice onset despite bite blocks anchoring the jaw at abnormal degrees of opening; also with Bell-Berti's (1975) evidence that some American English speakers use muscular action to expand the pharynx to sustain glottal airflow in voiced stops, while others allow it to expand passively; and with the finding of Bell-Berti *et al.* (1978) that American English speakers could be sorted into two categories according to genioglossus activity in front vowels – decreasing activity corresponding either to decreasing vowel height (i:>ɪ>e:>ɛ) or to the tense vowel/lax vowel distinction (i:>e:>ɪ>ɛ); and with the presence in one but absence in another speaker of interarytenoid muscle activity in controlling glottal opening, measured by Sawashima *et al.* (1978).

More clearly indicative of auditory goals is the finding of Harshman *et al.* (1977), using factor analysis of vocal tract cross-sectional area (the 'configurations' themselves, note) over a set of vowels, that different speakers used different proportions of the two principal 'movement' factors (possibly as a consequence of anatomical differences, they suggest). This study is complemented by that of Perkell (1979), who shows (through direct palatography) considerable variation across subjects in tongue-palate contact for particular vowels; he contends that his results, along with those of other authors, suggest (1979:375)

that each individual does what is necessary to produce an appropriate acoustic output.

Delattre (1967) uses x-ray and spectrographic evidence to show that some American English speakers achieve a retroflex quality without in fact raising the tongue tip, but by bunching the tongue – the so-called 'molar' *r*. Lieberman (1967) produces evidence that different speakers producing similar fundamental frequency curves can have different patterns of subglottal pressure variation, and suggests they may therefore be compensating with different patterns of laryngeal tensioning (e.g. 1967:80–1, 85–6). Most telling is the finding of Riordan (1977) that if lip rounding is artificially prevented from occurring on rounded vowels, speakers nevertheless achieve a lowering of formants by compensatory larynx lowering. An auditory goal is being achieved as best possible by an alternative implementary strategy.

Input to the phonetic representation will be from the integration rules, already discussed, and from the long term strands. The input from the latter will be in the form of a value in each of the phonetic dimensions which will be stated at the beginning of an utterance. A long term value may, of course, be reset during the course of an utterance for communicative effect. A distinction may exist between two kinds of long term value: *null* versus *non-null*. A null value would be the equivalent, in Tatham's (1969:18) categories of articulatory event, of a 'controllable intrinsic event' when it is not in fact being controlled; that is, a null value instructs the vocal apparatus to perform in the long term in the way most 'natural' to it (consistent of course with the requirements at any point of the primary strands). For example, in terms of larynx height, it is assumed that there is a larynx position of least effort given the satisfaction of the other strands, and this would be permitted by a null value; a speaker may, however, produce a raised larynx quality, which would result from a specific non-null value, counteracting the most 'natural' articulatory implementation. Note that a non-null value need not be communicative; it may be a *default* value which the speaker habitually adopts, making an extrinsic contribution to his voice quality, but which has no communicative value in the speech community and is merely informative of his identity. Thus, at the level of mapping from communicative intent onto the long term strands, values may be distinguished as *default* versus *determined*, the latter resulting from the mapping of some aspect of communicative intent.

Figure 2.5 gives a very schematic impression of part of a phonetic representation – no claim is made about the correctness, and certainly not the comprehensiveness, of the dimensions shown. Although the dimensions are labelled in acoustic terms, they should be interpreted as their equivalents in the transformed auditory space. (For instance, the F_1 and F_2 dimensions would represent not peaks in dB on a Hz scale, but, to the best approximation discovered by recent empirical work (see e.g. Bladon and Lindblom 1981), peaks in sones (perceptual loudness units) on a Bark (auditory critical band) scale after smoothing by a function emulating the spreading of energy distribution along the basilar membrane; subject

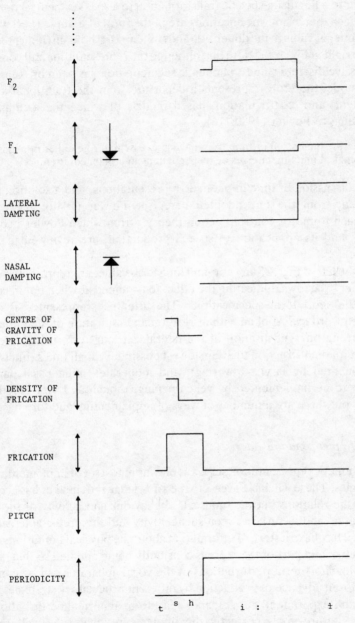

2.5 Schematic impression of part of a phonetic representation

further to a linguistic-specific transformation to a speaker-neutral domain.)

In each dimension specifications are in the form of a duple (v, t) where v is the integer value in the dimension and t its temporal domain (indicated from left to right in Fig. 2.5). Note that although the representation still consists in successive discrete values, phonemic segmentation has been broken down. The model therefore represents a departure from the traditional kind of 'segment' and 'coarticulation' based models of which the assumptions, according to Fowler (1980:116),

exclude the dimension of time from having an essential role either in defining the phonological units themselves or their relations in a planned utterance.

For a discussion of time in phonetic representations, and a solution rather different from the one adopted here, see Fowler (1980); the general approach to motor control, 'action theory', from which Fowler's solution stems, and its application to speech production, are reviewed in Nolan (1982c).

At the left of Fig. 2.5 any non-null long term values are represented on the diagram by arrows, indicating the effect to be aimed at when not in conflict with the short term specifications. The utterance represented is of the English word *teal*, spoken with affrication and aspiration of the initial stop and strong pharyngalisation of the lateral; all long term values are null, except for an instruction to attain lowest possible F_1 at all times (likely to be implemented by larynx lowering), and moderately high nasal damping (likely to be implemented by velic opening, though as Laver (1980:77ff) points out there are a number of ways of implementing auditory nasality).

2.3.8 *Implementation rules*

The phonetic representation serves as one input to a set of implementational strategies. These will have access to the knowledge the speaker has acquired about the relations between muscular behaviour and activity of the vocal apparatus, and in turn between such activity and the predictable acoustic result. They have a store of information about the physical limitations of the apparatus, and part of this store is constantly being updated so that, where possible, short term perturbations of the vocal apparatus can be compensated for in advance of production by different articulatory strategies (as in Riordan's experiment, above); and, apart from abnormal perturbations, to achieve future goals correctly the implementational rules will require feedback from present and past activity of the apparatus (for example very different muscular activity will be required to produce the [i] in the two sequences [ci] and [qi]).

If the whole point of the implementational rules is to achieve identical auditory effect for (presumed) identical phonetic representations in the face of individuals' diverse vocal apparatus, it seems at first paradoxical to claim (note the diamond in Fig. 2.4) that the implementation rules contribute speaker-specific acoustic features. The reason, however, is that strategies will strive to implement as accurately as possible certain 'primary' auditory specifications in the phonetic representation; different implementation strategies may achieve these equally well, but have different 'secondary' effects. A possible example of this is the tongue-tip versus molar strategies for achieving auditory retroflex quality (see Delattre, above p. 55); a curling up and back of the tongue will tend in an intrinsically 'natural' gesture (if not 'controlled' or 'resisted' for phonological reasons) to cause following alveolar sounds to become retroflex, which is not the case after molar *r*. In this case different implementary strategies for an effect of high priority lead to different secondary consequences where the phonetic representation has a high tolerance. Another situation to consider might be the juxtaposition of two targets of equal priority but conflicting value, where a number of transitional strategies will be equally tolerated. These matters are discussed more specifically in Chapter 3 on speaker-specific coarticulatory behaviour.

2.3.9 *Physical constraints*

The vocal apparatus itself is perhaps the most obvious source of phonetic differences between speakers. What it is essential to recognise, however, is that it does not determine particular acoustic characteristics of a person's speech, but merely the range within which variation in a particular parameter is constrained to take place. Thus it is certainly true to say that the dimensions of a person's vocal tract, or the length and mass of his vocal folds, will in some sense 'determine' his formant frequencies and fundamental frequency, respectively, and may even define 'optimum' values for him in these parameters (compare the notion of a 'null' long term specification); but the *plasticity* of the vocal tract is such that his scope for variation in these parameters is considerable (e.g. by raising/lowering the larynx, and imposing a greater/lesser degree of tension on the vocal folds). An indication of the direction and magnitude of the acoustic variation possible from an individual speaker, though even then not its furthest limits, will be apparent in Chapter 4.

There is, in fact, no acoustic feature which escapes the plasticity of the vocal tract. Nasals such as [m], [n] are often spoken of as if they did, since nasal resonances are thought of as depending on the nasal cavity of which the dimensions cannot be wilfully altered. But the spectrum of a nasal depends not just on the nasal cavities, but on the complete pharynx-nasal tube and oral sidebranch; changes in tongue body position will therefore alter (especially the frequency of the antiresonances in) the complete output spectrum.

Is this tantamount, then, to claiming that there are in fact no 'intrinsic features' which 'derive solely from the invariant absolutely uncontrollable physical foundation of the speaker's vocal apparatus' (Laver 1976:57)? It means rather that intrinsic features in general take the form of ranges within which variation may take place, and of complex interactions: for example, though a person may lower his formant frequencies by lowering his larynx, muscular interdependencies may occasion an alteration in phonation type (see Chapter 4); or the top end of an individual's frequency range may only be attainable both with a change of phonation type to falsetto, and a raising of the larynx (affecting formant frequencies) consequent upon having to tension the vocal folds in an extreme way.

Intrinsic features may be classified along a continuum of permanence. Some factors underlying them, such as the size, mass, composition and innervation of the organs of speech, change only slowly through time (e.g. as the result of ageing). Others, such as states of health (colds, laryngitis, etc.) last days or weeks, whilst effects of fatigue and diurnal rhythms, emotional states, and experimental phonetic intervention, are even more transient. For references to the effect on voice quality of a variety of intrinsic factors see Laver (1979).

An independent cross-cutting classification of intrinsic constraints divides them into *configurational* and *dynamic* constraints. Configurational constraints comprise the physical limits on the size and shape of the vocal tract, and the relative position of the articulators. Under configurational constraints would also be included differences of composition of the vocal tract – for example, the acoustic boundary effects at the walls of the vocal tract might vary according to the thickness of fatty tissue in the boundary walls. The main acoustic dimensions which have limits imposed on them by intrinsic constraints are formant frequencies and bandwidths, fundamental frequency, presence and frequency of antiformants (particularly in the case of blockage of the velic port), and intensity and frequency distribution of fricative energy (dependent, for instance, on dentition).

Dynamic constraints impose upper limits on the rate and acceleration of articulators, and on the rate of change of vocal tract configuration, including upper limits on the transmission of neural impulses. Little is known about such constraints, but it is reasonable to assume that different speakers may have differential agility in speech production, in the same way that speed of movement and coordination differ in other physical skills such as gymnastics or playing a musical instrument.

2.3.10 *Mapping of communicative intent*

It is time now to consider the ways in which communicative intent is mapped onto the resources of the linguistic mechanism which has been outlined above. The crucial importance of this mapping from the point of view of speaker recognition lies in the need to be aware of potential changes in the phonetic signal of a particular speaker according to his communicative intent and in interaction with the situation in which he is speaking. As noted in 2.2 there has been a very inadequate amount of attention paid to this mapping in speaker recognition work.

2.3.10.1 *Cognitive intent* The cognitive part of communicative intent provides perhaps the main exception to this neglect, since it is readily apparent that a change in the cognitive meaning of an utterance, causing a change either in selection of lexical items and/or their syntagmatic sequencing, will cause utterances to be phonetically non-equivalent. Speaker verification schemes, therefore, require the speaker to produce some pre-agreed sequence of words, which is then compared with a stored reference token or tokens of the same words; and in legal applications for speaker identification, attempts are made to elicit the same sequence of words from the suspect as occur at some point in the recording of the criminal (e.g. Bolt *et al.* 1979:75; Tosi 1979:110).

Cognitive intent is also mapped indirectly onto the suprasegmental strand, since syntactic structure is one of the factors which determines the choice of intonation patterns (intonational 'words'). However, it cannot be assumed that a particular syntactic structure will be associated with a given intonation pattern, since choice of intonation pattern is also determined partly by, for example, affective factors – as Crystal points out (1969:3) the two patterns '*What are you ‚doing?* and '*What are you ‚doing?* are equally possible, but the second is

generally more serious and abrupt in its implications – at least for British English – than the more friendly and interested [first pattern].

In general, cognitive intent seems not to be mapped either into the realisation rules of the two primary strands – increasing the frontness of the realisation of a vowel phoneme, reducing the pitch movement of a fall–rise nucleus, using persistent lowered larynx voice or a high pitch range seem unlikely to change the 'factual, propositional' content of an utterance (see 2.3.3). However there may be exceptions; there may be processes which in fact change or override the cognitive meaning of a lexical item; for example, the lexical entry for *wonderful* would be unlikely to contain a meaning such as 'bad', but it is quite possible to utter *Oh yes he's a wonderful cook* in such a way (perhaps with reduced pitch range throughout, heavy nasalisation, and creaky voice) that it makes little sense to consider the cognitive intent of the speaker to be derivable from the literal meaning of the words – in fact a meaning may be reversed.

2.3.10.2 *Affective intent* The affective part of communicative intent, the attitudes and feelings that a speaker wishes to convey, is mapped in complex ways. Some are not of direct concern for the phonetic aspects of speaker recognition – choice of lexical item may be influenced, and of syntactic structure, but these will be obvious in the everyday sense of resulting in a 'different utterance'.

From the phonetic point of view, affective information is first and foremost thought of in terms of mapping onto the suprasegmental strand. The mapping involves both direct influence on the choice of discrete contrasting intonation patterns ('intonational words') at the level of the intonational lexicon (which is reflected, for example, in the guidance to learners about attitude conveyed, given in respect of the various contrasting tone groups of their analysis by O'Connor and Arnold (1973)) and also mapping into the realisation rules where less discrete suprasegmental effects are specified; for example, a high fall nucleus according to O'Connor and Arnold (1973:125) conveys in statements 'a sense of involvement', but it is not counter-intuitive to suggest that the degree of involvement may be reflected in the size of the pitch movement of the high fall.

Affective information may also be mapped into the long term strands. A speaker may replace his default value for phonation type, for example, by one determined by the attitude he wishes to convey – a speaker with a normally creaky phonation type might adopt a more breathy phonation type in order to convey sympathy; and in the suprasegmental strand a speaker with a default pitch range which is narrow might broaden it in order to communicate enthusiasm.

The significance of these mappings from the point of view of speaker recognition is that they underlie phonetic properties which may be selected as speaker-specific parameters; yet unless the affective communicative intent of two otherwise similar utterances is the same (highly unlikely in the case of a recording of a sequence of words used in the commission of a crime and the same sequence of words recorded in a police station) there is no guarantee that affective mapping will not confound identification or elimination based on those properties.

2.3.10.3 *Social intent* A simplistic, and perhaps popular, view of social information in speech would suggest that social (including geographical) group membership within a language community is reflected in the use of certain phonetic features; and that by extracting these features it is possible to assign an individual to a particular group. Whilst this would not count as identification of an individual, it would at least be part of a process of subclassification of speakers, and therefore constitute a useful component of the process of speaker recognition. Presumably this is what Bolt *et al.* (1979:67) have in mind when they write

Training in the performance of voice identification should include more extensive instruction in related scientific disciplines than is usually included at present. . . For example, a knowledge of dialectology would show how shifts in vowel color could produce important differences between voices being examined by listening.

It is, however, necessary to reinterpret what they actually say, which seems only to make sense if 'produce important differences' is replaced by 'constitute differences of social significance'.

It is indeed true that dialectology (concerned predominantly with regional variation, and often in rural communities) and more recently sociolinguistics (concerned with social stratification of language, so far particularly in urban areas) have recorded many phonetic differences between the speech of different groups. However, if such differences were purely in the linguistic system which a speaker of a dialect or sociolect has at his disposal compared with a speaker of another, then the differences would be merely informative rather than communicative, and have no place in the present discussion.

But one of the most striking discoveries of the type of work in sociolinguistics which Labov pioneered is that each speaker has control over a range of styles of speech – Labov (1972:208): 'As far as we can see, there are no single-style speakers' – and, most significantly for speaker recognition, that the sociolinguistic variables along which speakers of different social strata will employ different values are the same variables along which stylistic variation takes place; Labov (1972:240):

The same sociolinguistic variable is used to signal social and stylistic stratification.

Fig. 2.6, adapted from Labov (1972), shows this situation schematically. The lines each relate to a particular independently defined socioeconomic group; the vertical axis shows that each higher social grouping uses a higher percentage of a prestige form; and moving from left to right shows how in each class use of prestige variants increases with the formality of the context. (Labov elicited speech under the following situations of increasing formality, or likely attention to speech: interviews, reading a text, reading

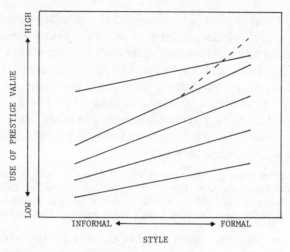

2.6 Schematic representation of the use of a prestige value of a sociolinguistic variable according to class and style

word lists, and reading minimal pairs of words; and he also attempted where possible to obtain as the least formal style recordings of casual conversation when the informants no longer had their attention focussed on the fact that they were being recorded. A detail of Fig. 2.6 which is not of direct concern here is that at the most formal end of the style-range a lower group may surpass a higher group's usage of a prestige value – in Labov's data the 'Lower Middle Class' and 'Upper Middle Class' respectively. He terms this phenomenon 'hypercorrection', and it is indicated by the dotted line. Apparently this behaviour only occurs when the variable in question is involved in a linguistic change in progress (1972:Ch. 5).) In fact two points are of significance for speaker recognition. Firstly, for many variables, such as the use of /n/ versus /ŋ/ in the *-ing* suffix in New York (Labov 1966) and in Norwich (Trudgill 1974a), a speaker in a given context does not produce either 100% or 0% of the variable; as Trudgill (1974b:40) puts it in relation to another of the socially significant New York variables, presence versus absence of postvocalic *r*:

the researcher could not predict on any one occasion whether an individual would say *cah* or *car*, but he could show that, if he was of a certain social class, age, and sex, he would use one or other variant approximately x percent of the time, on average, in a given situation.

Labov (1972:101) exemplifies this kind of variation by giving the order of occurrence of values for one informant in each of two styles (the variable is the *th* sound of words like *thing*, where $[\theta] = 1$ and $[t] = 2$); casual speech:

1221221111; careful speech: 221111111111112121. (Whether the apparently random remaining variation can be explained by assuming that each individual word has its own index which interacts with the context and at a threshold resultant value switches *all* occurrences of *that word* discretely from one category to another, as suggested by Kerswill (1980) on the basis of data from Cambridge English on replacement of final [t] with glottal stop, remains to be further explored.) From the viewpoint of speaker recognition, this means that the occurrence of a value of a variable in a limited sample of speech cannot be taken as predicting its reliable occurrence throughout all the speech of that speaker in the given context.

The second point is that, since sociolinguistic stratification and stylistic variation are taking place along the same dimensions (Labov 1972:240)

it may therefore be difficult to interpret any signal by itself – to distinguish, for example, a casual salesman from a careful pipefitter.

As a concrete example (from Labov 1972:103ff) the indices for post-vocalic *r* (higher indices show greater proportion of -*r* actually pronounced) for two informants were: Miriam L. (lawyer) – casual speech 32, careful (interview) speech 47; Doris H. ('lower middle class') – casual speech 00, careful speech 31. Thus both speakers, from different strata, attain virtually the same value (31/32) but in different styles. So it is not the case that an individual has one all-purpose manner of speaking which immediately pins him down to a particular group, but rather he has control over a stylistic range which overlaps the stylistic range of at least some other groups. From the perspective of speaker identification, it is not acceptable to assume *a priori* that, for instance, suspects interpret the provision of samples for voice comparison as a context of equivalent formality to the circumstance in which the incriminating recording was made – at the very least, it is implicit in work within Labov's paradigm that awareness of being recorded itself induces a different style of speaking. It is not clear on what basis the problem of style-shifting has been ignored in discussions of the feasibility of speaker recognition.

So far in this discussion the focus has been on those variables which a speaker may manipulate, and may therefore be considered as communicative (whether the speaker is communicating his allegiance to a particular group, or his understanding of the formality of a particular context). Not all variables, however, are of this type; Labov (e.g. 1972:314) draws a distinction between *indicators* and *markers*.

Indicators are linguistic features which are embedded in a social matrix, showing social differentiation by age or social group, but which show no pattern of style shifting and appear to have little evaluative force [for the speakers

65

themselves]. . .*Markers*. . .do show stylistic stratification as well as social stratification. Though they lie below the level of conscious awareness, they will produce regular responses on subjective reaction tests.

The variables mentioned above are examples of markers; Labov cites the merger in American English of the vowels of *hock* and *hawk* in the speech of some, according to region, class, and age, but which nonetheless does not undergo style-shifting, as an indicator.

Further, certain markers may attain social recognition and be the subject of comment among speakers themselves – these Labov calls *stereotypes*. In terms of the present model, a marker would result from the mapping of social communicative intent at some point in the linguistic mechanism resulting in a *determined* value; an indicator would be the product simply of a particular speaker's *default* value at some point in the mechanism – a default value, of course, within the limits set by the particular variety of which he feels himself to be a speaker.

A specific aspect of the social context in which a person is speaking requires further comment, namely the other participant(s) in the interaction. The context must in fact take its definition in part from the participants' interpretation of their interpersonal relationship and relative status; it is not enough for a speaker to know that he is in a situation, such as a chance meeting on the street, where casual conversation might be the norm, in order for him to know what style to adopt – he also needs to assess his relationship to the other person, as for example his friend, his boss, or his subordinate and junior. As Brown and Levinson (1979:314) point out, a specially important distinction in this respect concerns whether the two participants feel themselves to be members of the same group or not (which itself is dependent on context – even the shop steward and the manager may feel that common nationality overrides their normal outgroup relationship when they are stranded in a foreign airport):

It seems a reasonable hypothesis that if both parties to an interaction are drawn from one group then it is likely that the social relationship obtaining between them will be organized around nongroup (or subgroup) identities – sex, kinship, role, personality, or whatever the relevant criteria may be. On the other hand, if the parties belong to different groups, then their group identities are likely to be the ones that (at least in large part) determine their relationship. So the distinction between ingroup and outgroup relationships is fundamental to the organization of interaction for any two parties.

An instance of ingroup versus outgroup interaction relevant to the present topic might be the (tapped telephone) conversation of a criminal with his colleague, versus the verbal interaction of a suspect with a policeman or 'voiceprint' expert. In response to the ingroup/outgroup nature of his relation to the other participants the speaker may choose to make his speech more similar to that of the other (*convergence*), or in the case of desired dissociation, more dissimilar (*divergence*) – see, for example, Giles *et al.* (1979:369); further, the degree of convergence may even change during the time course of an interaction with one individual, and according to the topic of conversation (see Douglas-Cowie 1978). It may be that convergence is a very basic part of the human communicative ability, since Lieberman (1967:45) reports evidence that when talking with a parent, a ten-month-old boy lowered the fundamental frequency of his babble compared with when he was alone, and that he lowered it more with the father than with the mother. Crystal (1975:79) suggests that 'This "vocal empathy" seems a normal adult phenomenon also'. Although there seem to have been few if any studies of this kind of convergence, which may be only minimally sociolinguistic in that it involves extrinsic accommodation to a partially intrinsically determined feature of the other's speech, it cannot be ignored in a theory of speaker recognition, and is ripe for research.

The phonetic mapping of a speaker's vocal intent, and likewise the existence of variety-specific default values ('indicators'), is not confined to any one part of the language mechanism; although the majority of sociolinguistic studies have concentrated on the realisation of segments (and on what in the present model would have to be regarded as differences in the phonemic composition of lexical items), the suprasegmental strand is equally implicated (see e.g. Pellowe and Jones 1978; Knowles 1978) and increasing attention is being paid to the long term 'voice quality' reflexes of these strands (e.g. Labov 1972:40; Trudgill 1974a:185ff; Esling 1978; Knowles 1978).

The percentage of phonetic features which are subject to manipulation by the speaker as sociolinguistic markers, and subject to variation according to his interpretation of the context, is hard to estimate; however it is clear from the work published over the last 15 years in sociolinguistics that such markers are far from being isolated phenomena – at least in urban communities. The case presented above that they constitute a problem for speaker recognition may turn out to be overstated, but the onus is properly on those who claim parameters to be successful in identifying speakers in the laboratory to demonstrate that these parameters are resistant to the kinds of variation that occur in different social contexts – particularly since this variation, as is inevitable on the one hand from the ambiguity with respect to class and style which characterise markers, and on the other from the definition of 'convergence' phenomena, will have precisely the effect of making one speaker sound more like another.

If speaker recognition is to be reliable and efficient, then in theory the problems posed by stylistic variation might be circumvented in two ways. Firstly, knowledge of the ways a community operates with its markers might be used to 'normalise' the value obtained in some dimension for a particular speaker in a given context. This solution seems improbable, given the difficulty in practice of knowing how a speaker interprets any given social context (other than circularly through the way he speaks), and the complexity of discovering the way in which markers operate in a community (especially when the problems posed by speakers who have spent time in other communities and as a result have been affected by other linguistic systems are taken into consideration). The second solution would be to ensure that speaker recognition parameters derive only from features of speech which are inert with respect to social context – that is, from indicators (in Labov's sense), or from features which are uncorrelated with social stratification. However, it may be that further exploration of the phenomenon of convergence will be required to ascertain that features do in fact exist which are inert to all aspects of social context in its broadest sense.

2.3.10.4 *Accentual versus personal information in speech* Here it is appropriate to consider the division sometimes made of information in the speech signal over and above cognitive information into *accentual* versus *personal* (e.g. Ladefoged 1967:104). It should be clear by now that the notion of accent, as a subdivision of a language associated with a particular speech community, and defined by the cooccurrence of a static set of phonetic/phonological properties, is no longer tenable, given the variability of some at least of those properties according to context. Two other possibilities exist.

The term accent could be restricted to the set of properties which occur at some point in the stylistic continuum for a particular speech community – possibly at the least formal style since (for English at least, due to the wide spread of certain prestige forms of pronunciation) it is here that the greatest diversity would be manifest. This then produces the problem of labelling what it is that the speakers of that community are speaking in more formal contexts, which is nevertheless distinct from the pronunciation of other speech communities.

A more promising possibility is to consider an accent to consist in the complete stylistic range of pronunciations controlled by members of a speech community. Under this interpretation it might be feasible to maintain a distinction between accentual information, determined by the community-agreed sociolinguistic system, and personal information, where the speaker has chosen idiosyncratic values within the tolerances allowed by the 'accent'. However this presumes that all the speakers have equal control over the stylistic facilities provided by the 'accent' in this broad sense; that is, that their stylistic repertoires are equivalent. This is clearly not the case; as pointed out by Brown and Levinson (1979:309) membership of particular groups in the community will restrict a speaker to subparts of the total range of variation:

A. . .way in which group or category affiliation can be signalled by the code that a speaker utilizes derives from the fact that different groups within the speech community may command different subsets of the total linguistic resources available in the community.

Moreover, the restriction of repertoires of pronunciation does not end at group level, but carries on down to individual level; occasioned by differences in education, breadth of linguistic contact, and so on.

Three points may be made in relation to individual repertoires. Firstly, even given a complete and correct description of the system of social and stylistic variables available to members of a speech community it would still not be possible to extrapolate from a recording of a speaker in one social context to his performance in a different one, since it will not be known how far his flexibility is hampered by repertoire restrictions. Secondly, it is apparent that a contributory factor to speaker idiosyncrasy, and indeed one which may not be insignificant when listeners categorise speakers, is the stylistic flexibility of the speaker – the extent of the subpart of the 'accent', in the broad sense, that he controls. (For example, a labourer may not achieve much convergence towards his bank manager's speech during an interview at the bank, despite a sense that this is required of him; the labourer's brother, on the other hand, attending university, may be equally 'at home' in a relatively formal interview style or the informal style appropriate when working alongside his brother on a building site during his holiday; and in turn the bank manager, forced to seek employment on the building site after being caught with his fingers in the till, may discover inadequacies in his repertoire.) And thirdly it follows from the fact that one facet of personal quality finds its definition only within the systematic stylistic relationships of the 'accent', that a sharp division between the two kinds of information is not feasible.

2.3.10.5 *Self-presentation* Turning now to the exploitation of phonetic parameters in order to communicate a self-image to others, Scherer (1979:200) explains

actors [= participants in interactions] often use behavioural cues for the presentation of self and, given the importance of speech in social interaction, it is not surprising that speech cues are prime candidates for self-presentation purposes.

'Self-presentation' as used below may turn out to be too umbrella-like a term, intended as it is to include aspects of the view of self from bio-physical characteristics through to personality dimensions such as extroversion–introversion, yet it seems to provide a useful category of communicative intent distinct from the communication of purely short term emotions and attitudes (affective intent), and from the communication of information about interpreted positions within a purely social matrix.

At one end of the continuum speakers may manipulate, within the intrinsic constraints of their own vocal apparatus, characteristics of speech which over the population as a whole will be correlated with bio-physical characteristics. A person wishing to communicate a self-image of a large physique might therefore adopt low formant and fundamental frequencies as would normally be expected from a person of that physique; similarly the voice correlates in terms of formant frequencies and fundamental frequency of maleness and femaleness (see e.g. Coleman 1971, 1976) may to some extent be adopted by a speaker within his intrinsic limits. It seems probable that these kinds of information, closely related as they are to intrinsic limitations on vocal capability, will be mapped onto the long term strands – Scherer's (1979) discussion of personality markers (including both intended and unintended) in 'vocal aspects' of speech is confined to long term properties.

At the other end of the continuum, more indirect culturally mediated relationships exist between personality dimensions and phonetic dimensions. Among those in the work cited by Scherer (1979) are positive correlations (for American male speakers) between (mean) fundamental frequency and self-attributions (on inventories and rating scales) of achievement, task ability, sociability, dominance, and aggressiveness (p. 154); (for German male speakers) between mean fundamental frequency and self-ratings of adjustment, orderliness and lack of autonomy (p. 156); between extroversion and intensity (p. 158); and between breathy voice and introversion, neurotic tendency, and anxiety. It appears that more complicated interrelations may exist, abstract aspects of personality being mediated in their mapping by the sociolinguistic mechanisms: Douglas-Cowie (1978:47–51) reports that the degree of convergence (in terms of three segmental variables) of rural dialect speakers to an outsider's standard pronunciation in interviews 'is often clearly related to their social ambition rather than their social status in traditional terms', 'social ambition' being assessed from ratings made by the other informants, all informants knowing each other well. Pellowe and Jones (1978:111) note how one female informant's self-image in respect of age is reflected in her choice of the suprasegmental primes they were studying:

amongst women there is an *age trend* which indicates that younger women are realising rises in more and more tone units in which their elders would have realised falls . . . This is a trend which seems to be socially significant for members of the speech community. It seems, for example, to be a behaviour being emulated by *Ar* who in terms of her age should have had a value of +15% or so but who in fact has a value of −26%. (We know independently that *Ar* goes dancing, listens to pop music and reads teenage magazines.)

The sociolinguistic mechanism may also provide means for expression of sexual identity, though rarely as clearly as in Darkhat Mongolian (Trudgill 1974b:89) which has a different vowel system for men versus women; but in many instances (though not all) Trudgill (1974b:91) notes that 'women consistently use forms which more closely approach those of the standard variety or the prestige accent than those used by men'.

2.3.10.6 *Interaction management* According to Duncan (1973:34), speakers may produce three kinds of signal in their attempts to manage the progress of 'speaking turns' in a dialogue:

(a) a turn signal; (b) a turn-claiming suppression signal; and (c) a within turn signal.

The cues for the latter two involve body movements and syntax in the data analysed by Duncan, but intuitively it seems possible that a speaker will increase his pitch or loudness to 'fight off' an attempt at interruption by another speaker. 'Turn signals', whereby the speaker indicates that he feels he has completed his 'turn' and is prepared to allow the other to speak, were found to involve cues including particular intonation patterns, a 'drawling' of certain syllables, and a drop in pitch or loudness.

Lehiste (1975) found similar cues correlating with judgments of whether excerpted sentences had been read paragraph-initially (or in isolation), or paragraph-finally − high fundamental frequency peaks cued isolation and paragraph-initial judgments, and low fundamental frequency, perhaps with laryngealisation (creaky voice), paragraph-final judgments. It may be that the organisation of a read text, or a monologue, into 'paragraphs' has an affinity with the management of verbal interaction between two or more participants.

Further research should increase understanding of the cues speakers rely on to direct the progress of an interaction; and it may then be more possible to assess whether the increase in within-speaker variation they occasion, along, for example, fundamental frequency parameters, constitutes a problem for speaker recognition.

2.4 Summary and discussion

In the preceding sections an attempt has been made to formulate a model which reveals the bases of speaker-specific information in the speech wave, and the sources of its variability – the two being in a symbiotic relation. The model is undoubtedly inadequate in many respects, and in some controversial; but if it appears complex, this is not in itself a shortcoming, for it correctly reflects the immense complexity of the linguistic mechanism and the sophistication of the human communicative ability.

As a starting point the frequently quoted dichotomy between 'organic' and 'learned' sources of between-speaker differences was taken. The inadequacies of this dichotomy, previewed in 2.2, should now be clearer. The first of these is that the 'intrinsic' component of speaker idiosyncrasy is in the form not of absolute values, but of limitations on the variation which a speaker can induce in his vocal apparatus; the data in Chapter 4 amply demonstrate the plasticity of the vocal apparatus and its acoustic consequences. Within-speaker differences can also be caused by changes in intrinsic constraints, due to changes in state of health, etc., but these are not considered in detail here.

If all other sources of idiosyncrasy are lumped together under the heading of 'learned', then it is apparent that, at the very least, different kinds of learning are involved. At the lower end of the model, the speaker acquires by trial and error, rather than by learning through direct imitation of what cannot by its nature be accessible to him, a set of implementational strategies for achieving appropriate auditory phonetic effects. Chapter 3 investigates coarticulatory differences between speakers, which may result from acquired strategy differences at this level. Although the notion is not tested here it is conceivable that it is these strategies below the phonetic representation which are least susceptible to volitional alteration by the speaker.

At higher levels the speaker learns, on the basis of the language use he is exposed to, and arguably also on the basis of innate preconceptions as to the nature of language, a complex mechanism of expression. This mechanism serves for the mapping of different aspects of the communicative intent of the speaker, and this mapping is such that many parts of the mechanism – segmental and suprasegmental, short and long term, primes and realis-ational rules – can be affected by one aspect (e.g. social) of the communicative intent.

At each point where communicative intent is mapped there may be thought of as existing default values which are peculiar to the speaker, though they (normally) fall within the range permitted by the particular variety of the language he speaks. The point in a hyperspace defined by all a speaker's default values might be thought of as constituting his extrinsic personal quality; but this point is a purely fictional abstraction, because in any utterance a speaker will be mapping communicative intent in such a way as to replace some default values by determined values – for example a speaker may have a long term default value of non-nasalisation, and a default value of [ä] for /æ/, but may change these to nasalisation and [æ] when communicating an attitude of irony in a social context where he is converging to a speaker with a different pronunciation.

Within-speaker variability is clearly of concern in speaker recognition, but experiments based on the assumption that this variability results purely from random intrinsic changes in time, for example by getting subjects to read a passage several times over a few months, will not permit theoretically sound extrapolation to the real world. The way a speaker speaks on a given occasion is the result of a complex interaction between his communicative intent, the language mechanism he controls, and the context in which he is speaking. It may be that the within-speaker variation that results is trivial compared with the gross acoustic similarity of utterances from the same vocal apparatus; it may be that the parameters used in 'voiceprint' and automatic speaker identification schemes are just those which are inert to social context, attitude of the speaker, interaction management etc. (however great a coincidence this would be); but these hypothetical states of affairs need to be demonstrated, not assumed *a priori* as at present, if techniques of speaker recognition are to be acceptable outside the laboratory. In the real world, speakers communicate rather than merely exercise their vocal apparatus.

3

Short term parameters: segments and coarticulation

3.1 Introduction and survey

This chapter is concerned with the use of parameters for speaker recognition which are based in the short term strands, and specifically the short term segmental strand. Such parameters require the isolation of portions of the speech signal of limited duration corresponding to the acoustic exponents of abstract primes such as phonemes, or intonation nuclei, and are therefore most likely to be employed in semi-automatic speaker recognition schemes (see 1.1.2) where a human operator performs the *speech* recognition task of identifying the acoustic events corresponding to linguistic units.

In fact, it appears that no work in speaker recognition has yet attempted such a procedure with suprasegmental primes, perhaps because of the less discrete nature of suprasegmental systems, because of the variability of the temporal span of suprasegmental realisations in relation to segments, and also no doubt because of the influence of alphabetically written language, which focusses attention on the segmental strand. However in principle it should be possible for analysts to agree on the identification of a suprasegmental prime (such as a fall–rise nucleus) in samples of speech, and then submit it to automatic acoustic analysis and parameter extraction.

Atal's (1972) work on speaker recognition using pitch (here = fundamental frequency) contours might be construed as based on comparison of complete 'tunes' or 'intonational words' across speakers; he had 10 speakers record the same sentence six times, and used as primary data the pitch contours over complete utterances (time normalised), which were then reduced to 20-dimensional vectors by means of the Karhunen–Loève transformation. Closer consideration, however, reveals not only that this interpretation is inaccurate, but also that the experiments suffer from a neglect of the linguistic mechanism underlying the pitch contours. The interpretation is inaccurate because no attempt appears to have been made to ensure that the tunes used by the different speakers were in any sense linguistically comparable. Crystal (1975:8), for example, reports an experiment where 30 speakers were asked to read four sentences;

considering merely one intonational variable, the position of the nucleus, there were as many as seven different solutions by various speakers for a given sentence, and no sentence had fewer than three different nucleus placements. Furthermore Crystal's sentences were grammatical, semantically non-ambiguous and non-anomalous sentences of English, whilst Atal's 'sentence' was *May we all learn a yellow lion roar*. It will be recalled from 2.3.5.1 that nucleus placement and selection of nucleus type are partially determined by syntactic, and by affective, factors; it is unlikely that 10 speakers will have come to the same conclusion about the 'meaning' of so semantically anomalous a sequence, and hence about the intonation pattern to use on it; therefore the process of across-speaker comparison would be linguistically equivalent to experimentally 'recognising' different speakers on the basis of recordings of them saying each a different word – a capability which is clearly of more relevance to *speech* recognition.

Wolf (1972) measured fundamental frequency at a number of points in utterances, and found these measurements to be among the most efficient at distinguishing speakers. However, again the data derive from read sentences, and the measurement points were defined in terms of segmental events rather than events internal to the suprasegmental strand, so it is not certain that linguistically equivalent suprasegmental measurements were being compared. It seems clear that scope remains for work on short term aspects of the suprasegmental strand which pays more attention to its linguistic structure.

A number of investigators have used the acoustic exponents of segmental primes (phonemes) as the basis of recognition, in systems which require an operator to isolate the relevant acoustic events. Höfker (1977) reports on an experiment which rank ordered 24 German phonemes spoken in isolation on their ability to discriminate 12 speakers. The three nasals /n/, /ŋ/ and /m/ performed best. Wolf (1972) also found two nasal spectral parameters, one from /m/ and one from /n/, this time extracted from read sentences, to be ranked second and third among a number of segmental parameters (behind fundamental frequency parameters – but see above). The nasal cavities are a part of the vocal tract which cannot be altered at will, and, further, there is variation between individuals in their structure and size; but whilst these variations will be reflected in the resonant frequencies of the nasals of different speakers, expectations of constant acoustic cues to identity must be tempered since the nasal tract is not a resonator independent of the rest of the vocal tract – see 2.2. Not all researchers have found nasals clearly superior; Paul *et al.* (1975), using a semi-automatic speaker identification scheme involving visual and aural isolation of phonetic events, ranked 13

American English phonemes in the order /ʊuimɪəɔŋŋʌɚˈɑɛ/ (1975:57). All the rankings discussed so far have circumvented the problem of changes caused in a segment by its phonetic environment – Höfker by using phonemes uttered in isolation, Wolf by using equivalent measurement points in the same sentence read by different speakers, and Paul *et al.* (in the ranking quoted) by using segments with the same environment at either side.

Glenn and Kleiner (1968) describe an experiment involving identification based on the spectrum of nasal sounds in different environments in test and reference data. Words containing /n/ were recorded by 30 speakers reading from a list. Three spectrographic sections taken midway through each occurrence of /n/ were manually quantised into 25-element spectral vectors over the frequency range 1–3 kHz. The three vectors were then averaged to give a speaker 'sample'. A reference vector was formed by averaging 10 samples from each speaker; and in the identification trials, a test vector was judged as having come from speaker X if the angular separation between the reference vector of X and the test vector was smaller than the separation between the reference vector of any of the other speakers and the test vector.

If just one speaker sample was correlated with the thirty reference vectors, a correct identification rate of 43% was obtained. This rose to 93% if the average of 10 speaker samples was used for correlation, and further to 97% if the relevant population of speakers was reduced to 10. These results indicate that quite accurate speaker identification can be achieved on the basis of spectral information taken from individual segments of an utterance, in this case nasals. It is noted by the authors (1968:372) that no account was taken of the phonetic environment of the nasals. If the tests had been restricted to exponents of /n/ in a single environment, or if the effect of coarticulation could somehow have been factored out, it might be expected that within-speaker variation would have been reduced and as a result some of the errors eliminated.

The investigation of nasal parameters in this respect was carried further by Su *et al.* (1974), who examined the effect of coarticulation between the nasal and the following vowel. Recordings from a number of speakers of /hə'CVd/ sequences, where C is /m/ or /n/ and V one of six vowels, were fed into a filter bank. The digitised sampled outputs of the first 25 filters (250–3681 Hz) were used to form spectral vectors, from which samples of the nasal segments were then manually selected.

If no coarticulation had been present in the data, the mean spectrum of /m/ or /n/ followed by front vowels, and that followed by back vowels, would have coincided. In fact, samples from /n/ before front and back vowels formed a single cluster, but samples from /m+front V/ clustered separately from those from /m+back V/, indicating greater coarticulation. This reflects the articulatory fact that in /m/ the tongue is totally free to take up the position of the following vowel, whereas in /n/ it is at least constrained to make contact with the alveolar ridge.

It was found that the detailed clustering of /m/, though always exhibiting the separation, differed from speaker to speaker. A speaker could therefore be characterised by the extent of his coarticulation, quantified as the separation between his samples of /m/ before front, and before back, vowels. Identification experiments with four, and 10 speakers, who were characterised by the difference between their mean /m/ spectra before front and back vowels, achieved 100% identification. Nasal coarticulation, which may be an expression of implementational strategy (see 3.5.2), was claimed by the authors to be a better clue to identity than nasal spectra alone.

3.2 The experiments: aims and structure

3.2.1 *Experimental aims*

The work reported here has a twofold aim: to assess the usefulness for speaker recognition of the acoustic realisations of two English consonant phonemes which have received rather less attention than the nasals; and to gauge how far coarticulation should be taken into account to make fullest use of the speaker-dependent information provided by these phonemes.

The definition of coarticulation given in Daniloff and Hammarberg (1973:239) is accepted here:

we can define coarticulation as the influence of one speech segment upon another; that is, the influence of a phonetic context [environment] upon a given segment.

For the present purposes it is the manifestation of this influence in the acoustic spectrum of sounds which is most important.

3.2.2 *Choice of segments*

The consonant phonemes to be dealt with are /l/ and /r/. A number of considerations led to this choice.

3.2.2.1 *Acoustic grounds* As noted, investigators of segment-based parameters have frequently found useful information in nasal spectra; a nasal consonant with oral occlusion forward of the uvular region has a spectrum with resonances defined by the pharyngeal-oral-nasal cavity system, and antiresonances caused by the shunting of sound transmission by the side chamber, that is the oral cavity behind the occlusion.

The status of the nasals is unique, since no other sounds involve the coupling of a large resonator separate from the normal acoustic pathway from glottis to lips; but in laterals, produced with a central occlusion and a bilateral or unilateral passage, there are introduced into the spectrum antiresonances (or zeros) which interact with the resonances of the oro-pharyngeal system. The major zero occurs in the 2–3 kHz region and is dependent on the length of the shunting cavity behind the apical closure (Fant 1960:164). The zero has the effect of reducing the level of, or cancelling completely, the third formant of the lateral (which is dependent on the mouth cavity in front of the apical constriction and will be centred on the 2.3 to 2.6 kHz region); and of providing high frequency emphasis in the spectrum starting at a value 40% above its centre frequency. F4 occurs around 3 kHz, and is probably dependent on the cavity system behind the apical articulation; the problem arises as to whether to call this peak the third formant in cases where the 'true' F3 has apparently been cancelled out by the antiresonance (see 3.3.2). F_1 may be expected between 200 and 400 Hz and is dependent on the complete cavity system; a lowering of F_1 results from any narrowing of the lateral passage. F_2 is dependent in a complex way on the cavity system behind the apical articulation, and will be considerably affected by the location of a secondary stricture in this cavity system, as in velarisation. An F_2 as low as 800 Hz might be expected in a strongly pharyngalised lateral, and as high as 2 kHz in a palatalised lateral.

English /r/ is generally realised as a frictionless continuant, and has a vowel-like spectrum. Characteristic of [ɹ] as opposed to [l] is the 'lower frequency of F_3 and/or F_4' (Fant 1973:63). O'Connor *et al.* (1957:34) conclude from their synthesis experiments, however, that considerable variation of the formant frequencies is permissible:

we placed the second formant onset frequency of /re/ between 840 and 1560 cps, but we did not say that any particular value between these extremes gave a 'better' /re/ than any other.

We believe this is the most realistic way of stating our findings, since, in different idiolects and dialects, there are many phonetically discriminable sounds which are nevertheless readily identifiable as /r/.

This points to an area of high auditory tolerance in English, where different speakers may be left free by the culturally shared language system to adopt rather different auditory goals.

As well as the interaction of antiresonances with the formant structure, laterals also share with nasals the property of undergoing appreciable articulatory change under the influence of adjacent, notably following, vowels. Coarticulation in /l/ has been shown for American English by Lehiste (1964) and for British RP by Bladon and Al-Bamerni (1976). Both these studies found that first and second formant frequencies of allophones of /l/ were shifted in the direction of the equivalent formants of adjacent vowels; though the effect was most marked in syllable-initial /l/, much less marked in the darker (velarised or pharyngalised) syllable-final allophone, and scarcely manifested in the syllabic allophone; Bladon and Al-Bamerni (1976:149):

[l] coarticulates much more freely than [ɫ], while [ɫ]. . .is the most resistant of the three.

In the present study, investigation has been limited to the syllable-initial allophone, since most coarticulation occurs here, and therefore this allophone perhaps gives hope for a greater range of degrees of coarticulation amongst a population of speakers than do the coarticulation-resistant dark allophones; and since this course allows for closest comparison with the study of Su *et al.* (1974) on nasal coarticulation, as they dealt with syllable-initial nasals in /hə'CVd/ sequences.

The coarticulatory behaviour of /r/ is dissimilar; this phoneme was not examined by Bladon and Al-Bamerni, but Lehiste (who was studying American English, and therefore had the opportunity to study syllable-final allophones of /r/, absent from RP) states (1964:61):

The data reported . . . indicate that the initial allophones of /r/ are not significantly influenced by the following vowel nucleus. The final allophones, on the contrary, appear to depend to a considerable extent upon the vowels associated with them.

The inclusion in the present study of (syllable-initial) allophones of /r/ could not, therefore, be based on an expectation of extensive coarticulation, or of wide differences between speakers in degree of coarticulation; nevertheless it was felt that as liquids, /r/ and /l/ group themselves together, and moreover, as the possibility exists of producing a range of secondary articulations which is as wide for the alveolar/postalveolar approximant /r/ as for the alveolar lateral /l/, it was possible that some speakers might be found in a larger population who exploited this possibility.

3.2.2.2 Phonological grounds In Trubetzkoy's terms, /l/ and /r/ participate in an isolated bilateral opposition. The opposition is bilateral because the sum of the phonological properties common to /l/ and /r/ are common to only these phonemes (unlike the common properties of /p/ – /t/ which are also common to /p/ – /k/); and it is isolated because the relation between /l/ and /r/ is not repeated in any other opposition (unlike /p/ – /t/ which is 'proportional' to the oppositions /b/ – /d/ and /m/ – /n/); Trubetzkoy (1969:73):

German [and equally English] /r/ stands in a relation of bilateral opposition only to /l/. Its phonemic content is very poor, actually purely negative: it is not a vowel, not a specific obstruent, not a nasal, nor an /l/. Consequently it also varies greatly with respect to its realization.

In simple terms, the speakers of a speech community can afford variety in their realisation rules for /r/ without risking overlapping with other phonemes; it is not surprising then that in German, alveolar realisations stand in free variation with uvular, or that in English, a variety of realisations are encountered. Admittedly a uvular articulation must in English be regarded as a narrowly circumscribed dialectal feature (being used only in Northumberland and possibly some areas of Scotland) or as a rare and generally considered 'defective' substitute in a few other speakers. But on the other hand, there is a common tendency, particularly in the South of England, to articulate /r/ with considerable stricture at the lips, either in addition to, or to the exclusion of, the alveolar/postalveolar constriction. Whilst regarded by many as a defective substitute for lingual /r/, labial /r/ is common enough even within speech of broadly RP type to put it on a much more established footing than the uvular variant. Gimson (1980:207) sums up /r/ variation:

There are more phonetic variants of the /r/ phoneme than of any other English consonant. . . In RP, too, the degree of labialization varies considerably. Although for perhaps the majority of RP speakers the lip position of /r/ is determined by that of the following vowel, some speakers labialize /r/ whatever the following vowel. In some extreme cases, lip-rounding is accompanied by no articulation of the forward part of the tongue, so that /r/ is replaced by /w/. . . Finally [in certain regional pronunciations], the degree of retroflexion of the tongue for [ɹ] may be greater than in RP.

Probably more common than replacement of /r/ by /w/ is an articulation without participation of the apex or blade of the tongue which is yet distinct from labial-velar [w] by virtue of being a labio-dental, rather than bilabial, (frictionless) continuant, and possibly by lacking the velarisation of [w]. This is the labio-dental approximant [ʋ].

It has also been noted by Delattre (1967) that some speakers of American English produce /r/ without any raising of the tongue-tip, but achieve an acoustic effect identical to that of a retroflex /r/ by virtue of a 'bunching' of the tongue. If it is the case that speakers are using different implementation strategies to achieve identical auditory goals (Delattre does not in fact present frequencies for formants above F3, or formant amplitudes), the strategies may still have different 'secondary' effects – see 2.3.8.

Thus there is considerable scope for individuality in both realisation and implementation of /r/; further, differing degrees of coarticulation between /r/ and following syllabic nuclei may be expected, since speakers who abialize /r/ whatever the following vowel' (Gimson 1980:207) will presumably exhibit less variation in the consonant's formant frequencies according to following syllabic nucleus than those for whom 'the lip position of /r/ is determined by that of the following vowel'.

.2.2.3 Criteria other than between-speaker variability The evidence adduced so far to support the choice of /l/ and /r/ has been oriented towards criterion *1* of section 1.1.5, that is, between-speaker variability. Parameters deriving from these phonemes should fulfil, at least in part, three of the remaining criteria.

Criterion *4* requires that a parameter should occur frequently in speech, since it is of little practical value being able to identify a speaker by a feature he is unlikely to produce. In Table 3.1, reproduced from Gimson 1980:217–18), the frequency of occurrence of /l/ and /r/ compares favourably with that of nasals.

Table 3.1 Frequency of occurrence of English consonant phonemes

	%		%
/n/	7.58	/b/	1.97
/t/	6.42	/f/	1.79
/d/	5.14	/p/	1.78
/s/	4.81	/h/	1.46
/l/	3.66	/ŋ/	1.15
/ð/	3.56	/g/	1.05
/r/	3.51	/ʃ/	0.96
/m/	3.22	/j/	0.88
/k/	3.09	/dʒ/	0.60
/w/	2.81	/tʃ/	0.41
/z/	2.46	/θ/	0.37
/v/	2.00	/ʒ/	0.10

In the case of /r/, this high occurrence is despite the lack of any syllable-final /r/ in RP; this means that there is a relatively high frequency of realisations of /r/ belonging to a restricted subset of the possible positional variants (i.e. only pre- and inter-vocalic). This is important, even for varieties of English which have postvocalic /r/, since it seems unlikely that a parameter such as the amplitude spectrum of the /r/ phoneme', used irrespective of the appreciable difference in character found by Lehiste (1964) between initial and final allophones, would be particularly efficient. Similarly the *a priori* assumption is made that for speaker recognition the major extrinsic allophones of /l/ need to be treated separately.

Criterion *5* requires parameters to be robust in transmission. In the case of both the sounds under consideration the main concentration of spectral energy will lie within the normally quoted telephone band of 300 to 3500 Hz. Both these phonemes will be rated more highly in terms of robustness than some phonetic segments which have been examined for speaker identification, such as fricatives (Wolf (1972) included /ʃ/), and than other parameters that have been suggested as speaker-idiosyncratic such as the detailed shape of the glottal waveform, which, if it is to be recovered from recorded speech presupposes high quality recording.

Criterion 6, that of measurability, seems likely to be satisfied as well by parameters derived from /l/ and /r/ as by those from other segments previously used for speaker recognition, such as the nasals of Glenn and Kleiner (1968) or Su *et al.* (1974). If the parameters to be derived are formant frequencies, then there will be a complex of difficulties associated with measurement whether the measurement is performed by human or machine; but if, as is more likely in a practical speaker recognition scheme, attempts at formant extraction are abandoned and the parameters used consist in amplitude spectra represented as vectors, or in linear prediction coefficients, measurement appears to be relatively uncomplicated.

Criteria 2 and 3 (low within-speaker variability, and resistance to disguise) are more difficult to assess, however, without appropriate empirical work. It is apparent from 2.3.10 that a major source of within-speaker variability is the mapping of communicative intent. Pre-vocalic /l/ and /r/ have not been noted as social and stylistic 'markers' (see 2.3.10.3), and if in fact that they are not, then they may be inert to at least some communicatively determined within-speaker variation, and less susceptible to disguise strategies which involve imitating the speech of other social strata; but much more empirical (e.g. sociolinguistic) data is needed before firm predictions could be made.

3.2.3 *Structure of the experiments*

The experiments were organised as follows. A word-list was devised which included examples of words beginning with /l/ and /r/ and a number of speakers were recorded reading it. A second word-list including these words was then recorded by the same speakers three months later. Analysis was then carried out on the data from the first recording using a sound spectrograph (3.3), and on data from both recordings using computer-based facilities (3.4).

3.2.4 *Word-lists*

The words chosen aimed to provide three examples of both /l/ and /r/

occurring word-initially before each of 10 vowel phonemes – /iː ɪ e æ ʌ ɑː ɒ ɔː u:/. Monosyllabic words were chosen as far as possible, but in any case the syllable released by /l/ or /r/ always bore stress. In order to control phonetic environment as closely as possible, the following principles were observed: the syllable released by /l/ or /r/ should be closed by a plosive, or, as second choice, a fricative; the three examples of each syllable nucleus should be followed by consonants exemplifying the three broad place-categories labial, dental-alveolar, and velar; and those three consonants should exemplify both fortis and lenis types. Final nasals were rejected, since coarticulated nasality might produce marked changes in the vowel spectrum. Whenever a number of words might have fulfilled these conditions, nouns were chosen in preference to words of other grammatical categories. Nonsense words were avoided, the subjects being unfamiliar with phonemic transcription, necessary to indicate the pronunciation unambiguously.

The inventory of words is shown in Table 3.2. The word-lists presented to the speakers included this inventory plus a number of other words, ordered randomly, so as to minimise practice effects in the reading of the word-lists. The words were set out in six equal columns, and each column ended with an additional lexical item beginning with /l/ or /r/ which it was hoped would bear the distinctive 'column-final' intonation likely to occur at the end of each column, thus leaving items of interest with a more consistent, non-final intonation pattern.

Table 3.2 Word inventory

	y	z	x	y	z
eap	leak	league	reap	reek	reed
ip	lick	lid	rip	rick	rid
et	leg	led	wreck	rest	red
ap	lack	lad	rap	rack	rag
uck	lust	lug	rut	ruck	rug
ark	lard	large	raft	rasp	raj
ot	lock	log	rock	rob	rod
ord	lore	law	wrought	roar	raw
ook	look	look	rook	rook	rook
oop	loot	lose	roop	route	ruse

3.2.5 *Population of speakers*

The selection of the population of speakers to be used in experiments on speaker recognition requires care so that spuriously promising results,

founded on gross accent differences, may be avoided. The question is by n
means simple – see 2.3.10.4. It can be argued that the categorisation of a
individual by virtue of a different accent is part of a network c
categorisations which constitute speaker recognition (and it may indeed b
of use, for example, in criminal investigation). Nevertheless it is felt that th
best approach to an understanding of truly individual aspects of speec
production is to control accent variation; furthermore, speaker recognitio
techniques must clearly be able to discriminate between speakers from th
same community. Because of this a speech community was sought which wa
likely to be homogeneous. It was decided to record the members of a schoo
because in school a pupil is under considerable pressure to conform to th
norms of his peer group, and the pronunciation norm is no exception
Furthermore, the school selected – the Leys School, Cambridge – is in part
boarding school, which means that regardless of possible differences i
speech background at home, the young men recorded have spent well ove
half the year for the past few years within the same speech community. I
was decided to record 17-year-olds, as these would be the most mature wh
would still be available for recording at a later date.

3.2.6 *Recording*

The recordings were made at $7\frac{1}{2}$ ips using a Tandberg Series 15 tape recorde
and a Tandberg TM6 microphone. The microphone was supported a
approximately six inches from the lips of the speaker.

Fifteen subjects were recorded, though at the time of the secon
recording one of the 15 was not available. The subjects were given, prior t
being recorded, a copy of the word-list headed by the following instruction

Please read through the attached word-list. If you are in doubt about any of the word
(some of them are quite rare), ask before I record you. Don't worry that some of th
words appear twice.

Before a subject was recorded he would be asked if he had any doubt
concerning the word-list, and given the pronunciation of any words he wa
unsure of. He would then be asked to read the whole of the word-list. An
words which had been misread or contained hesitations were re-recorded a
the end.

In recording the words the subjects were asked to read each item twice
preceded the second time by the indefinite article (e.g. 'league, a league'
because prior to the main recordings some test spectrograms had bee
made, and it was found, particularly in the case of /r/, that the uppe
formants were easier to see when a vowel preceded the consonant. This ma

be due in part to production factors – /r/ is of quite short duration, and it takes some time for the amplitude of the vocal fold vibrations to build up, so that for some of its duration it may lack the amplitude in the higher harmonics for the relatively weak upper formants to be seen; and in part to visual factors – it is easier to trace a formant which is very weak through the middle of an /r/ if there is a strong indication of the formant and its transitional glides on both sides of the segment. In the computer-based investigation, the first utterance of each item is used, so it must be borne in mind that in 3.4 the consonants studied are in a slightly different environment (the C of /CV-/ instead of /əCV-/) from the ones in 3.3.

3.3 Spectrograph analysis

The sound spectrograph is an instrument capable of tracing a permanent record of the changing energy-frequency distribution of a complex wave through time. In its basic mode of operation, it will analyse 2.4 seconds of speech over a range of 80 to 8000 Hz with the choice of analysing filters of effective bandwidth 300 or 45 Hz. For a description of the spectrograph and its operation see Fant (1968).

3.3.1 *Making of spectrograms*

The equipment used was Cambridge University Linguistics Department's 7029A Sonagraph together with the plug-in unit 6075A Sona Counter. A standard format of spectrogram had to be decided on for the analysis of the data. The format adopted involved a three-stage process: firstly a wideband, scale-magnified spectrogram was made of the item – a 5000 Hz range was chosen, as it would include at least the first four formants of /l/ and /r/ and as clearly defined formants would be unlikely above 5000 Hz; secondly a narrowband section on the same scale was taken at a point defined during the consonant of interest, and this was reproduced on a blank portion of the same piece of paper by sliding it round the drum; and thirdly a section of the same kind was taken at a point after the first one such as to fall centrally within the following vowel – this was done by moving the sectioner pin a fixed number of divisions of the calibrated plate at the top of the drum. The result was a single sheet for each item which contained a wideband spectrogram and two narrowband sections all to the same scale. Tests performed with pure tones showed that wideband and narrowband scales coincided exactly, so it was possible to measure formants using the section in conjunction with the spectrogram.

The Sonagraph can generate its own calibration tone (of 50, 500 or 1000

85

Hz harmonics) and the accuracy of this was tested by comparing it with tones of known frequency. The internal 500 Hz calibration tone was found to be accurate (compared to the test tones) to within about 2% – that is, a 20 Hz discrepancy at 1000 Hz. This finding was reconfirmed a number of times during the making of spectrograms. Consequently a 500 Hz calibration tone was included on all spectrograms made, and this enabled accurate alignment of the frequency scale of the spectrogram with the calibrated template which was constructed for making measurements. The template was constructed on the basis of the calibration tone.

The points at which sections were to be taken were defined as follows. In items with initial /l/, the first section was taken at the end of the /l/ segment of the utterance (/əlV-/), so that the spectrum of the latter part of the segment was captured (including contributions from information as far back in time as the integration time of the filter (Fant 1968:184, 186)). The second section was then taken at a point 80 ms later if the subsequent vowel was a phonologically 'short' vowel followed by a fortis consonant, or 120 ms later otherwise. /æ/ was treated as a phonologically 'long' vowel because of its durational similarity to the long vowels in the speech of most of the speakers. In items with initial /r/, the first section was taken during the /r/ of the second utterance (/ərV-/) at the point where the third formant reached its nadir. The second section was taken so as to fall approximately half way through the vowel, the advancement of the pin being gauged with the help of an approximate durational measurement taken from the spectrogram.

A total of 2700 spectrograms and sections were prepared, comprising one spectrogram and two sections for each of 60 items (30 with initial /l/, 30 with initial /r/) from 15 speakers.

3.3.2 *Measurement*

The format of each spectrogram was such that measurement could be based on a combination of information from the time–frequency–intensity display and the two amplitude–frequency sections; the former gave the clearer indication of the general location of the formants, in part by showing their continuity through time, while the latter helped in assessing the centre frequency of the formant by displaying the relative amplitude of the harmonics.

It is necessary, despite the risk of circularity, to approach formant measurement with firm preconceptions about where the formants may be expected (on the basis of acoustic theory and previous investigation of the sound in question) to lie, so as not to be misled by 'spurious' formants – energy peaks which may be quite marked, but which do not fit into the normally found formant pattern for the sound (cf. Ladefoged (1967:84): 'This peak can be ignored, or regarded as spurious, only through knowing that it does not occur in the formant structure of other similar vowels'.) For example, in the present data speaker ACM's /i:/ often had a strong 'formant' visible at 900 Hz or so between the low F1, and F2 at around 2100 Hz, and this was disregarded only on the basis of knowledge of the general characteristics of /i:/. It might be argued that since this study aims to find differences between speakers, ACM should have been allocated an F_2 for /i:/ of 900 Hz, as this clearly marks him off from some (not all) other speakers. But a problem would arise. These extra peaks may be less reliable in their occurrence than the other 'true' formants, and if in some examples from ACM the energy at 900 Hz was not sufficient to be considered a peak, there would be great inconsistency in the values measured for his /i:/ – an inconsistency far greater than the real differences in spectrum shape since the overall distribution of energy might be very similar apart from a detailed difference in the 900 Hz region. For this reason it was decided to impose, in this part of the study, the expected formant framework on each sound as far as possible; and the differences discovered below within and between speakers are differences within that framework.

The actual values assigned to formants were estimates of their centre frequencies. If the harmonics dropped off in amplitude symmetrically on either side of the harmonic of highest amplitude in a particular region of the spectrum, then the frequency of this harmonic was taken as the centre frequency of the formant; in the majority of cases, however, peaks were asymmetrical, and in these cases the frequency chosen would lie between the highest and second highest amplitudes of harmonic, or even, in the case of marked skewness, beyond the frequency of the harmonic of second highest amplitude. The measurement of the first three formants of each sound (/l/ or /r/ and the following vowel) was attempted.

In the subsequent sections, only 13 speakers are used in the discussion of /r/. SH was left out because of an erratic tendency to use a tap, rather than the more usual approximant realisation of /r/. GRP was omitted, because the high damping of his upper formants combined with a relatively high fundamental frequency made measurements of even the first three formants unreliable. In 3.4, 14 speakers appear in the tables for /l/ and /r/ because speaker AS was unavailable for the second recording session.

In the case of /l/, the 'third' formant presented is, following Lehiste (1964), the third spectral prominence detectable. In most cases a marked antiresonance cancelled out the 'true' third formant (see 3.2.2.1), but speaker AM regularly exhibited such a peak (at around 2300 Hz) and accordingly his F_3 values are lower than those of the other speakers.

Although this procedure is apparently an exception to the principle, stated above, of ignoring peaks which fail to fit the expected formant framework, it is justified because acoustic theory makes no firm prediction of the extent to which the third formant will be cancelled in [l].

3.3.3 *Overall trends*

To deal first with the trends which emerge from the population of speakers as a whole, Table 3.3 presents the mean frequencies over all speakers of the first three formants of /l/ in each vowel environment, together with the first two of the vowel environment; and then the equivalent information for /r/. The third formant of the vowel environment is not shown because of

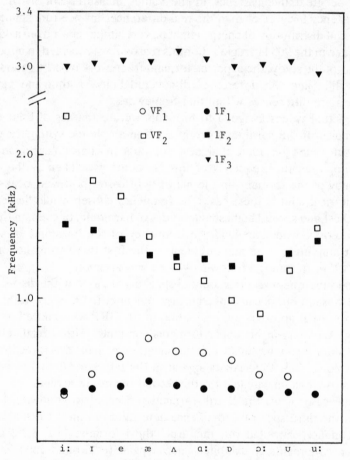

3.1 Means (over 15 speakers) of formant frequencies of /l/ and the vowel environments

difficulties encountered in measuring it particularly in the low back vowels /ɒ/ and /ɔ:/. The information from Table 3.3 is also displayed graphically in Figs. 3.1 and 3.2. These graphs have the ten vowel environments plotted along the x-axis in order round the vowel quadrilateral from close front through open to close back, so as to make the F_2 and F_1 trends optimally clear.

The first row of means in Table 3.3 are of the formant frequencies of the present study shown there; the second row are for values of initial /l/ and initial /r/ given by Lehiste (1964:Tables 2-III, 3-III and 3-XII), with only the nine of her vowel phonemes with equivalents among the present study's 10 included in the calculation (Lehiste's /i ɪ ɛ æ ə ɑ ɔ ʊ u/); and the third row (/l/ only) are from Al-Bamerni (1975) and relate to the present 10 British

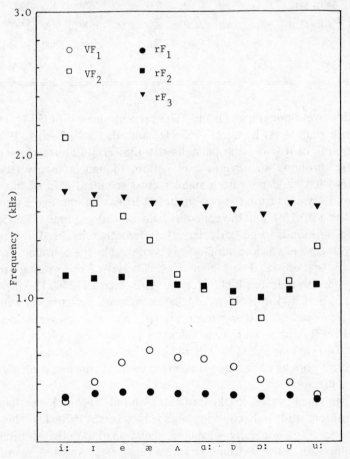

3.2 Means (over 13 speakers) of formant frequencies of /r/ and the vowel environments

Short term parameters

Table 3.3 Overall means (all speakers) of formants of initial /l/ and /r/, and their vowel environments; below, the mean (across vowels) of the means, and for comparison equivalent values from other sources (see text)

	lF$_1$	lF$_2$	lF$_3$	VF$_1$	VF$_2$	rF$_1$	rF$_2$	rF$_3$	VF$_1$	VF$_2$	
i:	340	1510	3010	310	2270	310	1160	1750	280	2120	
ɪ	350	1470	3040	460	1820	330	1140	1720	410	1670	
e	380	1410	3060	590	1710	340	1150	1710	550	1570	
æ	410	1300	3050	720	1440	340	1110	1670	630	1400	
ʌ	390	1290	3130	630	1230	330	1100	1670	580	1160	
ɑ:	370	1280	3080	620	1130	330	1090	1640	570	1080	
ɒ	370	1230	3030	570	990	320	1050	1630	520	970	
ɔ:	340	1290	3040	470	900	310	1000	1580	420	850	
ʊ	350	1320	3070	460	1200	320	1060	1660	400	1110	
u:	340	1410	2980	340	1500	300	1090	1640	320	1360	
MEAN	360	1350	3050	520	1420	320	1090	1670	470	1330	
MEAN	295	980	2600	580	1390	280	930	1360	380	1200	Lehiste
MEAN	365	1305	2780								Al-Bamerni

English vowel phonemes plus /ɜ:/. The present mean lF$_1$ (360 Hz) agrees well with that of Al-Bamerni (365 Hz) and also with Fant's (1960:164) measured F$_1$ of Russian non-palatalised /l/ (350 Hz). Lehiste's lower value (295 Hz) prompts no obvious explanation, though in theory (see Fant 1960:164) it should indicate a smaller cross-sectional area of the lateral passage. lF$_2$ values from the two studies of British laterals agree quite well (1350 and 1305 Hz), and the generally held view (e.g. Jones 1972:359) that American /l/ tends to be fairly dark (velarised/pharyngalised) even where British English has a clear allophone is borne out by the considerably lower mean lF$_2$ of Lehiste. The higher lF$_3$ (3050 Hz) of the present study as compared with Lehiste's (2600 Hz) and Al-Bamerni's (2780 Hz) is perhaps caused in part by the problem of locating formant peaks in what in many cases is a rather flat spectrum above 2500 Hz. Nevertheless Fant (1960:164–7) predicts an F$_4$ (equivalent to 'F$_3$' here and in Lehiste) of 2900 Hz for Russian non-palatalised [l] and of 3050 Hz for palatalised [lʲ], so that 3050 Hz may not be an unreasonable mean figure for the first peak above the major antiresonance.

Lehiste's mean values for the formants of initial /r/ are all lower than those of the present study – rF$_3$ considerably so (1360 versus 1670 Hz). This would seem to point to a generally 'weaker' articulation of /r/ in British English, in particular with a less extreme stricture (higher F$_1$) and less retroflexion (higher F$_3$).

Figs. 3.1 and 3.2 show clearly the relation between the formant frequencies of the vowel environments and the consonants preceding them. The clearest case of coarticulation is lF_2, which in almost every environment echoes the variation in VF_2. The range of variation in lF_2 is smaller than that of the equivalent #[l]V of Bladon and Al-Bamerni (1976:Fig. 2) – approximately 300 Hz as opposed to approximately 500 Hz – but this might be due to the preceding [ə] in the context used in the present study, and the inclusion in the means of some speakers who, as will be seen later, coarticulate very little. lF_1 can also be seen to vary with the F_1 of the vowel environment, within a range of 70 Hz. For /r/, the range of variation of F_2 and F_1 is smaller than for /l/, but scrutiny of the values in Table 3.3 confirms that within the limited range the variation is generally in the same direction as that of the equivalent formant of the vowel environment. Also shown are the high mean F_3 ('true' F_4) of /l/ and the low mean F_3 of /r/, this latter showing some tendency to follow rF_2.

3.3.4 *Speaker-specific results*

In this section the measurements obtained are examined to discover speaker-specific tendencies. Table 3.4 shows the means over all items of lF_1, lF_2, lF_3, and rF_1, rF_2, rF_3 for 15 speakers, and this information is shown graphically in Fig. 3.3 for /l/ and Fig. 3.4 for /r/.

Table 3.4 Means of consonant formant frequencies for each speaker over 30 items

	lF_1	lF_2	lF_3	rF_1	rF_2	rF_3
ACM	330	1240	3010	330	1160	****
AH	320	1430	2930	290	1010	1510
AHS	380	1280	2890	280	930	1440
AM	330	1380	2380	330	1040	1530
AS	420	1390	3010	370	1170	1690
GL	380	1460	2870	400	1370	2380
GRP	390	1440	2890			
JB	390	1250	3130	300	1060	1640
JR	340	1330	3340	280	1040	1480
JRC	370	1330	3510	320	1130	1930
ML	340	1430	3010	350	1080	1610
NL	350	1150	2970	300	1150	1660
PVE	360	1260	2850	340	1090	1480
SH	360	1360	3120			
TL	380	1520	3830	310	1000	1650
MEAN	360	1350	3050	320	1090	1670

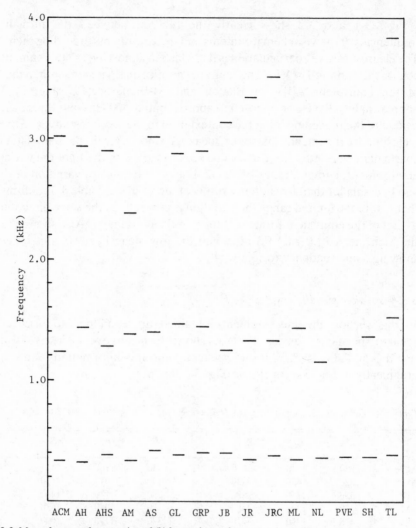

3.3 Mean formant frequencies of /l/ for each speaker

It can be seen from Fig. 3.3 that whilst the mean F_1 of /l/ lies between 320 and 420 Hz for all the speakers, F_2 and F_3 express different trends in individual speakers. Thus NL exhibits the lowest F_2 at 1160 Hz, and the rest of the speakers are ranged between this value and the 1520 Hz of TL's mean F_2. F_3 shows surprisingly wide variation, from AM (2380 Hz) to TL (3830 Hz). As mentioned above (3.3.2) AM was exceptional in that it was necessary to count as F3 of his /l/ the 'real' F3, which was not damped or cancelled out by a zero as in the case of the other speakers; but even if AM is excluded, the between-speaker variation is still around 1000 Hz.

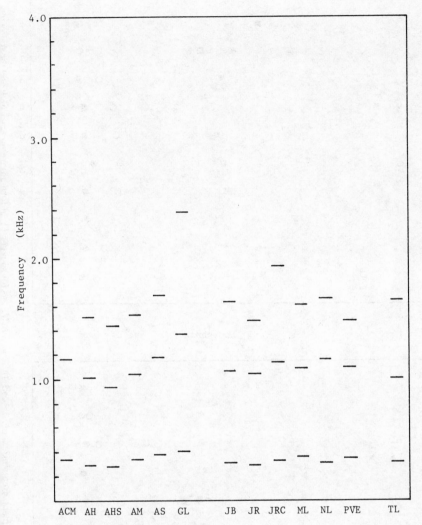

3.4 Mean formant frequencies of /r/ for each speaker

In regard to /r/ (Fig. 3.4), it is again F2 and F3 that show the marked variation between speakers. F_2 ranges from 930 Hz (AHS) to 1370 Hz (GL), and F_3 from 1440 Hz (AHS) to 2380 Hz (GL). It is visually apparent from Figs. 3.3 and 3.4 that there is a tendency for rF_3 to be low if rF_2 is low, whereas this is not seen in the case of /l/.

Turning now to coarticulation, Figs. 3.5 and 3.6 show two speakers (GRP and TL) who appear to exhibit a strong coarticulatory effect on lF2 by the following vowel. (A lesser coarticulatory effect in F1 is also discernible.) Figs. 3.7 and 3.8 (JB and NL), on the other hand, show F2 of /l/ to be very

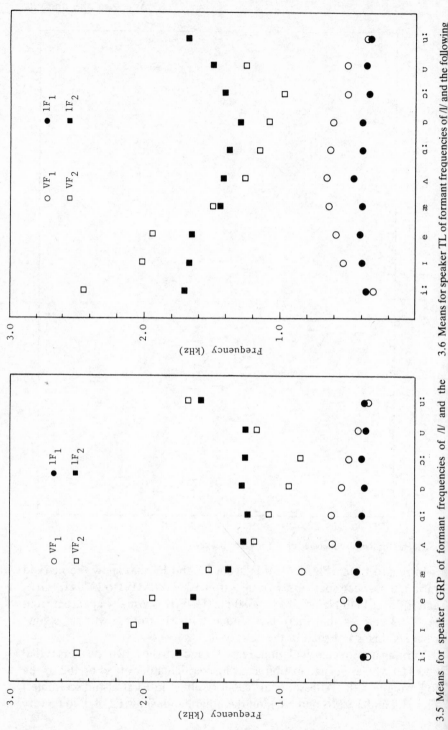

3.5 Means for speaker GRP of formant frequencies of /l/ and the

3.6 Means for speaker TL of formant frequencies of /l/ and the following

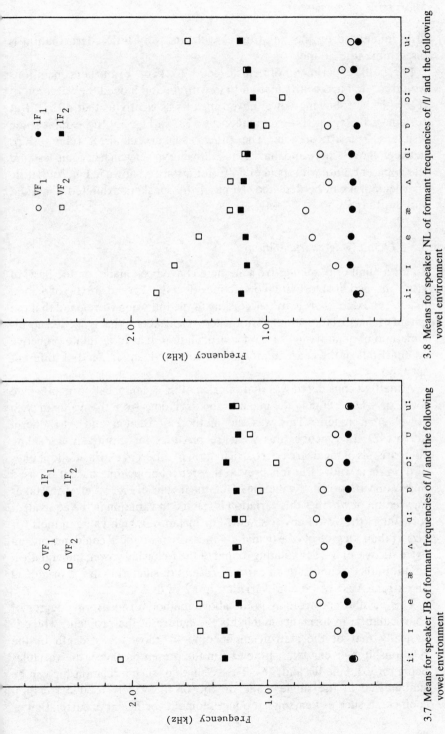

3.7 Means for speaker JB of formant frequencies of /l/ and the following vowel environment

3.8 Means for speaker NL of formant frequencies of /l/ and the following vowel environment

little influenced by the following vowel (and very little coarticulation is discernible in F1 either).

For /r/, the experiments of Lehiste (see 3.2.2.1 above) and her conclusions would foretell less coarticulation than with /l/, and indeed the variation of rF2 with the following vowel never appears as clearly as that of lF2. But certain of the speakers, exemplified by JRC in Fig. 3.9, do exhibit some visible rF2 coarticulation. The other speakers manifest relationships between the rF_2 curve and that of the following vowel which become less and less apparent, until with speaker PVE, for instance, shown in Fig. 3.10, little coarticulation can be detected. None of the speakers exhibited a marked variation in rF_1.

3.3.5 *Quantifying coarticulation*

So far a number of qualitative statements have been made, on the basis of visual inspection of formant plots, to the effect that F_2 (and also F_1) of /l/, and to a lesser extent of /r/, varies according to the following vowel, and that the extent of this variation is not uniform across speakers. What is needed now is a method of quantifying formant coarticulation so as to facilitate objective comparisons of the coarticulatory behaviour of /l/ and /r/, and of different speakers.

A method considered was that of calculating a 'canonical' formant value for /l/ or /r/, and finding the mean of the deviations from that value in each vowel environment. This was the method of Bladon and Al-Bamerni (1976:142). In practice, this measure provides for intuitively appealing comparisons of the degree of coarticulation of different extrinsic allophones of /l/ in their study. But it is prey to theoretical objection, since it is based purely on variation in F-values of /l/ (cf. the lF2 line of Fig. 3.5 etc.) and takes no account of whether this variation is related to variation in the equivalent formant of the vowel environment. For instance, a high value in mels (or Hz) of their 'degree of coarticulation' measure for F_2 of /l/ could indicate an extreme case of lF2 assimilating to that of the following vowel; but equally it could, in theory, indicate an extreme case of dissimilation in F2, or indeed an extreme case of random variation in F2 of /l/.

This possible shortcoming in the above method for measuring degree of coarticulation in formants highlights the nature of the problem, which is basically that of the statistician needing to know the strength of the relationship between two variables – in the present instance, the variables being for example lF_2 and VF_2. The strength of such a relationship can be summarised in the single value of one of the widely used correlation coefficients such as Pearson's product-moment coefficient of correlation or

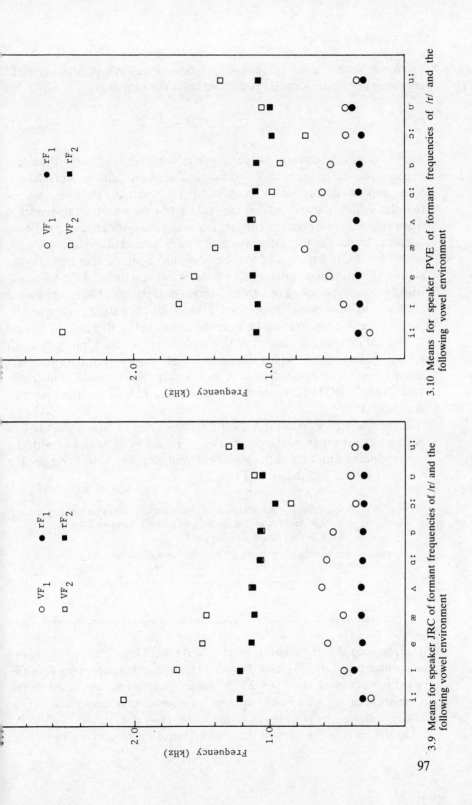

3.10 Means for speaker PVE of formant frequencies of /r/ and the following vowel environment

3.9 Means for speaker JRC of formant frequencies of /r/ and the following vowel environment

97

Spearman's coefficient of rank correlation. Pearson's product-moment coefficient of correlation (r) is derived from the formula

$$r = \frac{\Sigma(x - \bar{x})(y - \bar{y})}{ns_x s_y}$$

and the value lies between $+1$ (perfect positive correlation) and -1 (perfect negative correlation), with 0 indicating absence of (linear) correlation. Spearman's rank correlation coefficient (r_s) is essentially the same, except that the values of each variable are replaced by their rank number within that variable. Spearman's coefficient is a non-parametric statistic, and does not assume that the variables in question have normal distributions (Nie *et al.* 1975: 276). It was decided to use Spearman's coefficient to measure the degree of correlation between /l/ or /r/ formants and those of the following vowel because the values of a given formant over the list of 30 test items are not likely to be normally distributed. (Taking VF_2 as a strong example, the peak of the distribution will be near the lower end of its range at around 1000–1200 Hz, since a number of vowel phonemes (/ɑ: ʌ ʊ, possibly u: ɒ/) have F_2 in this region, whilst the middle, and upper end of the range will apply to rather few vowels – /i: ɪ/ and perhaps /e/. Computation (SPSS 'CONDESCRIPTIVE' subprogram) confirmed F_2 to have this 'positive skewness'.)

Using the SPSS NONPAR CORR subprogram, r_s was computed to evaluate the strength of the correlation of F_1 and F_2 of /l/ and /r/ with the corresponding formants of the vowel environment. The values of r_s for the complete corpus are shown in Table 3.5.

Table 3.5 Spearman coefficients of correlation between (across) formants of /l/ or /r/ and (down) of the following vowel, computed for data from 15 (/l/) or 13 (/r/) speakers

	lF_1	lF_2		rF_1	rF_2
VF_1	0.533		VF_1	0.305	
VF_2		0.575	VF_2		0.405

It can be seen that the highest correlation is that of lF_2 with F_2 of the vowel environment ($r_s = 0.575$), and the second highest is that of lF_1 with F_1 of the vowel environment ($r_s = 0.533$). A similar pattern emerges with /r/: the correlation of rF_2 with F_2 of the vowel environment is the stronger ($r_s = 0.405$), followed by rF_1 with F_1 of the vowel ($r_s = 0.305$).

On the basis of the present data, quantitative expression is given to the conclusion that /l/ assimilates more than /r/ to a following vowel, and this agrees with Lehiste's (1964:58) qualitative conclusions on her own data. Her conclusion that 'The data suggest that the following vowel has but little influence on the initial allophone of /r/' may be a little strong, since some correlation between the two main quality determining formants of /r/ and those of the vowel has been shown above, even if rather less than found in /l/; there might of course be a difference between American and British English in this respect.

3.3.6 *Speaker-specific coarticulation*

Table 3.6 presents the correlation coefficients r_s for each speaker between F_1 and F_2 of the consonant in question with the equivalent formants of the following vowel. All except seven of the coefficients are significant at the 0.05 level, and 37 achieve significance at 0.01.

From Table 3.6 it can be seen that, whilst it is far from clear that any speakers could be labelled strong or weak coarticulators in general, there is nevertheless a wide range of values for any particular formant. Taking F2 as the formant of primary interest as regards coarticulated vowel quality, Fig. 3.11 presents the 13 coefficients for both lF_2 and rF_2 (omitting the two speakers whose /r/ data were not used) rank ordered by descending value. This fails to show which speaker exhibited which value, but demonstrates clearly that in the cases of both /l/ and /r/ the values of the coarticulation

Table 3.6. Formant correlations as a measure of coarticulation for individual speakers

	lF_1 with VF_1	lF_2 with VF_2	rF_1 with VF_1	rF_2 with VF_2
ACM	0.706	0.684	0.531	0.638
AH	0.765	0.794	0.535	0.355
AHS	0.048	0.551	0.192	0.365
AM	0.572	0.375	0.339	0.260
AS	0.674	0.871	0.516	0.816
GL	0.906	0.752	0.540	0.888
GRP	0.586	0.856		
JB	0.552	0.316	0.264	0.546
JR	0.565	0.757	0.516	0.715
JRC	0.605	0.384	0.291	0.732
ML	0.653	0.750	0.764	0.500
NL	0.459	0.645	0.051	0.695
PVE	0.526	0.803	0.318	0.272
SH	0.499	0.766		
TL	0.730	0.885	0.594	0.548

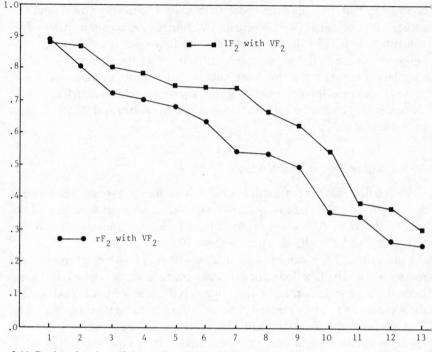

3.11 Rank ordered coefficients of correlation (r_s) for 13 speakers

coefficient vary across a considerable part of the possible range. It also demonstrates the trend towards a generally lower degree of coarticulation in rF_2 than in lF_2.

A further point of interest is revealed by the rF_2 coarticulation coefficients: the three speakers who were judged auditorily to have strongly labial realisations of /r/ – GL, JRC and ACM – had the first, third and sixth highest coefficients of correlation. It seems likely that the high rF_2 coarticulation of the labial realisations reflects a general 'weakness' in these sounds, as does the high rF_3 of GL and JRC (see Fig. 3.4) which results in a spectrum more like that of a neutral vowel than in the case of the other realisations of /r/.

3.3.7 *Efficiency of formant parameters*

The formant measurements were also examined from the point of view of treating each /l/ or /r/ formant as a parameter which might contribute to a speaker recognition algorithm based on a number of such parameters. This is the approach of Wolf (1972) who tested 31 phonetic attributes such as F_1

and F_2 of [ə] in *the*, the high frequency spectrum shape of [ʃ], and prevoicing in [b], to find 'efficient' acoustic parameters for speaker recognition. As a means of assessing efficiency, Wolf uses (as do Pruzansky and Mathews (1964), and others) the F ratio of analysis of variance. This may be thought of as the ratio of the variance of the speaker means in a particular parameter to the mean of the speaker variances:

$$F = \frac{\text{variance of speaker means}}{\text{average within-speaker variance}}$$

For the present purposes, the author wrote a computer program to implement the formula quoted by Wolf (1972:2047):

$$F = \frac{n}{m-1} \sum_{j=1}^{m} (\mu_j - \bar{\mu})^2 / \frac{1}{m(n-1)} \sum_{i=1}^{n} \sum_{j=1}^{m} (x_{ij} - \mu_j)^2$$

where x_{ij} is the value of the parameter in the ith utterance by the jth speaker, $i=1. \ldots .n$, $j=1. \ldots .m$;

$$\mu_j = \frac{1}{n} \sum_{i=1}^{n} x_{ij}$$

is the estimated mean for the jth speaker; and

$$\bar{\mu} = \frac{1}{m} \sum_{j=1}^{m} \mu_j$$

is the estimated overall mean.

A shortcoming of the present assessment of formant parameters, as indeed of Wolf's study, is that the parameter measurements are culled from a single recording session and so exclude medium and long term within-speaker variation. The computer-based analysis in the subsequent sections will, however, take into account data from the two recording sessions separated by three months. The characteristics of the present data are similar enough to those of Wolf to allow at least a general comparison; Wolf recorded 22 speakers who uttered each feature 10 times; in the present study the F ratio computation was performed on data from 15 (/l/), 13 (/r/), or 12 (/r/, F_3) speakers, who had each produced 30 examples of each parameter. The relevant results are shown in Table 3.7.

Comparison with Wolf's F ratio values indicates that despite the within-speaker variation in formant values in /l/ and /r/ occasioned by

Table 3.7 F ratio values of formant parameters

Parameter	lF_1	lF_2	lF_3	rF_1	rF_2	rF_3
F ratio	17.7	21.6	77.8	46.4	59.4	216.9
No. of speakers	15	15	15	13	13	12

coarticulation, the between-speaker differences are strong enough to give reasonably high values. Wolf's parameters attain values from 84.9 (a fundamental frequency parameter) down to 10.2 (for a spectral feature in [æ]). Less than one third of his values are higher than the 46.4 of rF_1 in Table 3.7, and five have values less than that of lF_1.

It is clear from Table 3.7 that the /r/ parameters are more 'efficient' as judged by the F ratio than the /l/ parameters. This is probably because of less within-speaker variation, resulting from the lower coarticulation of /r/, rather than because of appreciably greater between-speaker variation. As might be expected the third formants, which are much less prone to coarticulatory variation (see for instance Figs. 3.1 and 3.2), provide more efficient parameters than the first and second formants. As explained above (3.3.2), lF3 in the case of all speakers except AM is a formant (nearly) continuous with F4 of the following vowel; it may be that the much higher efficiency of rF_3 compared with lF_3 is related to this difference in the 'true' nature of these parameters; but also to an artefact of the formant extraction process. In speakers such as JR and JRC, the higher end of the /l/ spectrum is often lacking in clear peaks, and very slight peaks in this flat part of the spectrum have to be identified as lF3; these minor peaks occur rather unsystematically, with the result that considerable variation in the lF3 value is recorded which in fact reflects nothing more significant than a characteristically flat part of the spectrum. It is therefore certain that the high variance of lF3 within certain speakers, resulting in a mean of within-speaker lF_3 standard deviations (over 15 speakers) of 165 Hz as compared with a mean of within-speaker rF_3 standard deviations (over 12 speakers) of 90 Hz, has produced a disproportionately low F ratio of lF_3. If a more representative way of characterising the upper part of the /l/ spectrum, where F3 and F4 often appear to merge, can be found, then this might well prove an efficient parameter.

3.4 Computer analysis

The subsequent sections describe the analysis made using the computer-based facilities made available by Cambridge University Engineering

Department. The equipment consisted of an Interdata 80 laboratory computer with hard disc unit, and a laboratory-built interface and analog-to-digital converter. Programs available included one – 'M80' – which had been developed by Steve Brooks in connection with a deaf speech training project, and which provided for speech analysis based on both Linear Prediction and Fast Fourier Transform, as well as convenient display of speech waveforms and derived spectra. Fourier analysis yields an amplitude spectrum which shows the harmonic structure of the laryngeal source. A smooth spectral envelope of a speech sound free of the harmonic peaks caused by the source can be obtained by the 'cepstrum' method. This involves taking the inverse Fourier transform of the log amplitude spectrum, thereby separating the fundamental information which can then be excised; the remaining information (relating to the transmission characteristics of the supralaryngeal tract) can then be converted into a smooth spectrum by application of an inverse Fourier transform. This method is computationally laborious, involving three Fourier calculations. A less costly analysis technique is linear prediction (LP); this essentially statistical technique involves the computation of an optimum inverse (digital) filter, the reciprocal of which defines the smooth spectrum of the speech sound. An explanation of these techniques, and further references, are given in Wakita (1976), and a thorough treatment can be found in Rabiner and Schafer (1978). Although the LP model is an all-pole model, comparison with spectrograph sections and cepstral spectra suggested that it succeeds in approximating well the peaks and overall shape of the spectra of laterals, despite their antiresonance(s).

3.4.1 *Isolation of phonetic events*

The tapes of the word-lists from both sessions (henceforward referred to as Session A (SA), and Session B (SB)) were played in one item (without the indefinite article) at a time, the waveform being low pass filtered to 5 kHz, sampled at 10 kHz, and digitised with 12-bit resolution. At this sampling rate M80 allowed 0.5 seconds of digitised speech to be held in memory and displayed 25.6 ms at a time. A linear prediction spectrum computed on the part of the waveform in view could also be displayed simultaneously, and this combination of waveform and spectrum made it possible visually to locate the boundary between /l/ and the following vowel. Three 25.6 ms frames of the waveform, the last being located shortly before the transition from the /l/ to the following vowel, were then recorded on disc.

This procedure was repeated for each item, speaker and recording session. A similar procedure was carried out on the /r/ items, except that the

103

transition between /r/ and a following vowel is gradual and lacks the clear correlates of a breaking of apical constriction (e.g. the step up in F_1) useful for segmenting /l/. With /r/, the first frame which gave a well-defined spectrum, and two subsequent frames within the next 20 ms, were stored.

3.4.2 *Identification trials using spectral information*

In the first stage, log spectra computed from samples of /l/ and /r/ were used in simulated speaker-identification trials. This involved computing a reference spectrum for each speaker by averaging each point in the spectrum over a number of items for a given speaker. The spectrum covered the range 0–5 kHz, was represented by 128 points, and was normalised by the area under the curve before further calculation to neutralise amplitude differences between recordings. 'Test' samples, consisting in the first instance of the mean of the spectra from the three stored waveforms of a single item (e.g. *league*), were then compared with the reference spectrum for each speaker, and were identified as having been spoken by the speaker of the nearest reference. This procedure was carried out for each item in the test corpus.

The use of two measures of the similarity of test and reference spectrum was explored; the first, the angular separation or correlation of the two spectral vectors, is given as

$$r_{rt} = (R \cdot T)/(|R| \cdot |T|) \tag{1}$$

and is the measure adopted by Glenn and Kleiner (1968). The second is a distance measure of the form

$$d_{rt} = [\sum_{k=1}^{n} (r_k - t_k)^m]^{1/m} \tag{2}$$

where the vectors have n elements. The standard Euclidean distance is given by m = 2; m = 1 and m = 3 were also tried. It was quickly found that no systematic difference in identification rates resulted from the use of these different measures, except for a tendency towards slightly higher rates with m = 3 in (2). In the subsequent discussion the values given result from (2) with m = 2.

A few identification trials were made in which the log spectra used resulted from the cepstrum method described briefly in 3.4. Identification rates were similar to those obtained with LP log spectra; LP analysis based on the autocorrelation method with the model order set to 14 is henceforward assumed unless otherwise stated.

104

For the identification trials, the available data had to be partitioned into test and reference corpora. In the first condition all 30 items for each speaker from one session were used to form the reference, and the items from the same session used (one by one) as the test items. Although this meant that the test item was included in the formation of the reference, it can be concluded from the similarity of the results in the third condition (see below) with those of the first that its influence was not sufficient to boost the identification rates unnaturally. The second condition resembled the first, except that test items were taken from the other session. In the third condition, the corpus was split into three parts, corresponding to the columns titled *x, y,* and *z* in Table 3.2 above; each column in turn supplied the test items, while the reference was formed from the items in the two remaining columns. In tables, *x, y, z* indicate values where items taken from columns *x, y* or *z* were used as test samples (and *U* (Undivided) indicates that no subdivision of the corpus took place). The third condition was used with test and reference corpora from the same session and from different sessions. Identification results under these conditions using LP spectra are presented in Table 3.8 for both /l/ and /r/.

In Table 3.8, rows contain values for particular session conditions; and the columns indicate which subset of the items comprised the test corpus (*U* indicates all the items). Means for within- and across-session conditions are given at the ends of each of the pairs of rows; means for subdivision conditions at the foot of columns; and the overall identification mean for each phoneme at the bottom right corner.

From the overall means of Table 3.8, it appears that /r/ gives a slightly better identification rate (48.8) than /l/ (43.9), subject to qualifications discussed below, but that they contain generally similar amounts of speaker-idiosyncratic information – which is in accord with Höfker (1977) who, of the 24 isolated German phonemes investigated, found /r/ and /l/ to give sixth and ninth best identification.

Table 3.8 Percentage correct identification using LP spectra

REF/TEST	/l/					/r/				
	U	*x*	*y*	*z*	MEAN	*U*	*x*	*y*	*z*	MEAN
SA/SA	59.1	52.9	52.9	59.3 ⎫	53.3	61.7	57.9	57.1	57.9 ⎫	61.1
SB/SB	54.1	56.4	45.7	45.7 ⎭		63.3	62.1	65.0	63.6 ⎭	
SA/SB	30.2	38.6	30.7	23.6 ⎫	34.6	36.9	39.3	34.3	36.4 ⎫	36.3
SB/SA	38.8	37.9	37.9	39.3 ⎭		36.4	27.9	41.4	37.9 ⎭	
MEAN	45.5	46.4	41.8	42.0	43.9	49.6	46.8	49.5	48.9	48.7

Examination of the column means reveals that the average of 20 items provides a reference which is not improved on markedly, if at all, by increasing the corpus to 30 items (column *U*); it must be noted, however, that both the 20- and 30-item corpora span the complete range of vowel environments, and so theoretically provide an optimum basis for a reference. The row means, in contrast, show a marked deterioration in identification rates when test and reference corpora come from recording sessions separated by three months, a factor neglected by many studies; averaging all within- and across-session conditions, identification drops from 53.3 to 34.6 (/l/), and 61.1 to 36.3 (/r/) when this time factor is introduced.

The within-session correct identification percentages of 53.3 and 61.1 compare favourably with that of 43.0 given by Glenn and Kleiner (1968) for /n/ – but less so than at first glance; they used 30 speakers instead of the present 14, and so their rate is equivalent to 12.9 times better than chance identification, compared with 8.6 for /r/ and 7.5 for /l/. It would not, however, have been expected that /l/ and /r/ would have equalled the strongly idiosyncratic nasals in identification ability. (A further point to note is that they filtered their recordings to simulate telephone bandwidth.)

The identification rates of /r/ depend to some extent on the distinctiveness of the three speakers using strongly labial realisation (see 3.3.6). This can be seen if, for example, their average rate for within-session trials, 85.6, is compared with the equivalent average for the remaining 11 speakers – 54.2. No group so clearly 'more distinctive' can be found with /l/ – the average rate for the 'best' three speakers for /l/ is only 64.9, leaving the remainder with an average rate of 54.2. This raises the question of whether it is reasonable to include in the assessment of a parameter for speaker recognition speakers whose realisation rules for the segment differ (the [v]–[ɹ] distinction must be present at the level of the phonetic representation – speakers are quite aware of it even to the extent of commenting on it, and it is not an implementational distinction as may be the bunched versus retroflex alternatives for [ɹ]). If such speakers are operating with a different set of linguistic (realisational) rules, should they not be excluded from the 'homogeneous' speech community argued for in 3.2.5? An answer to the question of principle is not straightforward; but in the present case it is reasonable to include such speakers in the population since, firstly, speakers who use labial /r/ are widespread within otherwise homogeneous accent communities, and no valid independent criteria could be found to segregate them into a separate accent community; and secondly, in a practical speaker recognition scheme to reject /r/ would be to discard potentially valuable speaker-specific information.

Table 3.9 Percentage correct identification with test LP spectra computed
from 1, 2, 5 or 10 test items

No. items averaged	/l/		/r/	
	within session	across session	within session	across session
1	53.3	34.6	61.1	36.3
2	80.2	48.0	77.4	46.5
5	92.3	59.5	93.5	51.5
10	98.8	66.1	96.7	50.6

Next, the effect of averaging a number of test samples was explored.
Table 3.9 shows the average correct identification percentages for /l/ and /r/
within and across sessions with the reference vector formed as before in the
various conditions, but with the test sample computed as the average of 2, 5
and 10 items. (Because more test items were used, conditions SA/SA *U* and
SB/SB *U* were omitted so that there would be no commonality between test
and reference corpora.) Recalling the order of the vowels /iː ɪ e æ ʌ ɑː ɒ ɔː ʊ
uː/, then the test samples were computed from items with vowels five places
apart (for 2 items averaged, e.g. /iː/+/ɑː/, /ʊ/+/æ/), two places apart (for 5
items averaged), or with one each of the vowels (for 10 items averaged).

The information from Table 3.9 is displayed graphically in Fig. 3.12. It is
apparent that a considerable improvement in accuracy results from
averaging two items to produce the test sample, and that further averaging
produces diminishing returns. Fig. 3.12 highlights the inferiority of
identification across sessions; and it is at first curious to note the way in
which /r/ identification across sessions falls behind that of /l/ as test averaging
increases. But in fact this trend is also apparent within sessions, but then falls
behind when two or more items are averaged. The probable explanation lies
in the greater coarticulation of /l/. High coarticulation will result in
confusions of the kind where, for example, a coarticulatorily palatalised
(single-item) test sample from one speaker may be attributed to another
speaker, whose reference, as a result of a habitually more palatalised
articulatory setting, is itself 'palatalised'. If such confusions are indeed
significant in /l/, they may be expected to be alleviated by the kind of
item-averaging using different vowel contexts described above. With /r/ on
the other hand, coarticulatory confusions may be of little significance, and
the confusions caused primarily by random variation in articulation. Here
test averaging will make only a 'statistically-based' as opposed to a
'phonetically-based' improvement (combined with a statistically-based
improvement). If coarticulatory variation is responsible for the poorer

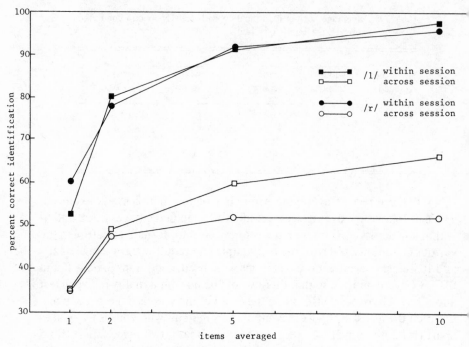

3.12 Identification rates averaging items to form test sample

performance of /l/ compared with /r/ in the one-item, within-session condition, then, because this variation (unlike random variation) should not increase between sessions, the improvement of /l/ relative to /r/ in the between-session condition is not surprising. However, it still remains to be explained, looking at the /r/ between-session rates, why so little ('statistically-based') improvement occurs when more than two items are averaged.

3.4.3 *Quantifying coarticulation (computer method)*

In order to examine in more detail the question of coarticulation and its speaker recognition potential, LP log spectra computed from the stored waveforms for /l/ and /r/ were employed in a procedure based on that of Su *et al.* (1974). Degree of coarticulation was estimated by finding the Euclidean distance between a vector representing the mean consonant spectrum before front vowels and one representing the mean consonant spectrum before back vowels; that is, for each speaker:

$$\text{DISTANCE } (\bar{C}_f, \bar{C}_b) = \{ \sum_{k=1}^{n} [\bar{c}_f(k) - \bar{c}_b(k)]^2 \}^{1/2}$$

where
$\bar{C}_f$ is a 128-point mean spectrum formed by averaging all the speaker's consonant tokens in front vowel environments, and $\bar{c}_f(k)$ is the kth element of that vector;
and
$\bar{C}_b$ is the equivalent mean spectrum, with elements $\bar{c}_b(k)$, for the consonant in back vowel environments.

A program was written by the author to effect this computation, allowing for different placements of the boundary between 'front' and 'back' vowels.

Table 3.10 shows the values of the DISTANCE measure for /l/ and /r/ for each of the 14 speakers based on the data from the first and the second recording sessions, and grouping the vowels: front /iː ɪ e æ ʌ/; back /ɑː ɒ ɔː ʊ uː/.

Whilst there is a little variation between the two sessions, it can be seen that in general a speaker with a large DISTANCE value, suggesting substantial coarticulation, in one recording will also have a high value in the other recording. In /r/, AM and GRP are perhaps exceptions to this. Inspection of Table 3.10 reveals the expected lower coarticulatory distance of /r/ compared with /l/ – their means over all speakers and both sessions being 99

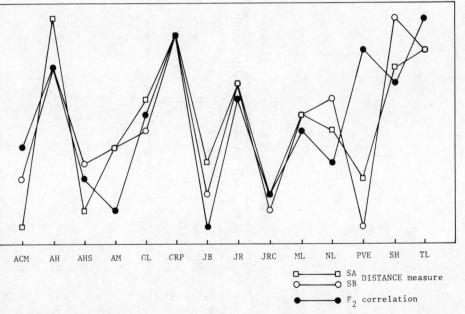

3.13 Rank ordering of speakers by /l/ coarticulation

Table 3.10 Values of the DISTANCE measure of coarticulation for the 14 speakers – high values indicate high estimated coarticulation

		ACM	AH	AHS	AM	GL	GRP	JB	JR	JRC	ML	NL	PVE	SH	TL	MEAN
/l/	SA	71	267	110	123	147	253	127	199	115	145	136	121	229	236	160
	SB	127	206	128	133	139	209	103	176	99	151	170	90	254	209	
/r/	SA	151	124	56	37	159	201	57	79	126	75	80	100	97	65	99
	SB	134	114	43	91	146	139	59	55	164	58	64	83	141	67	

and 160 respectively. It is of note that only three speakers – ACM, GL and JRC – have higher average coarticulation (DISTANCE) values for /r/ than for /l/; and these are just the three speakers judged auditorily to have labial realisations of /r/.

The present estimate of coarticulation can be compared with the one, based on correlation between formant frequencies of consonants with those of associated vowels, suggested in 3.3.5. This can be done by rank ordering the speakers in terms of greatest to least coarticulation, as determined by each measure. Table 3.11 presents such a ranking (1–14 in the case of /l/, 1–12 in the case of /r/, as determined by the values available) of the speakers.

For /l/, with the curious exception of PVE, there is fairly close correspondence between the rankings obtained by the measure based on correlation of its second formant with that of the following vowel, and those obtained by the present method. Fig. 3.13 gives an impression of the extent of this correspondence. Table 3.12 shows the correlation between the DISTANCE measure for either session and the formant correlation coarticulation measure.

Fig. 3.14 presents the same information from Table 3.11 for /r/. As might be expected for a sound where coarticulation is more restricted than in /l/, the reliability of the ranking appears lower than in Fig. 3.13. Apart from AM and JR there is good agreement between the two sessions' DISTANCE

Table 3.11 Rank ordering of speakers by coarticulation as assessed by formant correlation and by the DISTANCE measure

	/l/			/r/		
	F2 Corr.	DISTANCE		F2 Corr.	DISTANCE	
	SA	SA	SB	SA	SA	SB
ACM	9	14	11	5	2	3
AH	4	1	4	10	3	4
AHS	11	13	10	9	11	12
AM	13	9	9	12	12	5
GL	7	6	8	1	1	2
GRP	2	2	2			
JB	14	10	12	7	10	9
JR	6	5	5	3	6	11
JRC	12	12	13	2	3	1
ML	8	7	7	8	8	9
NL	10	8	6	4	7	8
PVE	3	11	14	11	5	6
SH	5	4	1			
TL	1	3	3	6	9	7

Table 3.12 Spearman correlations of different measures of /l/ coarti-culation

	F2 Corr		DIST SA	0.675	(p<0.01)
Correlation of	F2 Corr	with	DIST SB	0.594	(p<0.02)
	DIST SA		DIST SB	0.858	(p<0.01)

Table 3.13 Spearman correlations of different measures of /r/ coarti-culation

	F2 Corr		DIST SA	0.566	(p<0.05)
Correlation of	F2 Corr	with	DIST SB	0.252	(p<0.02)
	DIST SA		DIST SB	0.732	(p<0.01)

ranking; but rF_2/VF_2 correlation ranking tends to deviate from the other rankings. Correlations between measures are given for /r/ in Table 3.13. Probably the coarticulation of /r/ is too slight to yield as reliable ranking of speakers as /l/.

3.4.4 *Identification trials using coarticulation*

That coarticulation of /l/ and /r/ varies from speaker to speaker has been demonstrated, but the question remains whether this variation is reliable

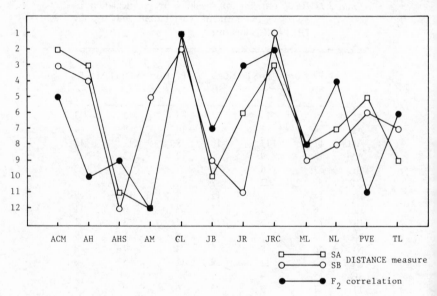

3.14 Rank ordering of speakers by /r/ coarticulation

enough to be used for speaker identification to the extent that Su *et al.* (1974) found nasal (specifically /m/) coarticulation to be. To test this, a speaker-identification exercise was simulated. The utterances were divided into test and reference corpora in the way described in 3.4.2. In condition *U*, 30 items would be available for calculating the reference coarticulation value for each speaker, and 30 for the test value; in conditions *x*, *y* and *z*, a value based on 10 items would be tested against references based on 20 items.

Following Su *et al.*, identification was performed using the following distance measure based on vector correlation:

$$c_{rt} = (D_r \cdot D_t)/(|D_r| \cdot |D_t|)$$

where

r is the reference speaker, t the speaker being tested;

D is the difference between the mean front and back spectra of the speaker in question $= (\bar{C}_f - \bar{C}_b)$

so that c_{rt} is a measure of the similarity of the coarticulation (i.e. of the difference between the mean consonant spectra in front and back environments) of speakers r and t. For each of the 14 test speakers t, 14 values of c_{rt} are obtained – one for each reference speaker r – and the reference speaker giving rise to the highest c_{rt} (maximum 1) is taken to be the identity of the test sample's speaker. The program developed performed each identification trial nine times, the first time with the 'front-back' boundary placed after /i:/ (/i: + ɪ e æ ʌ ɑ: ɒ ɔ: ʊ u:/); and in each subsequent trial the boundary moved on one vowel in this series. The best results were obtained with the division /i: ɪ e æ ʌ + ɑ: ɒ ɔ: ʊ u:/, and these are given in Table 3.14.

As can be seen in Table 3.14, high rates of identification can be achieved using /l/ coarticulation – up to 85.7 within sessions and 71.4 across sessions, and, more reliably, an average rate of 58.3 within sessions and 53.6 across. It

Table 3.14 Percentage correct identification using coarticulation

REF/ TEST	/l/ U	x	y	z	MEAN	/r/ U	x	y	z	MEAN
SA/SA		85.7	64.3	64.3	58.3		35.7	42.9	21.4	32.1
SB/SB		42.9	50.0	42.9			28.6	28.6	35.7	
SA/SB	71.4	50.0	50.0	42.9	53.6	42.9	21.4	14.3	28.6	24.1
SB/SA	50.0	57.1	42.9	64.3		35.7	14.3	14.3	21.4	

is not easy to explain the apparently better reference basis provided by SA. It is encouraging to note the smaller deterioration caused by the time factor as compared with previous identification trials. A much less satisfactory picture is presented by /r/, with average within- and across-session rates of 32.1 and 24.1. Apparently, despite the evidence of some coarticulation taking place in /r/, as expected the range is not sufficient reliably to differentiate speakers. The dissimilarity in identification rates between /l/ and /r/ using coarticulation contrasts with the similar results obtained from the two phonemes using straightforward spectral comparison.

In all cases the identification rate of /l/ in Table 3.14 is considerably better than chance (7%), but falls short of the 100% identification rate claimed for /m/ coarticulation by Su *et al.* (1974). Various factors may contribute to this lower accuracy: the greater number of speakers in the population in the present study (14 compared with Su *et al.*'s maximum of 10); the less ideal recording circumstances (their recordings were made in a sound-treated environment); and the fact that /l/ is an alveolar, and so allows less freedom of tongue body coarticulation than a bilabial (Su *et al.* found /m/ to exhibit around three times the coarticulation of /n/).

Despite the possibility of attaining a high level of identification using coarticulation, it has to be recognised that the practical value of this method is severely limited by the large and specialised test, as well as reference, corpus required. At first sight the use of /l/ coarticulation looks promising in its identification ability across sessions, achieving a rate of 53.6 compared with 34.6 by spectrum comparison (Table 3.8). But this is not comparing like with like, because the latter figure is attained with a test corpus of just one item (see Table 3.9 and Fig. 3.12). If five items, suitably chosen to be representative of the range of vowel environments, are averaged to form the test sample, then the spectrum identification rate overtakes that of the coarticulatory method with 59.5 to 53.6 (though the same does not apply with /m/, since here coarticulation apparently identifies with 100% accuracy); and if the data base for the two methods is the same, that is with the test spectrum, like the coarticulation value, computed from 10 items, the spectrum identification rate is appreciably higher (66.1). Likewise, when the equivalent 10-item test corpus is used within sessions, the coarticulation based rate of 58.3 compares most unfavourably with the spectrum based rate of 98.8. This suggests that the use of coarticulation will not be the most efficient way, as implied by Su *et al.*, of using segmental information in segments exhibiting strong coarticulation, but that research would more profitably seek ways of neutralising the within-speaker variation attributable to coarticulation, with a view to improved identification by ordinary spectral comparison.

.5 Conclusions

.5.1 *Practical conclusions*

pectral information from initial allophones of /l/ and /r/ has been shown to ield moderate identification rates on material recorded by a homogeneous roup of untrained speakers. Whilst the deterioration found when test and eference items came from recording sessions three months apart is onsiderable, there is little reason to suppose that the deterioration would e less marked for other segmental parameters, or indeed non-segmental arameters, examined under similar conditions. It is likely then that, though f lower value than nasals, /l/ and /r/ are worth incorporating in a speaker lentification scheme making use of segmental information.

At first sight /l/ and /r/ appear to provide similar speaker-specific iformation (in agreement with Höfker (1977) who gave a similar efficiency anking to the two equivalent German phonemes spoken in isolation). But loser examination reveals dissimilarities, which may indicate different reatments of the two segments in speaker recognition.

/l/ was shown to exhibit a greater degree of coarticulation than /r/. This nderlay the markedly better performance of /l/ compared to /r/ when lentification was based on coarticulatory distance between each speaker's onsonants in front and back vowel environments, as suggested by Su *et al.* 1974). As pointed out in 3.4.4, however, such a method scarcely lends itself ɔ practical identification, because of the large and highly sophisticated test, s well as reference, corpus that it presupposes.

The recognition of the differing characteristics of /l/ and /r/ nevertheless ears on the design of a speaker recognition system using both segments, or he choice of one or the other for incorporation into such a system. /l/ is etter suited to cases where a reference corpus covering a wide range of owel environments is, or can be made, available, together with test items epresenting at least two dissimilar vowel environments. /r/, whilst erforming less well than /l/ overall, will be less sensitive in cases where eference and test corpora are limited, in the sense of providing only a few on-equivalent vowel environments – that is, in the cases where the oarticulation of /l/ would be most detrimental.

.5.2 *Theoretical conclusions – coarticulation*

'he concluding sections of Chapter 3 return to the theme outlined on p. 3, hat the close attention to between-speaker differences entailed in work on peaker recognition should provide stimuli and challenges for phonetic heory. In so far as this is the case, the relationship between theoretical

phonetics and the discipline of speaker recognition is shown to be symbioti
rather than merely one where the latter has to take account of the forme
The discussion deals specifically with idiosyncrasy in coarticulation.

3.5.2.1 *Theories of coarticulation* As pointed out by Kent and Minif (1977:116)

Coarticulation is a conceptualization of speech behaviour that implies (1) discre
and invariant units serving as input to the system of motor control, and (2) ;
eventual obscuration of the boundaries between units at the articulatory or acoust
levels.

Much attention has been paid over recent years to coarticulatic
phenomena, in the hope of uncovering details of the way in which speec
production is organised, and what the significant units of that organisatic
are; for critical surveys, see Daniloff and Hammarberg (1973), Kent ar
Minifie (1977) and Hammarberg (1976). The interest was partly sparked c
by Kozhevnikov and Chistovich (1965) who claimed, briefly, th
coarticulation phenomena occurred within a so-called 'articulatory syllabl
consisting of a vowel and all the consonants preceding it (the boundaries «
'articulatory syllables' will not, therefore, necessarily correspond 1
traditional syllable divisions – for example, CVC.CV could only t
CV ‖ CCV in terms of articulatory syllables).

Evidence from investigations of a number of phonetic properti«
including nasality, lip rounding, and jaw opening, has shown coarticulatic
effects not to be strictly confined within such a unit; one of the cleare
counter-examples, as pointed out by Nolan (1978:50), inheres in the data «
Lehiste (1964) from American English /r/ and /l/. She found that prevocal
/l/ was susceptible to quality change according to the adjacent vowel, whic
postvocalic /l/ was not – schematically ‖l$\overleftrightarrow{V}$ and $\overleftrightarrow{V}$‖l, where the double b;
indicates the (here correctly predictive) 'blocking' effect of the articulato
syllable boundary; but the findings for /r/ were exactly the reverse, so th
the articulatory syllable makes precisely the wrong predictions – ‖r$\overleftrightarrow{V}$ a
$\overleftrightarrow{V}$‖r. The power of the articulatory syllable construct is severely reduced
two contradictory articulatory syllables (CV for /l/ and VC for /r/) have to I
postulated.

Problems of a different kind undermine the articulatory syllable and oth
approaches which seek universal control principles for coarticulato
effects. It appears that some coarticulatory behaviour is language-specifi
In some cases assimilation between adjacent segments can be viewed ;
limited by phonological requirements; thus Ní Chasaide (1977) showed th
in Irish, which has three (or marginally four) lateral phonemes
contrasting quality, coarticulation with adjacent vowels is minimal cor

pared with that of the one English lateral. In other cases the behaviour is phonologically unmotivated – an example may be velar stops in English which seem not to coarticulate very much with preceding vowels (compare [k̟iːp] and [kɒd] with [piːk] and [dɒk]).

At this stage it seems reasonable to seek an account of coarticulation which, if perhaps less elegantly global, actually accommodates the data. One possibility is suggested by Bladon and Al-Bamerni (1976) to account for their demonstration that three extrinsic allophones of RP /l/ coarticulated with adjacent vowels to different degrees – [l] more than [ɫ], and syllabic [ˌɫ̩] least of all. They postulate that attached to each extrinsic allophone is an index of *coarticulation resistance* (1976:149):

Coarticulation on RP /l/ takes place freely from either direction, but the direction itself is unimportant. Antagonistic vocal tract adjustments apart, coarticulation is inhibited only by coarticulation resistance (CR) at some point in the succession of speech events. Each extrinsic allophone (and indeed each boundary condition) is assigned a value for CR by rules which in some instances may be language particular and in others quasi-universal. The CR value would be represented as a numerical coefficient attaching to a phonetic feature, say [3 CR], along the lines proposed by Chomsky and Halle (1968) for all other phonetic specifications in the phonological system.

The CR value assigned by the (realisation) rules will be correlated with phonological factors; in the case of Irish laterals, for example, the CR value will be higher (and hence the segment's coarticulation less) than that of the lateral in English because of the need to keep the three phonemes distinct. Bladon and Nolan (1977:193) present evidence that speakers who use a laminal articulation for /s z/ and an apical articulation for /t d l n/ adjust the articulation of a non-fricative to that of /s z/, rather than vice versa, when they occur in a cluster. /s z/ would have a high CR value (though the same might not be so for a language which had a less rich fricative series than English) which, combined with the rather precise articulation required to achieve the correct aerodynamic conditions for auditorily adequate /s z/, would cause the implementation rules to modify the non-fricative.

The concept of coarticulation resistance seems closely in accord with the position of Tatham (1969:17; see 2.3.4.8 above) who argues that in addition to controlled, extrinsic events, and inevitable, intrinsic events

there will be effects which occur or tend to occur *unless there is a specific command for them not to occur*.

The CR value constitutes just such a limitation on otherwise naturally occurring events – specifically the adjustment of adjacent segments to each other.

3.5.2.2 *Revision of 'coarticulation resistance'* Although it accommodates the differences in coarticulatory behaviour between different languages, and between different extrinsic allophones of a phoneme in the same language the theory of coarticulation resistance as presented in Bladon and Al-Bamerni (1976) falls short in at least two respects.

Firstly it cannot be the case as implied there that a single CR value attaches to an extrinsic allophone. For example, in a study demonstrating a least some tongue *body* coarticulation of fricatives and stops with adjacent vowels, Amerman and Daniloff (1977:111) suggest that

except for the regions of contact or constriction, tongue body shape may not be any more precisely specified for the. . .fricatives than the. . .stops.

It is therefore proposed here that a number of CR values attach to each segment. However, it will be recalled from 2.3.7 that in the present model the phonetic representation does not consist in segments, but in series of specifications (in a number of phonetic dimensions) taking the form (v,t) where v is the integer value in the dimension and t its temporal domain; significant temporal relationships thus inhere in the phonetic representation (see Fig. 2.5). It is now proposed that rather than being duples, specifications are triples of the form (v,r,t) where r indicates the resistance of the value v to perturbation. For example, from Fig. 2.5 it will be recalled that [s] is putatively specified for a particular spectral 'density of frication', which, following the arguments of Bladon and Nolan (1977), would be protected by a high r value; other dimensions such as 'centre of gravity of frication' might have lower r values, so that a speaker would be at liberty to produce a 'low pitched' or 'high pitched' [s] if this facilitated integration with an adjacent vowel. In implementational terms, the tongue tip and blade would have little freedom, whereas the tongue body would be free to vary. The somewhat contrasting coarticulatory behaviour of blade and body are in this way accounted for.

Interestingly, and linking with the discussion below, Amerman and Daniloff (1977:110) found that their two subjects, who also produced /t d/ in the same environments as /s z/, differed in relative coarticulation of the sounds; one coarticulating increasingly in the order /s z t d/, the other in the order /d s t z/.

The second shortcoming of the original formulation lies in the way it handles the kind of between-speaker variation in coarticulation investigated in this chapter. Bladon and Al-Bamerni (1976) mentioning the work of Su et al. (1974:150) on speaker identification using nasal coarticulation claim that 'there seem to be cases where CR is assigned on a highly idiolectal basis'. However they seem thereby to be envisaging incorporating into the phonetic representation information which is not part of the culturally shared language system, but rather concerns individuals' strategies for achieving common goals. It is preferable to assume that, beyond linguistic constraints, coarticulatory solutions are not specified in the phonetic representation but, where the latter allows latitude, are determined by alternative implementational options.

A concrete proposal for the implementation mechanism will clarify this position. Fig. 3.15 shows schematically two adjacent triples in a dimension of the phonetic representation. It might for instance represent the auditory correlate of F_2 for the canonical 'clear' [l], and a following [i].

A speaker knows that he cannot implement a step between values, and in

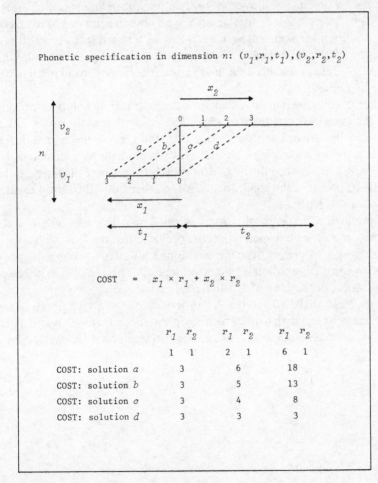

3.15 Coarticulatory implementation strategies

fact (given his knowledge of articulator dynamics) that the transition cannot be sharper than the slope of the dotted lines $a - d$. The problem is where to locate the transition.

Each of the solutions $a - d$ has associated with it a *cost*, which the speaker aims to minimise. The cost is the sum of two terms, one for each triple involved. Each of these terms is the product of the coarticulation resistance r, and the time x by which the specification is 'eaten into' by the transition. (In fact the cost computation will involve more than merely adjacent segments as in the present simplified example, and it is likely that it should include a weighting factor to make transitions more expensive as they approach the maximum rate, in accord with the readiness of speakers to anticipate a specification over more than one preceding specification.)

In cases where r_1 and r_2 are the same, a number of solutions have an equal cost, and each speaker will be free to choose his own strategy. This is the analogue of the lateral plus vowel sequences investigated above, where different speakers reliably exhibited various degrees of vowel influence in a preceding lateral.

When one r value is greater than the other, the various solutions no longer have the same cost, as shown on Fig. 3.15 by the columns for $r_1, r_2 = 2, 1$ and 6, 1; and the greater the difference in r, the greater the cost difference between the solutions. Irish laterals plus vowel might be specified 6, 1 for r_1, r_2 where a low cost could only be attained by perturbing the lateral quality as little as possible; the consequence is the heavily diphthongised nature of the vowels in Irish.

A prediction made by this mechanism is that in cases where a clear disparity in r exists between adjacent specifications, the 'cost slope' will be steep enough to prevent speakers adopting alternative solutions, and so between-speaker variation would be minimised. This remains to be tested – for instance, in the case of Irish laterals.

Regardless of the correctness or otherwise of the above proposals, the point remains valid that idiosyncrasy in coarticulatory behaviour is data which cannot be ignored in formulating theories of speech production.

4

Long term quality

4.1 Introduction

This chapter approaches the characterisation of the acoustic exponents of the long term strands (see 2.3.2). Firstly (4.2), there is a review of the use of long term suprasegmental properties in speaker recognition; in fact, this work has been confined largely to the dimension of fundamental frequency, which is robust in transmission and amenable to automatic extraction.

Sections 4.3 and 4.4 then attempt to sharpen understanding of the acoustic correlates of segmental long term qualities, as exemplified by the categories of Laver's (1980) descriptive framework for voice qualities. there is a brief survey in 4.3 of speaker recognition techniques based on the long term spectrum, which exploit such properties; 4.3 also outlines a descriptive framework for long term qualities ('voice qualities'); and demonstrates the relationship of terms in that framework (both laryngeal ('phonation type') and supralaryngeal) to the long term spectrum.

In 4.4, an alternative approach to the acoustic categorisation of the supralaryngeal qualities is then explored in some detail. The work in this section and the previous one relies primarily on data from one speaker (supplemented by data from a second) exemplifying different supralaryngeal qualities. Such a limitation may be unexpected in the context of speaker recognition, which normally concerns itself with differences between speakers. In the study of long term qualities, however, it seems that knowledge of acoustic correlates is still at such a rudimentary level as to justify the imposition of the strictest limitations on the data utilised. The limitation to single speakers factors out (most kinds of) intrinsic variation in the data; in terms of the model presented in Chapter 2 the 'physical constraints' (2.3.9) of the vocal tract are controlled for. Only by adopting such a limitation will a clear picture emerge of what constitutes the acoustic correlates of the range of long term speech settings and their perceptual equivalents.

Concentration on a single speaker should also illustrate a recurrent theme of this dissertation – the enormous plasticity of any vocal tract and hence the potential for variation in its output.

4.2 The long term suprasegmental strand

4.2.1 *Introduction*

The suprasegmental strand of speech, as explained in 2.3.2, involves contrastive patterns having a domain (potentially) greater than that of a segment; it is taken traditionally to consist in modulation of the physically measurable dimensions of fundamental frequency, amplitude (or equivalently here 'intensity', or 'gain'), and duration.

Although two contrasting suprasegmental patterns may be established on a stretch of utterance as short as a syllable, there are characteristics of a person's voice in these dimensions which, whether extrinsic or intrinsic, may be regarded as pervading the whole of his acoustic output, or at least some appreciable part of it on a particular occasion, and cannot be attributed to realisations of one particular element in the linear sequence of supra-segmental patterns. Familiar impressionistic descriptions such as a 'high (pitched)/monotonous/loud/soft/drawling voice' are mostly a perceptual response to such characteristics. More rigorously defined terms have been developed by Laver *et al.* (1981) in the application of Laver's (1980) kind of voice quality framework to the description of pathological speech; auditory judgments are made along six-point scales on, for instance, the mean, range, and variability of pitch and loudness.

The following two sections survey briefly the ways in which the long term aspect of the suprasegmental strand has been exploited in work on speaker recognition, and the third draws attention to a type of parameter which appears to have largely escaped notice in such work.

From the point of view of criterion 5 (1.1.5), robustness in transmission, both fundamental frequency and duration have the attraction that they resist distortion by telephone and similar transmission lines which could have a severe effect on spectral properties (for fundamental frequency, see for instance McGonegal *et al.* (1979) cited in 1.1.5 above). Tape recorder speed could of course be a confounding variable; but the absence of energy in the region below around 300 Hz in which the fundamental is likely to be found is not a problem given F_0-finding techniques such as those of Snow and Hughes (1969), Miller (1968, 1970), and the widely used 'cepstral' method, which rely on the interval between higher harmonics. For a comparison of the performance of F_0-finding algorithms, see Rabiner *et al.* (1976). Amplitude, on the other hand, will clearly be affected by many factors, from the distance of the speaker from a microphone, to the settings of the controls on the measuring apparatus. The utterance-internal amplitude relationships might also be subject to distortion according to the dynamic range of the equipment involved.

4.2.2 *Atemporal long term suprasegmental parameters*

The simplest parameters related to the long term suprasegmental strand are those based on the whole of a speech sample, information from the time base having been discarded. If, for example, the fundamental period is measured of successive (pitch-synchronous, or fixed-length) frames in the utterance, a statistical distribution of fundamental period (or its reciprocal, fundamental frequency) can be built up. It will often approximate a normal distribution, and its deviations therefrom can be used in its characterisation. A similar treatment is possible with amplitude measurements.

Jassem (1971:59) claims that

Among the many features that distinguish individual voices there are two that are related to the range of tones used in speech. We refer to them as 'pitch' and 'compass'. PITCH is the position of the range of tones used by the speaker along the frequency scale and COMPASS is the width of that range.

He goes on to suggest that an appropriate measure of 'pitch', in this sense, is the arithmetic mean value of a long term F_0 distribution, and of 'compass', the F_0 interval between $\pm 2\sigma$ around the mean. Additionally, statistical measures of the skewness and kurtosis of the distribution, based on its third and fourth moments, will show respectively whether the speaker's most-used fundamental value (the mode) is below, at, or above the mean, and whether the distribution is narrower (leptokurtic) or wider (platykurtic) than the normal distribution. Green (1972), in an attempt to recognise speakers on the basis of conversational speech, characterised them by the first four moments of their fundamental frequency distribution.

A recurring question in relation to long term parameters is that of the length of speech sample required to obtain a genuine characterisation of the speaker. For F_0 statistics of this kind, there seems to be a convergence of opinion that within-speaker variation between speech samples reduces with increasing sample length up to around one minute, and thereafter rather little. Mead (1974:8) found, for the difference-moment parameters explained in 4.2.3 below, that

sampling error is negligibly small for samples containing more than approximately 75 seconds running speech. . .[and that]. . .mean parameter standard deviations have converged to within a factor of two of their 'large sample values' for. . .stretches of approximately thirty seconds duration.

Similar values (around 70, and 40 seconds respectively) emerge from the study of Markel and Davis (1979), and these figures bracket those of Steffen-Batóg *et al.* (1970) – 50 secs, and Horii (1972) – 60 secs.

Green's method proved to be (Mead 1974:4)

of only moderate value for recognition, the separation obtained between different speakers being quite small.

A limiting factor, as always, is the relation of within-speaker to between-speaker variation, and in a study on variation in fundamental frequency Atkinson (1976:440) found that

the intraspeaker variability was essentially as great as the interspeaker.

He suggests that the within-speaker variation can be assigned to two types: a 'static' component, involving the shifting up or down of the F_0 contour as a whole, and a 'dynamic' component affecting parts of contours relative to others. His claim that

The static component basically appears to be a random variable affecting the initial value of F_0 at the onset of phonation for the entire utterance,

is interesting as it implies empirical disconfirmation of Crystal's (1969:143) hypothesised 'pitch constant' for a speaker:

For any speaker, the first prominent syllable of a tone-unit is articulated at or around a stable pitch level for the majority of his tone-units.

Only 1 per 200 tone units in Crystal's data were perceived as having involved onset variation. However, a definitive assessment of the claim would require an experiment including a systematic analysis of the intonational properties of the data, as opposed to Atkinson's purely mechanical F_0 registration.

In general, measures based on the mean and deviation of F_0 have proved to be among the more successful long term measures in speaker recognition, second only to long term spectral properties. Markel *et al.* (1977:337) found on the basis of between-speaker to within-speaker variance ratios that

the rank ordering of parameter sets in importance was shown to be spectral, fundamental frequency, and then gain.

Doherty and Hollien (1978) ranked three vectors, LTS (23 elements consisting of the long term averages of the outputs of 23 one-third octave band pass filters), SFF (2 elements – mean F_0 and the standard deviation of F_0) and ST (2 elements – the total time a speech signal [i.e. phonation, apparently] was present, and a measure of rate of segmental articulation) in that order, on their performance in speaker identification tests.

In fact ranking of individual features by Markel *et al.* (1977:Table 1) reveals that whilst mean F_0 has a variance ratio similar to that of all but the best of the long term average linear prediction reflection coefficients, the standard deviation of F_0 is a worse parameter even than the gain standard deviation. They point out (1977:336) that this goes against the suggestion of Mead (1974), extending the work of Green (1972), that the first four moments of F_0-based distributions may be suitable parameters. In the opinion of Markel *et al.* higher order moments magnify errors in the automatically extracted F_0 contour to a damagingly high degree. Further, Markel and Davis (1979) show F_0 to be less stable across recordings made over at least 10 weeks than a long term spectral parameter.

Perceptually, the importance of F_0 in speaker recognition is well attested. Precise conclusions are difficult to draw from experiments such as those of Pollack *et al.* (1954) and Shearme and Holmes (1959). The former found that to achieve equivalent levels of speaker identification, subjects required a sample of whispered speech (lacking F_0) three times as long as of voiced speech; but clearly here characteristic source-spectrum features, and possibly vocal tract transmission information, are also being lost. Shearme and Holmes found that subjects were still able to achieve 69% correct verification when samples from eight speakers had had their laryngeal source substituted by a monotone using a vocoder; but it is not clear what decrement this represents compared with unmodified speech, as this was not tested. But in a later experiment Matsumoto *et al.* (1973:435) used a multiple correlation analysis to find the relationship between the personal quality of sustained vowels, represented in a multidimensional space derived from perceptual confusions in speaker discrimination tasks, and a number of acoustic parameters of the stimuli; they concluded that

the relative contribution of the mean fundamental pitch frequency to the perception of the personal quality of voice is the largest among all parameters.

Abberton (1976), presenting real and synthesised laryngographic signals to listeners, found that the most important cue to speaker identity was mean F_0.

This very perceptual salience may, however, render F_0 statistics vulnerable under conditions of mimicry and disguise (criterion *3*, 1.1.5). In mimicry, it appears that, although adjustment may take place in the direction of the mean F_0 of the target speaker, an exact match is not achieved; Hall and Tosi (1975:107) reported that in pairs of a 'real' voice and a professional attempt at mimicry: 'in all cases, average fundamental frequencies differed', and Endres *et al.* (1971) found that whilst imitators try to adapt the mean frequency of their voice to the person being imitated, they generally do not succeed in striking the exact frequency.

In disguise, however, the speaker has the advantage as his goal is any set of F_0 characteristics but his own: and it appears it is easy for him to alter his own. The results above indicating F_0 change in mimicry carry over to the disguise question since one strategy of disguise is to mimic another's voice; and in an experiment where speakers were encouraged to adopt a disguise of their choice, Doherty and Hollien discovered that the identification success of their SFF vector (comprising mean F_0 and standard deviation of F_0) reduced sharply under disguise (1978:5):

While the reduction due to stress is minimal, it is exceptionally severe when talkers attempt disguise. . .speakers appear to be conscious of pitch as a vocal attribute and frequently change it when attempting to disguise their voices.

4.2.3 *Time sensitive long term suprasegmental parameters*

The above long term suprasegmental measures have contained no temporal information – as Atal (1976:471) comments on the use of moments of the F_0 distribution:

Such a description retains information only about the variability of pitch in an utterance but not about the exact sequence of pitch variations as a function of time. For example, a particular sequence of pitch samples can be arranged in any arbitrary order without affecting the moments.

Two long term measures which do not discard all temporal information are investigated by Mead (1974). The first technique involves differencing the values of the F_0 curve. The first-order difference curve consists of the differences between each adjacent pair of values in the F_0 curve; the second-order difference curve consists of the differences between each adjacent pair of values in the first-order difference curve; and so on. Differences up to fourth order were computed, giving five curves including the original F_0 curve; each speech sample was characterised by the first four moments of the distribution of values in each of these curves (20 parameters in all).

The second technique exploits F_0-contour shape over longer time spans to overcome the statistical interdependence of adjacent F_0 values (1974:12). It involves approximating the F_0 curve with sections of straight line, and assigning each section to one of three clusters according to whether the line is level, ascending, or descending. Each line segment is also characterised in terms of its own mean F_0 value, and its length in time. Each cluster is then described by its mean and standard deviation in the three dimensions (slope, mean F_0, and length), giving 18 speech-sample parameters, plus three others which are the proportions of the line segments allocated to each cluster.

In a straight forced-allocation closed identification test the difference-moment parameters yielded a marginally better performance, whilst in an open test based on a 'fixed radius' threshold in the parameter hyperspace, the line-segment parameters gave fewer ambiguous decisions. It is not known whether these parameters would be more resistant to disguise than those derived from standard F_0 statistics.

A technique similar, in that it extracts long term statistical information about repeated F_0 time-base patterns, has been used by Fourcin (e.g. Fourcin and Abberton 1976) as a method for identifying laryngeal pathologies and monitoring recovery. It uses a laryngographic recording as input for F_0 tracking, but in a speaker-identification application it could be extended to audio signals, given an adequate method of pitch-synchronous F_0 tracking. A series of statistical distributions are computed, the first being the probability in the sample of periods of each given duration, the second the probability of two consecutive periods of each duration, and the third the probability of three such consecutive periods. Low probabilities of identical successive fundamental periods will result from voices which exhibit appreciable 'pitch jitter', the perceptual correlate of which may be a harsh voice quality (cf. Wendahl 1972). However, phonation types (such as harsh voice, breathy voice, etc.) are here regarded as belonging to the segmental strand (2.3.4.10), and F_0 statistics which reveal period to period (ir)regularity ('microperturbation' as opposed to 'intonation' in the terminology of Laver *et al.* (1982:193)) are perhaps no longer exploiting the suprasegmental strand.

4.2.4 *Time base long term parameters*

Between-speaker differences in this category arguably originate equally in the segmental as in the suprasegmental strand, since (relative and absolute) segment durations may contribute to them; but they will be dealt with here in 4.2 since the perceptual properties to which they relate, such as rhythmicality, have traditionally been regarded as suprasegmental or prosodic properties.

A number of casual terms exist to describe overall impressions of speech which have to do with timing factors, such as 'rhythmical', 'clipped', 'drawling'. Rhythm is always problematical, because inherently it must imply not only a time base, but also the occurrence of definable events along that time base – in the case of speech the events possibly being defined in any of or a mixture of the dimensions of intensity, periodicity, or spectral properties.

In a section on rhythm Crystal (1969:4.11) defines three analytic dimensions: *rhythmic/arhythmic, spiky/glissando,* and *staccato/legato.* Rhythmic/arhythmic refers to (1969:163)

our awareness that a stretch of utterance may comprise markedly regular, 'stress-timed' pulses, on the one hand, and markedly irregular beats on the other.

It is not clear, however, that his opinion that 'the perception of rhythmicity

127

is principally due to increased or decreased loudness on the stressed syllables of the utterance' would be generally supported, or testable; further, it seems to lead to overlap between this dimension and staccato/legato (below). Spiky/glissando concerns the relation between (successive strongly and weakly prominent) syllables (1969:164):

spiky utilises sharp and rapid [pitch] jumps between syllables, *glissando* utilises smooth and usually fairly slow glides,

while in the staccato/legato contrast, it seems, the contrast between strongly and weakly prominent syllables is heightened (staccato) or lessened (legato) by increasing or decreasing the loudness and duration differentials between them.

Laver (1980) does not include, in his framework for the description of voice quality, terms relating explicitly to time base phenomena; but in subsequent work on the application of the voice quality framework to pathological voice qualities (Laver *et al.* 1981) there are included in the perceptual dimensions (on which auditory ratings are made by trained judges) two 'temporal organisation features', 'continuity' and 'rate'; and separately a feature of 'rhythmicality'. These auditory judgments were also made on a control group of normal voices.

The correspondence between auditory judgments of time base parameters and acoustic correlates is notoriously problematical. A classical example is the auditory phonetic categorisation of languages as either 'stress-timed' or 'syllable-timed' (cf. Abercrombie 1967:97ff); to a first approximation, this implies that in some languages (stress-timed ones) the stressed syllables fall (or have a tendency to fall) on a regular rhythmic beat, the duration of intervening unstressed syllables being adjusted according to their number to facilitate this; in other languages (syllable-timed), all syllables tend towards a constant duration and so may be regarded as each falling on a regular beat. English, and French, respectively, are traditionally cited examples of the two types of language. However the notion of 'stress isochrony' (equal time between stressed syllables) implicit in stress-timing is hard to pin down in terms of acoustic correlates (see e.g. Lehiste 1977), and some writers retreat to viewing isochrony as purely perceptually imposed on the acoustic substance. Certainly instrumental investigation of the claims implicit in stress- and syllable-timing have conspicuously failed to support the distinction (see e.g. Roach 1982).

Even though differences between languages may be reflected (on a smaller scale) in differences between individual speakers of the same language, it seems that the stress- versus syllable-timing dimension is too elusive even in the former context to be of use in the latter. It is likely to be more productive from the point of view of speaker recognition to start from features which have well-defined measurable acoustic correlates – and then perhaps test their relationships to the complex perceptions of rhythm and rate.

The temporal vector ST of Doherty and Hollien (1978 – see above, 4.2.2), consisting of the total proportion of speaking time a signal was present, and rate of segmental articulation, was ranked as the least successful of three vectors tested. But other possible time base parameters would be worth exploring, such as syllable rate (reasonable instrumental approximation might be obtained by detecting peaks in the F_1 contour (Andrew Crompton, personal communication) since high F_1 corresponds to lack of obstruction in the vocal tract, and the succession of syllables reflects largely the successive openings of the vocal tract). The syllable rate could then be expressed as what are commonly known as speech rate (total speaking time including silent pauses divided by the number of syllables produced), or articulation rate (speaking time excluding silent pauses divided by the number of syllables produced) – see e.g. Scherer (1979:161).

Again, more interesting than a ratio between total voiced and total voiceless time in speech samples might be mean durations of the alternately voiced and voiceless stretches (preferably excluding pauses) of which the speech wave consists; the ratio between these means; and statistical distributions of each kind of stretch. This kind of measure seems the most probable acoustic correlate of Crystal's spiky/glissando contrast (above), for although Crystal discusses it in terms of pitch jumps versus slow pitch glides, this seems likely to correlate with shorter versus longer bursts of voicing (and hence presence of fundamental frequency and perception of pitch) in relation to the alternating stretches of speech. In more 'everyday' terms, 'clipped' speech would consist of relatively short (principally vocalic) stretches and relatively long intervening voiceless (principally consonantal) stretches, whilst 'drawled' speech would be perceived when the opposite relationship existed.

However, although speaker recognition parameters on this kind of basis are worth exploring, it must be appreciated that they will probably be as sensitive as any other long term suprasegmental parameters to variation due to the mapping of (especially affective) communicative intent.

To summarise the relationship between speaker recognition and the long term aspect of the suprasegmental strand, most writers have concentrated on the dimension of fundamental frequency. Those who have employed long term amplitude and duration parameters (e.g. Markel *et al.* 1977, and Doherty and Hollien 1978) have not found them as efficient in separating speakers. Mean fundamental is the most effective parameter at separating speakers, though in technical speaker recognition it is not more important than the best spectral cues (e.g. Markel *et al.* 1977), unlike the perceptual dominance ascribed to it by for example Matsumoto *et al.* (1973). Its perceptual salience may make it especially vulnerable to disguise attempts.

4.3 The long term segmental strand

4.3.1 *The use of long term spectra in speaker recognition*

Apart from exploitation of F_0 statistics, the methodology in speaker recognition which most clearly exploits long term properties centres on the use of long term spectra. These are overall spectra obtained by averaging the short term power spectrum over a sample of speech long enough for the effect of the spectral characteristics of individual linguistic segments no longer to be significant. The long term spectrum should then provide a characterisation of the speaker independent of the linguistic content of the utterance.

Tarnóczy (1962) presented average spectra obtained by the 'choral' method (see Tosi 1975, and below) and suggested their application in speaker recognition, but did not proceed to test his suggestion. Pruzansky (1963) tried identifying speakers by cross-correlating three-dimensional time–frequency–energy patterns, and, finding that identification rates suffered little when the time dimension was omitted in what was effectively the cross-correlation of long term spectra, concluded that the spectral distinctiveness of speakers is retained in such spectra.

Kosiel (1973) explored two statistical treatments of average spectra produced by bandpass filters, the first involving analysis of the spectral curves using orthogonal polynomials, and the second treating the spectra numerically as consisting of as many variables as there were frequency channels, and performing data reduction before computing Mahalanobis distances between spectra; she concluded that either method demonstrated sufficient individuality in the long term spectrum to justify its use in speaker recognition. Majewski and Hollien (1975), working with speech samples of 32 second duration from 50 American and 50 Polish males analysed by a one-third octave band spectrum analyser, used a Euclidean distance measure to compare the long term spectra, and obtained a high identification rate (in general higher for the Polish speakers). In a study using the same data base Zalewski, Majewski and Hollien (1975) found that cross-correlation of long term spectra yielded identification approximately equal to the Euclidean distance technique, and concluded that combining the two might result in a more powerful identification process.

Gubrynowicz (1973) used a bank of 15 one-third octave filters (160–4000 Hz) to produce vectorial long term spectra of newspaper text read by 15 males. He concluded that identification improved when the reference was an average of spectra from more than one recording, but that no great advantage was gained by spacing the recordings over longer time spans than a day. This finding does not conform with those of Furui *et al.* (1972) who claim it is necessary to base the reference on samples recorded over a long period (up to three months) to achieve good recognition of a later test sample. When the reference sample is based on short observation periods (e.g. 10 days), recognition is only high if the test item is produced within a few days to three weeks. Concerning the duration of sample needed to prevent the phonetic content influencing the spectrum, Furui *et al.* infer from identification and verification rates that 10 seconds of continuous speech is sufficient.

To investigate the effect of language spoken, Tosi (1979:90–1) used as his subjects 20 natives of Piedmont fluent in Italian, French and Piedmontese, and characterised their speech samples by deriving 'choral' spectra from them. This technique involves dividing the speech into sections and re-recording these simultaneously on a single tape loop, before processing by a one-third octave spectrum analyser. Tosi concluded that each speaker possesses 'relative invariances' in his or her choral spectra regardless of the language used. This finding does not directly contradict that of Majewski and Hollien (1975) and Hollien and Majewski (1977) who achieved less good identification for American English than the Polish speakers, and concluded that the power of the long term spectrum as an identification tool might be 'somewhat language dependent' (1977:979), since these authors used different populations for the tests in the two languages; nevertheless there is an indirect conflict because, whilst Tosi would presumably predict that if Majewski and Hollien's 50 Polish speakers turned out to be bilingual and subsequently recorded themselves in English, their identification rate would remain the same, Majewski and Hollien would expect the use of English to lower identification rates.

The sections of Hollien and Majewski (1977) unfamiliar to readers of Majewski and Hollien (1975) deal with the effects on identification of 25 American English speakers under normal conditions, under stress (when suffering electric shocks at random intervals), and when attempting to disguise their voices. Choice of disguise was left to the speaker, except that foreign accents and non-modal phonation types were discouraged. Identifications were computed from 80–10 000 Hz long term spectra, and also band limited (315–3150 Hz) versions simulating telephone transmissions. With the full bandwidth, identification dropped from 100% for normal speech to 92% under stress or to 20% under disguise; with the limited bandwidth, from 88% to 68% under stress or 32% under disguise.

The surprising facet here is that, contrary to the trend with the other two speaking conditions, band limiting appears to improve identification when disguise is attempted. The anomaly disappears when Hollien and Majewski rank the parameters by total number of confusions, rather than just considering correct identification; however this anomaly might still be more than a mere artefact. Virtually by definition, the spectrum within the telephone passband is subject to linguistic constraints, whereas the frequency range outside is presumably much less so. It would not be surprising, then, if the telephone passband provided less scope for radical disguise – hence higher identification rates when the range more amenable to disguise is omitted. It may be that on the parameters outside the telephone bandwidth a speaker, unconstrained linguistically, has freedom to achieve values to place himself outside the space bounded by the values of the speech of most normal speakers. Within the telephone band, however, his disguising attempts are linguistically constrained (he could not, for instance, articulate [i] all the time so as to produce a peak in the long term spectrum at 2 kHz; but he would have the option to produce one at perhaps 3 kHz or above – the so-called 'singing formant' – by lowering his larynx and causing the larynx tube to function as an independent resonator (see Sundberg 1974)).

The status of the anomaly is made even less clear by what is apparently a re-presentation by Doherty and Hollien (1978). Here the anomaly has vanished, unexplained, from the identification rates: (fullband) normal 100%, stress 72%, disguise 24%; (band-limited) normal 80%, stress 60%, disguise 20%. It must be inferred that these different values result from a change from a Euclidean distance measure (Hollien and Majewski 1977:975) to ' a discriminant analysis technique. . .one of pattern matching' (Doherty and Hollien 1978:4). Clearly a number of conflicts and confusions in this area remain to be resolved.

4.3.2 *The bases of recognition by long term spectra*

Lacking from these various studies is any detailed consideration of the bases of the speaker-dependent information in the long term spectrum which is being exploited. Hollien and Majewski (1977:976), after cautioning against too ready generalisation of their laboratory results to particular applications, state that

Nevertheless, the following experiments should extend the understanding of LTS as a cue for speaker recognition.

But whilst their experiments extend knowledge of how well the cue works under conditions of distortion, understanding of why it works, and hence the possibility of predicting theoretically the conditions which are most likely to affect its reliability, are not really brought closer.

A long term spectrum is a straightforward averaging of the short term spectrum (usually a power spectrum) of the acoustic output of the vocal tract. The spectrum is classically regarded as the result of the combination of a source function and a transmission function; in the case of a voiceless fricative the source will be a stricture causing turbulence somewhere in the vocal tract, and the transmission function will depend on the vocal cavities in front of and behind the stricture, and also on radiation effects at the lips, and damping by the cavity walls; in the case of resonants, which in terms of duration constitute the majority of speech, the source is laryngeal vibration and the transmission function depends on the configuration of the supraglottal vocal tract. Useful as this model has proved to be in its synthetic applications, it may be found inadequate because it ignores the effects of subglottal cavities, as pointed out by for example Fant *et al.* (1972) and Wakita and Fant (1978). From the point of view of speech production, however, it is reasonable to assume that for the speaker the foci of control in affecting the power spectrum of the sound radiated from the lips are the configuration of the supraglottal vocal tract (the subglottal vocal tract being relatively insusceptible to modification), and the activity at the glottis (dependent on its configuration and tension, and on pulmonically controlled aerodynamic factors).

The long term spectrum is determined by both intrinsic factors, resulting from the physical constraints of the speaker's vocal apparatus, and extrinsic factors, resulting from control exerted by the speaker (see 2.3.2). Additionally, it was suggested in 2.3.7 that a speaker may forward *null* values to the phonetic representation for implementation – abdicating potential control, as it were, and merely allowing his vocal apparatus to perform in the way it finds most natural.

It has been stressed repeatedly (2.2, 2.3.9, 2.4) that physical constraints do not determine absolute acoustic values in the output speech, but merely the limits within which variation can take place. Any speaker is therefore free to alter the properties of the long term spectrum, in at least the ways demonstrated below in 4.3.4. Intrinsic limitations do prevent certain combinations of incompatible long term specifications – for example, palatalisation with velarisation, or creaky with breathy phonation (see 4.3.3) – and speakers may be prevented temporarily or permanently from achieving values or combinations of values within the normal human range by for instance states of health and stress, but even here the range of possible adjustments is considerable.

Long term quality

Within the intrinsic limits, the speaker is free to exert extrinsic control over long term quality. He may in some instances choose to forward a *default* value to the phonetic representation – a value which, in default of a determined value resulting from a mapping of communicative intent, he habitually selects within the culturally acceptable range, and which is informative of his identity (see pp. 56 and 66). Otherwise he chooses a value in accord with some aspect of communicative intent – whether it be nasalisation to indicate an attitude of irony, whispery voice (conspiracy, perhaps), creaky voice to convey solidarity by convergence to the pronunciation of a speaker of a different class (cf. Trudgill 1974a:186) or whatever – which potentially affects the long term spectrum.

A question which deserves attention is the strength of the long term specifications with respect to short term specifications. Given that the phonetic dimensions of the long term specifications are the same as those of the short term specifications, conflicts may arise. Laver (1980:20) considers this question, and employs the terms 'susceptible' and 'non-susceptible' to refer to segments which can, or cannot, be affected by a long term setting. Non-susceptibility is of two kinds: where the parametric long term value is overridden by a short term specification, leaving the long term specification to apply vacuously – as in the case of a nasal segment in nasalised voice – or where the long term value is temporarily 'reversed' by the short term requirement – as in the case of an oral stop (with velic closure) during nasalised voice.

However it is likely that the interaction between long term requirements and those of the short term strands in cases of potential 'reversal' is more complex. The kinds of conflict which may arise are similar to those which arise through segmental juxtaposition, giving rise to 'coarticulation'. It is tentatively suggested here that the 'coarticulation resistance' value of a short term specification, which according to 3.5.2 governs its implementational adaptation to proximate specifications, may additionally govern its power to reverse long term specifications. In this way pressures in the phonological system would have the potential to inhibit the effect of long term specifications, in the same way that they inhibit coarticulation; such a mechanism, appropriately supported by evidence, might answer Crystal (1975:61):

'Secondary articulations' such as velarisation, palatalisation and labialisation are regularly cited in both phonemic and paralinguistic studies, but there does not seem to be any generally recognised means of integrating this information, and there is a basic lack of knowledge about the 'facts'. For example, does a language which uses velarisation as a normal phonemic distinctive feature also allow paralinguistic velarisation?

As an example, given the greater 'F$_2$' coarticulation resistance of the 'dark' as compared with the 'clear' extrinsic allophone of English /l/, it would be predicted that if a speaker for communicative effect adopted long term palatalisation the effect on the 'clear' allophone would be greater. To the extent that such predictions were borne out, so would the generality, and hence perhaps the explanatory power, of 'coarticulation resistance' be increased. The testing of such predictions, however, lies outside the scope of the present work.

The subsequent section demonstrates the potential a speaker has for perturbing a long term spectrum by his long term specifications. In theory any of these 'voice qualities', or combinations of them, might be recruitable in a particular community for communicative purposes, and certainly for disguise; a task for speaker recognition is to determine the kinds of variation which are in fact communicatively exploited.

4.3.3 *Componential analysis of long term quality*

A reason why knowledge of the acoustic correlates of long term qualities has lagged behind that of the acoustic properties of segments may have been the lack until recently of a coherent phonetic framework for classifying the former comparable to the traditional phonetic description of segments. In the short term segmental strand, categories of sound could be systematically specified and their acoustic correlates explored. Without a parallel framework for long term effects, it was not straightforward to explore their acoustic correlates. The provision of such a framework, superseding a largely heterogeneous and unsystematic collection of impressionistic labels for voice qualities, is due largely to Laver (1975; 1980). Starting out from Abercrombie's definition (1967:91) of voice quality as

those characteristics which are present more or less all the time that a person is talking: it is a quasi-permanent quality running through all the sounds that issue from his mouth,

Laver attempts to provide, for voice quality, a general phonetic descriptive framework (1980:7) 'applicable to the vocal performance of all human beings of normal anatomy and physiology'. The descriptive system (1980:7)

stands on an auditory foundation. But the auditorily-identified components all have correlates specified at each of the three other levels of analysis, all capable of instrumental verification – the articulatory, physiological, and acoustic levels.

As implied, the framework describes auditorily identified voice quality components in primarily articulatory terms, although of course in some cases knowledge is not advanced enough to permit confidence that the articulation postulated to underlie a particular quality is the only, or even primary, articulatory requirement. The long term articulatory trend underlying a voice quality component is known as a *setting*.

The research described in the following sections is directed towards the discovery of the acoustic correlates of the voice quality components. A brief summary of the framework follows to assist understanding of the subsequent sections; the details can be found in Laver (1980).

Fig. 4.1 indicates the structure of the framework. The primary trichotomy characterises a *setting* according to whether it is a function of the supralaryngeal vocal tract; of the phonatory mechanism of the larynx; or is a setting affecting the overall muscular tension of the whole of the vocal tract.

To provide a reference for the description of the supralaryngeal settings, a 'neutral configuration' of the vocal tract has to be defined. Laver makes use of the acoustic phonetician's idealised 'neutral vowel', resulting from a straight-sided tube, which will have formant frequencies

$$F_n = (2n - 1)c/4l$$

where c is the velocity of sound and l the effective length of the vocal tract. For an average male vocal tract of $l = 17.0$ cm, the formants will be spaced 1000 Hz apart: F_1 500 Hz; F_2 1500 Hz; F_3 2500 Hz and so on. In articulatory terms the supralaryngeal neutral configuration is thought of as a 'constellation' of settings as follows (Laver 1980:14):

– the lips are not protruded
– the larynx is neither raised nor lowered
– the supralaryngeal vocal tract is most nearly in equal cross-section along its full length
– front oral articulations are performed by the blade of the tongue
– the root of the tongue is neither advanced nor retracted
– the faucal pillars do not constrict the vocal tract
– the pharyngeal constrictor muscles do not constrict the vocal tract
– the jaw is neither closed nor unduly open
– the use of the velopharyngeal system causes audible nasality only where necessary for linguistic purposes.

Supralaryngeal settings which deviate from this neutral configuration may constitute longitudinal, latitudinal, or velopharyngeal modifications of the vocal tract.

Longitudinal settings involve physically lengthening or shortening the vocal tract at its inner or outer ends, the possibilities being lowering or raising of the larynx and protrusion or spreading of the lips.

Latitudinal settings are subdivided into labial, lingual, faucal, pharyngeal and mandibular categories. Labial settings comprise the various combinatory possibilities of horizontal and vertical expansion or contraction of the interlabial space, which may thus affect the labial cross-sectional area of the

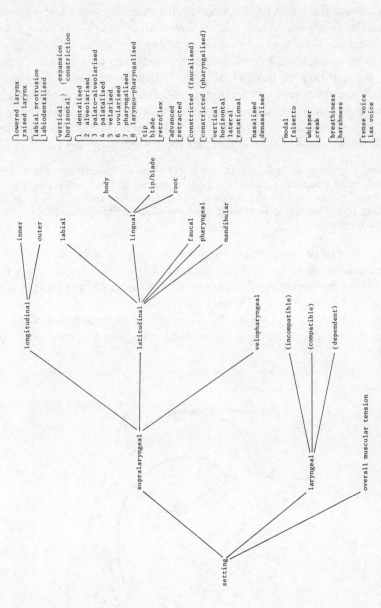

4.1 Summary of Laver's descriptive framework for long term qualities

137

vocal tract (and from the acoustic point of view alter its effective length). The classification might be simplified to, for example, four terms – spread, neutral, open rounded, and close rounded lip positions – in accord with traditional phonetic classification. Lingual settings are further subcategorised as involving tongue body, tongue tip/blade, and tongue root. Tongue body settings may be thought of as equivalent in nature though not in function to the secondary articulations of segmental phonetics, which create a reduction in the coronal cross-sectional area at some point along the vocal tract. Laver however rejects the traditional 'point of maximum constriction' classification of vowel articulations for the present purposes (1980:45):

> In describing [voice quality] settings. . .it is less a matter of specifying relatively fine distinctions of place of articulation than of stating general tendencies for the positioning of the bulk of the tongue. We can therefore profitably take as our reference point the long-term average speech position of the approximate centre of mass of the tongue.

Such a 'centre of mass' is purely notional, but it allows for convenient description of tongue body displacements from the neutral configuration in terms of the movement of this centre of mass towards an upper articulator as stylised in Fig. 4.2 (adapted from Laver 1980:Fig. 7).

Although the settings are analytically discrete and independent of each other, the interdependencies of the muscle systems of the vocal tract may

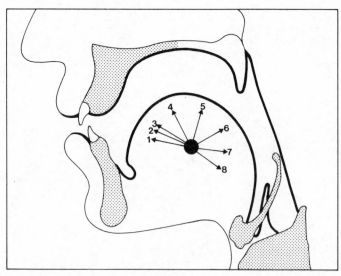

4.2 Sagittal section showing stylised radial displacements of the notional centre of mass of the tongue body in settings

cause interaction between settings – the pulling down and back of the body of the tongue may disturb the position of the larynx and mode of vibration of the vocal folds, and fixation of the velum to enable the palatoglossus muscle to achieve a velarised setting may result in denasalisation.

Latitudinal modifications in the tip/blade category involve a shift in the centre of mass of the body of the tongue 'merely as an "enabling" factor' (1980:49). Examples might involve consistent use of tip instead of blade, or vice versa, or of a 'retroflex' configuration. Laver suggests (1980:50–1) that the tip/blade system of settings is not an entirely independent system articulatorily, since the position of the tongue tip is dependent to some extent on the activity of the tongue body; and that perceptually its effects are limited to those segments where the tongue tip or blade is the active articulator (with the probable exception of the retroflex setting).

The slightly confused situation in this part of the framework is further complicated by a problem detailed in Nolan (1982b:2.1). Specifically, a dental setting, for example, in which all tip/blade sounds are articulated against the teeth, may quite easily be accompanied by a tongue body setting such as velarisation or pharyngalisation, a situation which in Laver's framework would require the tongue body to be shifted simultaneously in opposing directions. A better solution might be to replace palato-alveolarisation, alveolarisation, and dentalisation in the tongue body system with a single term, perhaps 'prepalatalisation', and use palato-alveolar, alveolar, and dental in combination with 'apical' (tip) versus 'laminal' (blade) to describe settings of the tip/blade area of the tongue.

The possibility of latitudinal modification by the tongue root, parallel to that of the tip/blade system in its independence from the tongue body, is mentioned by Laver; work by Laufer and Condax (1979) on the functioning of the epiglottis as an independent articulator in the production of pharyngeal sounds may indicate that other mechanisms may be responsible for independent modifications in this area.

Approximation of the faucal pillars, two muscular arches at the back of the oral cavity, may constitute an independently variable setting; it may additionally be correlated with high overall muscular tension, or nasality. The pharyngeal musculature itself may permit expansion and contraction of the pharynx independently of displacement of the body of the tongue. Finally within the latitudinal modifications are settings of the lower jaw. Whilst compensatory behaviour on the part of the articulators is possible, the neutral mandible setting (Laver 1980:65)

interferes least with the tongue and lips achieving a configuration of the vocal tract which most nearly approximates to an equal cross-sectional area along the full length of the vocal tract.

Commoner deviations are in the vertical, and horizontal (protrusion/ retraction) dimensions; a lateral displacement of the lower mandible with respect to the upper, or its tilting to one side, are also possible.

Velopharyngeal settings are discussed extensively in Laver (1980:2.3). Briefly, the complexity of the auditory quality labelled 'nasality' arises from the fact that, far from nasality being unequivocally caused by opening of the velic port, neither such opening, nor airflow through the nasal cavities, are necessarily guarantees of the presence of the auditory quality; and nor are the lack of such opening, or of airflow through the nasal cavities, necessarily guarantees of its absence, since it is possible that alternative side-branch resonators in the vocal tract (perhaps in the lower pharynx, such as the sinus piriformes) may cause the damping and zeros characteristic of nasality. However, because of the speculative nature of alternative mechanisms, Laver decides (1980:87) to retain the term 'nasal' and its derivatives in its traditional sense of 'control of resonance involving the nasal cavity by means of velopharyngeal action, unless there is indication to the contrary'.

Laryngeal settings are again identified auditorily, but here the labelling of categories is less clearly articulatory. Three kinds of laryngeal settings are isolated, given here in Fig. 4.1 the labels *incompatible, compatible,* and *dependent.* The basis of this trichotomy is the (in)ability of a laryngeal voice-quality component to occur alone, and to combine with others to form a 'compound' phonation type. The first category's settings, modal and falsetto, are 'mutually incompatible' in the sense that they cannot combine with each other, although they may combine with other settings. The settings of the second category, whisper and creak, are compatible with each other (whispery creak is a possible phonation type), and with terms from other laryngeal categories (e.g. whispery falsetto, creaky falsetto). All four of these settings have in common that they may occur alone, whereas those in the third category – breathiness and harshness – may only occur in compounds with other settings; hence the label used here – 'dependent'.

The neutral mode of phonation, modal voice, is one where (Laver 1980:14)

the vibration of the true vocal folds is regularly periodic, efficient in air use, without audible friction, with the folds in full glottal vibration under moderate longitudinal tension, moderate adductive tension and moderate medial compression (van den Berg 1968).

Further (Laver and Hanson 1981:59), the glottal pulse is approximately triangular, regular in amplitude and frequency (i.e. with only limited frequency jitter and amplitude shimmer), and the main excitation of the vocal tract occurs during the closing phase of the cycle. There is no aperiodic noise in the glottal source.

Falsetto, in contrast, requires high passive longitudinal tension ('stretching') of the vocal folds. The vocal folds are thinner, and vibration may be confined to their medial edges. Fundamental frequency is typically higher than in modal voice, though for a given speaker the two 'registers' will normally overlap to some extent.

Whisper requires the introduction into the pharynx of a high velocity jet of air, generally through a triangular opening between the arytenoid cartilages, though in weaker forms of whisper the opening may extend to the ligamental glottis. In creak (or 'vocal fry') the vocal folds are adducted along their whole length, and according to Catford (1977:98) 'air escapes in small periodic bursts through a very small aperture near the forward end of the vocal folds'. The folds are short and thick, and may be loaded by the ventricular folds (e.g. Hollien 1974b:135).

Breathiness results when both adductive tension and medial compression of the vocal folds are low, and longitudinal tension is generally within the lower part of the range. Because of these requirements it can only occur with modal voice, resulting in a phonation type which is inefficient in that a large volume of air escapes through the glottis in a short time, the open phase of the duty cycle being long, and the glottis in some cases not achieving any complete closure. Harshness results from a high degree of aperiodicity or frequency 'jitter' in the glottal wave (probably combined with amplitude 'shimmer'), which (Laver 1980:127) 'is heard as a component of auditory *quality* rather than of auditory pitch'. It is probably caused by extreme adductive tension and medial compression; severe harshness may stem from the additional loading of the ventricular folds (false vocal cords) onto the vocal folds, and this may be referred to as ventricular voice. Possibilities for combining the various laryngeal settings, to produce compound phonation types, will become apparent from the inventory of settings investigated in the next section.

Settings of overall muscular tension, finally, combine higher or lower than normal degrees of tension both in the supralaryngeal vocal tract and at the larynx. Lax voice will normally be associated with a breathy phonation type, and tense voice with harshness; supralaryngeally the walls of the vocal tract will be less rigid in lax voice, with possibly a tendency to velopharyngeal opening, whilst in tense voice they will be more rigid, and velopharyngeal closure probable. The glottal contribution to the spectrum of tense voice compared with lax voice will be greater energy in the higher harmonics because of sharper discontinuities in the glottal wave; and there will be less damping of particularly the lower formants of tense voice due firstly to the greater impedance of the rigid cavity walls and secondly to the smaller mean glottal area (see e.g. Wakita and Fant 1978:Table II-A-IV). Tense versus lax voice may also involve a greater versus lesser excursion of the articulators from a neutral position in the execution of a segment.

The complete descriptive framework is comparable to the Cardinal Vowel system in that verbal descriptions (auditory or articulatory) are inadequate to the task of teaching it – it can only be learnt by imitation; but mastery of the consensus as to the auditory referents of the labels enables verbal communication about characteristics of speech. The significance of the voice quality framework for speaker recognition stems from its provision of a tool for analysing and talking about otherwise descriptively elusive speaker-specific traits. Furthermore it provides the categories of long term effects which are needed if their acoustic properties are to be explored systematically.

4.3.4 *Correlates of voice qualities in the long term spectrum*

The material used in this investigation was a recording, made on high quality equipment in a sound-treated studio, of 31 voice qualities exemplifying the categories from Laver's framework. The speaker was John Laver. The supralaryngeal and laryngeal qualities, mostly simple, but including certain compound qualities, were as follows:

0 neutral
1 raised larynx
2 lowered larynx
3 labial setting with spread lips
4 labial setting with open rounding and protrusion of the lips
5 labial setting with close rounding and protrusion of the lips
6 retroflex
7 laryngo-pharyngalised
8 pharyngalised
9 uvularised
10 velarised
11 palatalised
12 palato-alveolarised
13 alveolarised
14 dentalised
15 nasalised
16 denasalised
17 close jaw setting
18 open jaw setting
19 modal

20 falsetto
21 creak
22 whisper
23 whispery voice
24 whispery falsetto
25 whispery creak
26 creaky voice
27 creaky falsetto
28 breathy voice
29 harsh ventricular voice
30 harsh ventricular whispery falsetto

The qualities were implemented in reading the first paragraph of the 'rainbow passage' (see 4.4.3.1) giving utterances of approximately 30–35 second duration.

An initial analysis was carried out as follows. The whole utterance was low pass filtered to 5 kHz and digitised with 12-bit resolution at a sampling rate of 10 kHz. A Hanning window was applied followed by an FFT, to a frame of 25.6 ms, and the squared real and imaginary parts of the spectrum summed to obtain the power spectrum for that frame. The procedure was repeated over the whole passage, advancing the frame by one frame-length (no overlapping) each computational cycle, and the mean power spectrum for the whole passage obtained; also the mean power spectrum for the first and second halves of the utterance separately. The mean spectrum was normalised by the total power, and the log taken. The term 'long term spectrum' will be used here to refer to the log of the normalised mean power spectrum.

Long term spectra were computed both over every successive frame, and also over voiced frames only, the decision on voicing being made by heuristically determined intensity and autocorrelation thresholds. In both cases visual inspection of the long term spectrum from first and second halves of an utterance bore out the quantitative finding of Furui *et al.* (1972) that as little as 10 (or in this case 15) seconds of speech will yield a fairly representative long term spectrum. However, even if the present 30 seconds of speech were inadequate to neutralise totally the effect of segmental content this would not be a serious problem as the spectra to be compared are derived from phonemically equivalent utterances.

Fig. 4.3 presents the long term spectra for complete utterances in each setting (except whisper). The horizontal axis shows frequency in kHz, and the vertical axis amplitude in dB. The solid trace shows the spectrum computed over all frames, and the dotted trace over only voiced frames; it is

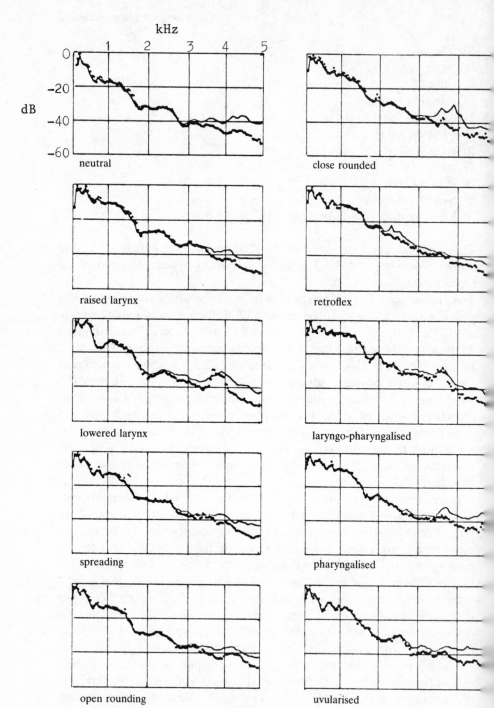

kHz

dB

neutral

close rounded

raised larynx

retroflex

lowered larynx

laryngo-pharyngalised

spreading

pharyngalised

open rounding

uvularised

4.3a Long term spectra of voice qualities (speaker JL)

144

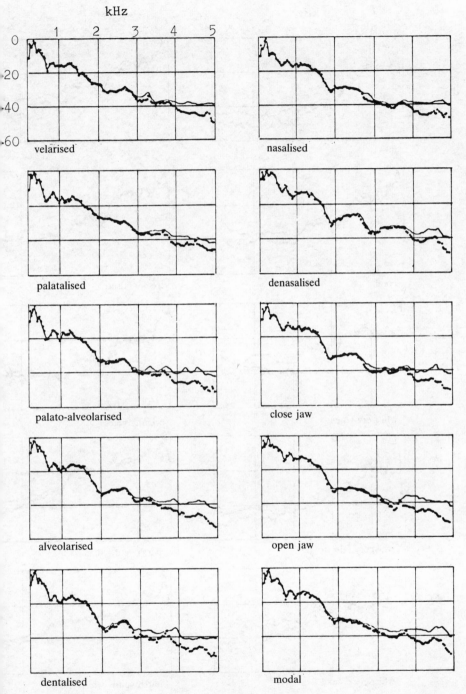

4.3b Long term spectra of voice qualities (speaker JL)

145

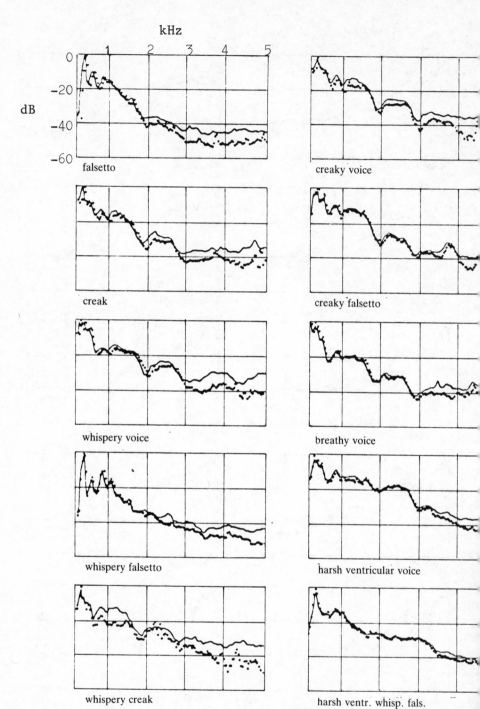

kHz

dB

falsetto

creaky voice

creak

creaky falsetto

whispery voice

breathy voice

whispery falsetto

harsh ventricular voice

whispery creak

harsh ventr. whisp. fals.

4.3c Long term spectra of voice qualities (speaker JL)

apparent that the main difference in these two conditions occurs above 2.5 kHz, presumably as a reflection of the effect of voiceless fricatives.

It is immediately evident from Figs. 4.3(a) and 4.3(b) that the long term spectrum is comparatively little affected by auditorily quite striking changes in supralaryngeal voice quality – for example between uvularised and palatalised, or between nasalised and denasalised settings. It is clear that some writers expect the long term spectrum to manifest formant characteristics; Frøkjær-Jensen and Prytz (1976:8):

Above the first formant region we normally notice some spectral discontinuity caused by the average levels of the second and third formant,

Sundberg and Nordström (1976:38):

As the peaks in the long term average spectrum are dependent on the time average of the formant frequencies we would expect that these peaks differ depending on the position of the larynx,

and such a view is coherent. What is not known is how far peaks and troughs in the long term spectrum, as well as its overall slope, may be determined by phonatory as opposed to resonatory characteristics, and how sharply a change in the frequency range of a formant will be visible in the long term spectrum. These questions will be considered below, in the light of findings on the effect of the settings on formant frequencies.

Fig. 4.3(c) shows the long term spectra of the laryngeal settings. It is apparent visually that the spectrum is more severely perturbed by changes in laryngeal as opposed to supralaryngeal setting – falsetto, whispery falsetto and breathy voice show the sharpest fall-off within the first 3 kHz, where harsh ventricular voice maintains a high energy level.

Before an attempt is made to quantify these impressions, equivalent long term spectra based on the same settings adopted by a different speaker may be compared. The author recorded the same text in these 31 qualities in Cambridge University Linguistics Department's recording studio. These utterances were judged by John Laver to be generally adequate implementations of the voice quality categories, with the following main criticisms: phonation type tended towards creaky voice rather than modal during supralaryngeal settings; most settings were accompanied by a slightly greater than neutral degree of nasalisation; modal voice with high fundamental frequency replaced falsetto in creaky falsetto; and harsh ventricular whispery falsetto approximated more to harsh ventricular creaky voice with high fundamental frequency.

The long term spectra of the utterances produced by the author are presented in Fig. 4.4; the trace relates to the mean spectrum computed over all frames. The same observation seems valid with this speaker that in

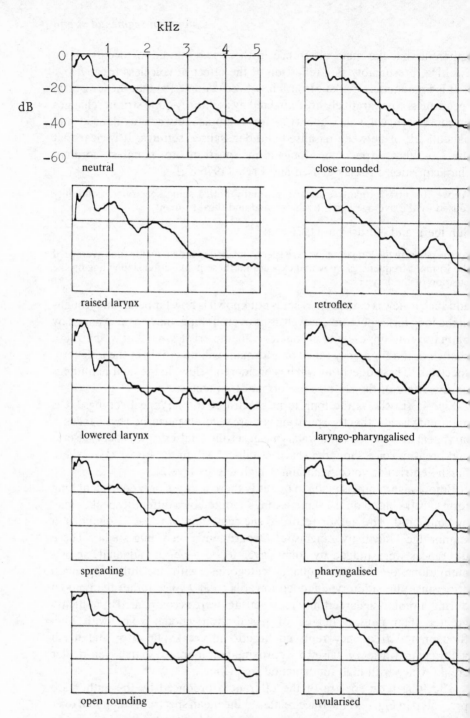

kHz

dB

neutral

close rounded

raised larynx

retroflex

lowered larynx

laryngo-pharyngalised

spreading

pharyngalised

open rounding

uvularised

4.4a Long term spectra of voice qualities (speaker FN)

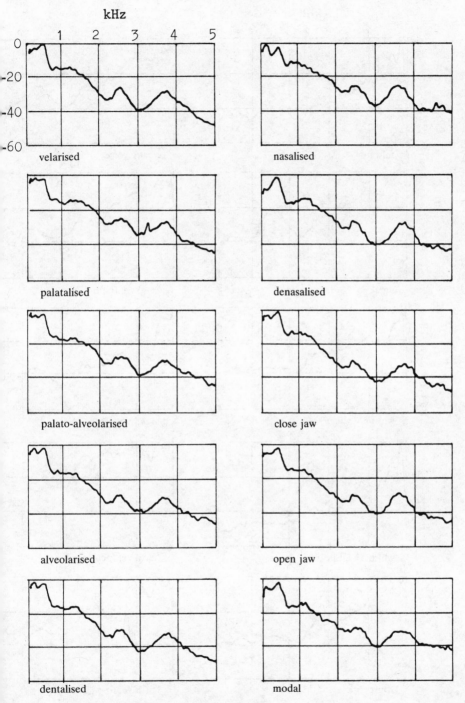

kHz

velarised

nasalised

palatalised

denasalised

palato-alveolarised

close jaw

alveolarised

open jaw

dentalised

modal

4.4b Long term spectra of voice qualities (speaker FN)

149

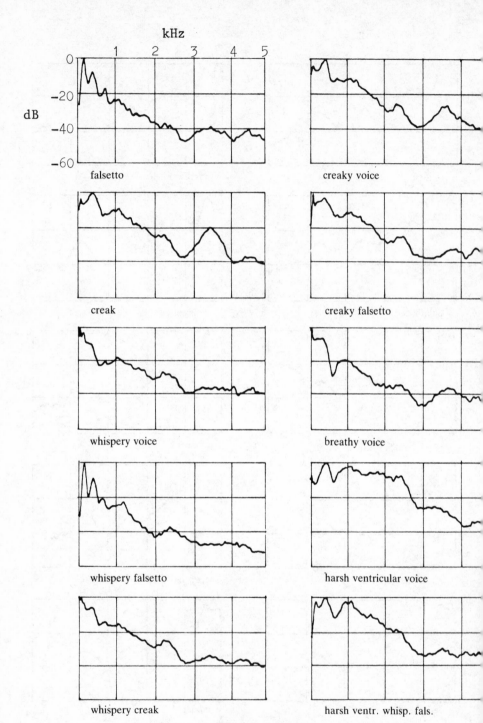

kHz

falsetto

creaky voice

creak

creaky falsetto

whispery voice

breathy voice

whispery falsetto

harsh ventricular voice

whispery creak

harsh ventr. whisp. fals.

4.4c Long term spectra of voice qualities (speaker FN)

150

general the spectral slope and shape remain fairly constant through the
supralaryngeal changes (apart from noticeable consequences from larynx
lowering, and, to a lesser extent, raising), but that spectral slope and
detailed structure are more affected by phonation type (Fig. 4.4(c)). A
regularly occurring peak at around 3.5 kHz is largely absent in falsetto,
whispery voice, whispery falsetto, whispery creak, creaky falsetto, breathy
voice, and the two harsh settings, but most strongly present during creak,
and also creaky voice. It is completely absent in whisper (not shown), in
raised larynx voice, and in lowered larynx voice, where the more steeply
falling spectrum indicates a concomitant change in phonation type. It is
possible therefore that this 3.5 kHz peak is a function of the waveform of the
creaky phonation type generally used (see above). The fact that it fails to
appear when the larynx is lowered or raised, however, when the
cross-sectional area ratio between the larynx and pharynx tubes might be
expected to be disturbed, opens up the possibility that it is a phenomenon
similar to Sundberg's (1974) 'singing formant' found at around 2.8 kHz and
resulting, he demonstrates, from the resonance of the larynx tube when the
cross-sectional area of this is sufficiently different from that of the pharynx
into which it inserts for it to act as an independent resonator. This
explanation is made less likely, however, by the failure of the peak under
larynx lowering – precisely the condition exploited by singers to produce it.

Two methods were applied to quantify differences between the long term
spectra. The first is based on that of Frøkjær-Jensen and Prytz (1976), whose
interest was to assess improvement in phoniatric patients through changes in
their long term spectrum. They used as a spectral measure the ratio of the
amplitude level above 1 kHz to that below, expressed in decibels. In the
present work a number of different ratios between upper and lower parts of
the spectrum were tried: above to below 1 kHz; 2 kHz; 3 kHz (with the
upper part in each case bounded at 5 kHz); 0.5–1 kHz to below 0.5 kHz; 1–2
kHz to below 1 kHz; 1.5–3 kHz to below 1.5 kHz; and 2–3 kHz to 1–2 kHz.
For each frequency condition the decibel value of the ratio of mean
amplitude in the upper versus the lower part of the spectrum was taken, that
is

$$\text{spectral ratio} = 10 \times \log_{10}(\bar{a}_u/\bar{a}_l),$$

where $\bar{a}$ is the mean amplitude in the upper or lower division of the
spectrum. The effectiveness of the measures was assessed by the standard
deviation of the values across the supralaryngeal settings, and across the
laryngeal settings (a higher standard deviation indicating better separation
of settings). No one measure proved clearly superior for both groups of
settings and both speakers, but the 'upper 1.5–3:lower 0–1.5' was generally

151

highly rated. Values for this measure are presented in Table 4.1, and shown graphically in Fig. 4.5.

Table 4.1 also shows the results of the second kind of measure applied to the spectra. This method attempted to find the straight line which would best match the 0–2.5 kHz part of the spectrum given a logarithmic frequency scale. Lines representing *n* dB/octave slopes, where *n* ranged from 0 to 30, were compared with the spectra and the distance computed from

$$\text{distance} = \sum_{k=1}^{m} |s_k - l_k|,$$

where s_k is the amplitude of the *k*th point in the spectrum and l_k the amplitude of the *k*th point in the straight line. The dB/octave slopes may be compared with a generally accepted value in normal speech of around −6 dB/octave (see e.g. Frøkjær-Jensen and Prytz 1976:Fig. 6). These values are plotted in Fig. 4.6. The approximation involved in this method should be borne in mind when considering, for example, the 0 dB/octave value for FN's harsh ventricular voice. In this instance the slight slope of the spectrum will have been offset by the lack of energy around 700 Hz – a region which will receive extra weight compared with higher frequencies by virtue of the logarithmic frequency scale.

Figs 4.5 and 4.6 bear out the impression gained visually that in general gross long term spectral changes do not result from supralaryngeal settings.

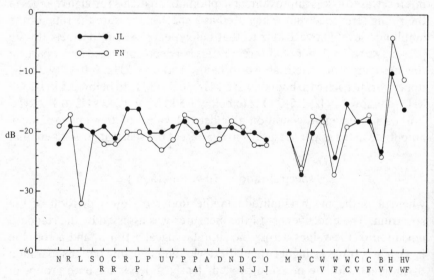

4.5   Long term spectra of voice qualities: amplitude ratios

Table 4.1 Measures of characteristics of long term spectra of voice qualities: (left) ratio in dB of upper (1.5–3 kHz) to lower (0–1.5 kHz) parts of spectrum; (right) best approximation to dB/octave slope of spectrum

| SETTING | upper: lower | | slope approximation | |
	Speaker JL	Speaker FN	Speaker JL	Speaker FN
neutral	−22	−19	−6	−6
raised larynx	−19	−17	−4	−3
lowered larynx	−19	−32	−5	−11
labial/spread lips	−20	−20	−5	−7
labial/open rounding	−19	−22	−6	−6
labial/close rounding	−21	−22	−5	−7
retroflex	−16	−20	−4	−5
laryngo-pharyngalised	−16	−20	−2	−5
pharyngalised	−20	−21	−4	−6
uvularised	−20	−23	−4	−6
velarised	−19	−21	−4	−6
palatalised	−18	−17	−4	−6
palato-alveolarised	−20	−18	−4	−6
alveolarised	−19	−22	−5	−6
dentalised	−19	−21	−5	−6
nasalised	−19	−18	−4	−6
denasalised	−20	−19	−4	−4
close jaw	−20	−22	−5	−6
open jaw	−21	−22	−5	−6
modal	−20	−20	−4	−5
falsetto	−27	−26	−9	−9
creak	−20	−17	−3	−4
whispery voice	−17	−18	−5	−5
whispery falsetto	−24	−27	−8	−8
whispery creak	−15	−19	−3	−6
creaky voice	−18	−18	−3	−4
creaky falsetto	−18	−17	−3	−4
breathy voice	−23	−24	−5	−8
harsh ventricular	−10	−4	−3	−0
harsh ven. whis. fals.	−16	−11	−6	−2

It is possible that the rather slight fall-off (−2 dB/octave) of JL's laryngo-pharyngalised voice may result from the high F_1, low F_2 characteristic of this setting (see 4.4.3), but on the other hand the production of a constriction in the lower pharynx tends to affect the disposition of the larynx and so may alter its mode of vibration (Laver 1980:46–7). A similar explanation may also be valid for, in the case of FN in particular, the less steep slope (−3 dB/octave) for raised larynx voice and very steep slope (−11 dB/octave) for lowered larynx voice (1980:28, 31); larynx lowering seems to induce breathy phonation, and for FN breathy voice also has a steep slope

153

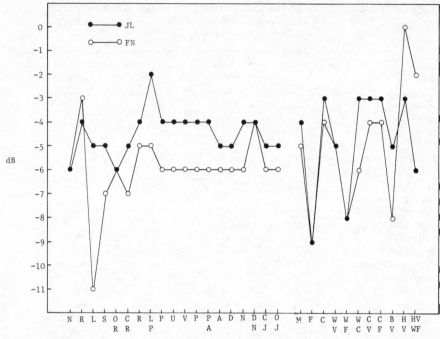

4.6   Long term spectra of voice qualities: slope approximation

(–8 dB/octave). There is a conspicuous absence of effect on the spectral slope measure, however, by for instance the change from pharyngalised to palatalised voice, which in terms of formant frequencies (4.4.3) are diametrically opposed.

The plots make plain the greater perturbation caused by phonation type. A falsetto or whispery component gives a tendency towards steep slopes, creaky and harsh components towards more level spectra. The slope discrepancy between the speakers in harsh ventricular whispery falsetto bears out the auditory criticisms (above) that FN's implementation lacked the whisper component and replaced falsetto by high F_0 creaky voice.

The significance of these findings for speaker recognition is the following. Beyond the segmental and suprasegmental strands, where speaker-specific information may reside, it is necessary to recognise secondary long term strands. Without such strands many general and unified statements about speech would not be possible, and facts could only be stated through piecemeal reference to individual segmental and suprasegmental elements. The long term strands also seem to correspond well with an aspect of auditory perception of speech in which auditory judgments about 'voice quality' can be made without analytic awareness of short term features. Such

154

judgments are undoubtedly an important part of auditory decisions about speaker identity, and it is not unreasonable to suppose that technical equivalents of these judgments could be of use in speaker recognition – indeed long term spectra have already proved successful to a degree in this (4.3.1). Taking segmental long term quality to depend on both supralaryngeal and laryngeal mechanisms, it is apparent that a technique which is sensitive to the acoustic reflexes of only one of these will not fully capture a speaker's voice quality. Section 4.4 explores a method of characterising the supralaryngeal components of long term quality.

4.3.5 *Dips in long term spectra*

The long term spectra of Figs. 4.3 and 4.4 manifest, as well as the gradient already discussed, certain fine structure. In particular there are quite narrow frequency regions, for example around 0.7 kHz in both speakers, where a spectral minimum can often be seen. These become more apparent in spectra with higher frequency resolution. Dips of this kind are well attested in other work with long term spectra, but their source is problematical. They are often attributed to properties of the pseudo-triangular glottal source waveform; Nolan (1980) argues, however, mainly on the basis of their stable frequency despite gross changes in phonation type in the present data, that this explanation is unlikely. Instead they might result from acoustic coupling to the trachea. At this preliminary stage such a suggestion can only be made very tentatively; but if it proves to be correct, it points firstly to the inadequacy for speaker recognition of the traditional source-filter speech production model, which ignores subglottal effects, and secondly to a possible stable cue to speaker identity of intrinsic origin, dependent on subglottal dimensions.

4.4 **Acoustic correlates of supralaryngeal qualities**

4.4.1 *Data and methods*

Although, as has been shown in 4.3.4, long term spectra of a passage read with different long term qualities bring to light differences between them, it is clear that particularly in the case of supralaryngeal qualities distinct auditory impressions are not captured by the long term spectrum. It has been demonstrated by Laver (1975:281ff; 1967) that simulation of perceptually recognisable supralaryngeal qualities can be effected by adjusting the frequency range of the first three formants of a terminal-analogue synthesiser. This seems to have been carried out, however, in a largely heuristic way without detailed knowledge of what the actual acoustic correlates of the different qualities might be. The aim of the work in this section is to provide such detail, which in future may serve as the basis of more specific hypotheses which could be put to the test by synthesis and perceptual experimentation, and to clarify the nature of the settings underlying the qualities by reference to existing knowledge of articulatory-acoustic relationships. In turn, this should facilitate both understanding of the potential for variability and disguise within an individual speaker, and the development of objective classification of voice types for speaker recognition purposes.

As data the recordings by John Laver, described in 4.3.4, were used. The method involved the use of a linear prediction pole-finding routine, developed in Cambridge University Engineering Department by Steve Terepin, supplemented by visual examination of spectrograms. At first sight it might seem attractive to have used such a program in a purely automatic way, obtaining as an overall characterisation of each quality the average of the frequency values of the first three or four poles in each successive analysis frame over the length of the passage. This would, unfortunately, yield meaningless results since there is no guarantee that the first four poles found will correspond in all cases to the first four formants as they are generally understood. It is a commonplace of spectrographic studies, reiterated above in 3.3.2, that only a predisposition (through knowledge of acoustic theory and practice) to find formants in the correct locations enables the investigator to discount spurious resonances. The incorporation of such knowledge, much of it necessarily linguistic, would result in an algorithm of as yet unattained sophistication. A second disadvantage with such an approach, even if it had been feasible, is that information about the effect of the settings on different classes of vowels would not have been recoverable. As will be seen below such information turns out to be of considerable interest and importance.

The method adopted was as follows. The speech was low pass filtered to 5 kHz, sampled at 10 kHz and digitised with 12-bit resolution before being stored on disc. The digitised speech was then input to the program mentioned above, which was based on the autocorrelation method of linear prediction and used a Newtonian method to locate the pole frequencies. Frames 25.6 ms long were Hanning windowed before being input to the program, in which the model order was set to 12 yielding six pole pairs. The frame moved on 12.8 ms each time, giving a processing overlap of half a frame. The values in Hz of the six located poles for each successive frame were printed at the start of a line, and the rest of the line was used to represent the spectral domain from 0 to 5 kHz. Asterisks were printed in positions corresponding to the poles, and in this way a representation comparable to a spectrogram was built up with frequency running from left to right, and time vertically down the line printer page.

Because of their radically different appearance these skeletal pole plots were at first visually interpretable only with difficulty. It soon became clear, however, after comparison with wideband spectrograms, that they could be 'read' with almost equal facility. Once features on the pole plots could be identified with confidence the analysis could go ahead. A number of points which it was hoped would be consistent from one quality to another were defined in terms of the pole trajectories; for example in the phrase *These take the shape* the trajectory of the pole corresponding to the second formant always rose to a peak during the [i:] of *These*, and the frame where it reached its highest value was defined as a measurement point. The values of the poles corresponding to the first three formants were then recorded as characterising the measurement point. Most measurement points were defined on the basis of one of the first two formants, and a few as a fixed proportion of the duration between two identifiable events. It must be borne in mind that since linguistic segments are implemented not as discrete acoustic units, but rather as quasi-continuously varying resonance patterns, the labelling of measurement points with phonetic symbols is a convenience and not a claim about their exact phonetic quality.

It may help to clarify the distinction between 'pole' and the various senses of 'formant'. The term 'pole' is used of any of the elementary resonances, specified by a frequency and a bandwidth, into which the complex transfer function associated with a particular vocal tract configuration can be analysed; equivalently, an electrical analogue of the transfer function can be constructed, in which a series of circuits, each with its own resonance (pole), form a network replicating the filtering effect of the vocal tract when a source waveform is introduced (Fant 1973:6). Mathematically the resonance is represented as a conjugate pole-pair in the S-plane. In the case of sounds in which the source is not at the terminal end of the vocal tract, or where sidebranch resonators are opened off the main acoustic pathway, the analysis/synthesis of the transfer function will be unrealistic without the inclusion of 'zeros' or 'antiresonances'. Usually the pole frequencies will correspond closely to the frequency of a peak in the transfer function; there may however be discrepancies when poles lie close to each other in the frequency domain. Two poles cannot coincide in frequency, except when the cross-sectional area of a constriction is reduced to zero (Fant 1960:39), but as two poles approach closely the resultant peaks in the transfer function may fuse into a single peak. The introduction of a weak pole (i.e. of wide bandwidth) in the proximity of a strong pole corresponding to a 'formant' in the transfer function of the vocal tract may not appear as a separate peak, but simply cause the original peak to be skewed slightly in its direction.

So far, then, two analytic/synthetic stages have been considered – the elementary resonances, and their combination in the complex transfer/ 'filter' function. The third involves the interaction of the glottal source. Two factors may cause minor disparities between the frequency of a peak in the transfer function and that in the resultant output spectrum: the source function in real speech may deviate from the idealised smoothly decrementing (classically – 12 dB/octave) source function and contain peaks or troughs which may interact with those in the transfer function; and unless the fundamental is low, the harmonics will be too widely spaced for the transfer function to be accurately recoverable. It is at this third stage, the output spectrum, that 'formants' are measured from spectrograms; the term is loosely applied either to peaks in the output spectrum or to peaks in the transfer function – Fant (1960:21):

Formants are labelled F1, F2, F3 etc., in the order they occur in the frequency scale. The notation F_1, F_2, F_3 etc., refers to the frequencies of the formants or to the frequencies of the corresponding vocal tract resonances.

In practice, the disparity between the peaks in the transfer function and those in the sound spectrum is usually insignificant enough to allow of a systematic ambiguity – Fant (1960:20):

The frequency location of a maximum in [the transfer/filter function] $|T(f)|$, i.e., the *resonance frequency*, is very close to the corresponding maximum in the spectrum $P(f)$ of the complete sound. Conceptually these should be held apart but in most instances resonance frequency and formant frequency may be used synonymously.

Similarly, the potential lack of correspondence between poles, and peaks in the transfer function, outlined above, is not serious enough in practice to cause problems in the present work. The discrepancy may be as great as 10 Hz at 100 Hz for typical speech bandwidths, but declines asymptotically as the pole frequency rises (Terepin 1980). Fant (1960:25) defines the F-pattern at any instance in time as

the resonance frequencies of the oral part of the vocal tract or those resonance frequencies that show a continuity with the oral resonances of an adjacent sound.

In the present work it was attempted to pick out, at the measurement points, those poles which corresponded to the first three terms in the continuously varying F-pattern; in doing so use was made both of 'syntagmatic' knowledge – the 'continuity' of the above quotation – since spurious poles tended to appear erratically and for short durations, and of 'paradigmatic' knowledge – expectations of where approximately the poles for a particular quality of vowel might be located. The first three frequency values were then, by a slight extension of the systematic ambiguity above, labelled F_1, F_2

and F_3. It should be remembered in the subsequent sections, however, that all references to formant frequencies obtained in the present experiments are strictly references to estimated pole frequencies.

Because the linear prediction method involves an all-pole model, in theory it is not applicable to sounds with zeros underlying their spectra. Measurement points in portions of vowels where coarticulated nasality might be expected were therefore avoided where possible.

4.4.2 *Preliminary analysis*

Initially a single sentence was selected from the passage, and its recording in 16 supralaryngeal qualities analysed. The qualities, together with the symbols used subsequently to represent them on graphs and which have some, perhaps tenuous, mnemonic value, were as follows:

N neutral
M modal
L lowered larynx
R raised larynx
Q labial setting with open rounding and protrusion of the lips
O labial setting with close rounding and protrusion of the lips
& retroflex
? laryngo-pharyngalised
P pharyngalised
U uvularised
V velarised
J palatalised
Z palato-alveolarised
A alveolarised
D dentalised

The sentence chosen was *These take the shape of a long, round arch, with its path high above, and its two ends apparently beyond the horizon.* Spectrograms were made of the complete sentence for all 16 voice qualities, and these were used in conjunction with pole plots to define and locate the following 16 measurement points:

location	definition
1 ði:z	highest F_2
2 teɪk	starting point of the vowel formants
3 ʃeɪp	starting point of the vowel formants
4 əlɒŋ	lowest F_1

159

location	definition
5 rɑʊnd	(realised as nearly a steady-state vowel) highest F_1 in the firs half (to minimise nasalisation)
6 ɑ:tʃ	highest F_1
7 wɪðɪts	highest F_2
8 pɑ:θ	first steady state value of (most nearly) steady-state
9 haɪə	highest F_2 (never as high as expected for [ɪ] or [i])
10 əbʌv	highest F_1
11 ɪts	highest F_2
12 təu:endz	starting point of the vowel formants – probably unrounde element of diphthongal realisation of /u:/
13 təu:endz	lowest F_2 – corresponding to most [u]-like point in the vowe trajectory
14 bɪɒnd	highest F_2
15 bɪɒnd	first value in high F_1 (nearly) steady-state
16 həraɪzn	middle value of high F_1 steady-state

After they had been obtained from the pole plots, the values for each of the first three formants were averaged over all measurement locations – these means are given in Table 4.2.

In Table 4.2 the value for F3 of laryngo-pharyngalised voice is left blank because of a measurement difficulty which also arose to a lesser extent with

Table 4.2 Means of F_1, F_2, F_3 for long term qualities (Hz): mp 1–16

		F_1	F_2	F_3
N	neutral	545	1365	2405
M	modal	535	1390	2470
L	lowered larynx	465	1300	2450
R	raised larynx	545	1285	2245
S	lip spreading	550	1375	2515
Q	open rounding	530	1340	2370
O	close rounding	515	1300	2195
&	retroflex	575	1315	2235
?	laryngo-phar.	575	1240	
P	pharyngalised	565	1265	2265
U	uvularised	535	1350	2490
V	velarised	515	1505	2560
J	palatalised	530	1515	2480
Z	palato-alv.	535	1475	2520
A	alveolarised	540	1455	2460
D	dentalised	535	1450	2480

pharyngalised voice: namely the absence on pole plots and spectrograms of a regularly occurring formant in the usual 2.3–2.6 kHz range. Instead a choice usually had to be made between a peak which was often quite weak (to judge from the spectrograms) at 2.0 kHz or just below, and a stronger peak in the 2.6–2.9 kHz region. In the case of pharyngalised voice the choice was easier since the lower peak was usually over 2.0 kHz and was more reliable in its occurrence than the higher peak, which in its turn was often well above an expected F_3, at around 2.8–3.0 kHz. This lower peak fits in well with an expectation of a downward shift in upper formants caused by pharyngalisation, one of the exponents of the Jakobsonian feature 'Flat' (cf. Fant 1960:219). This lower peak was therefore taken as F3 in pharyngalised voice, but F3 of laryngo-pharyngalised voice has been omitted from consideration because of its erratic behaviour.

The trends in Table 4.2 are made clearer in Fig. 4.7 which plots mean F_2

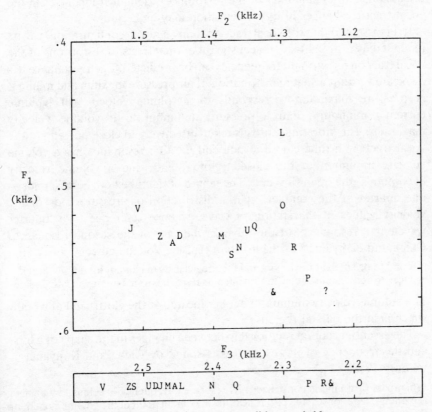

4.7   Means of formant frequencies for long term qualities: mp 1–16

against F_1 with the axes reversed in the way frequently used for vowel plotting because it produces relationships between vowels reminiscent of traditional 'vowel quadrilateral' diagrams; the inset to Fig. 4.7 places the settings in the F_3 dimension.

In Fig. 4.7, the settings are grouped into three clusters on the basis of F_2: palatalised, velarised, palato-alveolarised, alveolarised and dentalised with relatively high F_2 (at or above 1450 Hz); a central group comprised of modal, lip spreading, neutral, uvularised and open rounding with F_2 between 1340 and 1390 Hz; and a low F_2 group – retroflex, close rounding, lowered larynx, raised larynx, pharyngalised and laryngo-pharyngalised – below 1320 Hz. Differentiation by F_1 within the first two groups is probably not important; in the third group there is a wide (110 Hz) range of F_1.

Although there are certain anomalies in the F_2 F_1 plane, the general disposition of the qualities even on this very limited data base is much as might be expected according to acoustic theory. For the subsequent discussion, a brief summary of the relation of resonant frequencies in the vocal tract to changes in its configuration may be helpful.

If it is assumed that the vocal tract (in some 'neutral' configuration) can be modelled as a straight-sided acoustic tube, the effects of distortions of the vocal tract on its resonant frequencies can be predicted. Each resonance has associated with it a spatial distribution of air pressure maxima and minima. A pressure maximum corresponds to a volume velocity (or 'volume current') minimum, and a pressure minimum to a volume velocity maximum. The vibrating glottis is taken effectively to close one end of the vocal tract; in a tube closed at one end the first resonance has a volume velocity minimum at the closed (glottis) end, and a volume velocity maximum at the open (lip) end. The length of the tube here corresponds to one quarter of the complete spatial distribution of pressure and volume velocity values in the stationary wave, whence reference to a 'quarter wavelength resonance' of the tube. In the case of the second resonance, Chiba and Kajiyama (1958:146) state that the volume current

is found to be small at the larynx and then reaches its maximum for a time until it is reduced to zero; finally, at the mouth opening it reaches its maximum negative value.

The volume velocity minima, then, are located at the glottis and at a point which is in the palatal region.

The essential general relationship between changes in the shape of a tube and the frequency of its resonances is stated by Chiba and Kajiyama as follows (1958:151):

When part of a pipe is constricted, its resonance frequency becomes low or high according as the constricted part is near the maximum point of the volume current or the excess pressure.

That is, a constriction at a volume velocity maximum for a particular resonance causes a lowering of its frequency, and at a volume velocity minimum, a raising. Thus, for example, a constriction in the palatal region will optimally raise F_2, as in the vowel [i] (Fant 1968:239).

For the same reason that [i] is the vowel with the highest F_2 a shift in the 'centre of gravity' of articulation in a direction towards close front would be expected to entail a raising of F_2. The evidence of Fig. 4.7 is in accord with this; palatalised and palato-alveolarised voice, and to a lesser extent dentalised and alveolarised, all having high F_2. That velarised voice has almost as high an F_2 as palatalised (1505, 1515 Hz) is a little unexpected considering the widespread view that a 'velarised' lateral has a low F_2, but it is in accord with Fant (1960:219):

a narrowing of the tongue passage causes a shift down of F_2 only when it is located in the posterior half of the model, i.e. in the pharynx. At the uvula the effect is nil, and it is the opposite in the mouth cavity.

It is probable that 'velarisation' as applied to secondary articulations is used to cover superimposed vowel qualities ranging from [ɨ] round the periphery of the vowel area even to [ɑ] (strictly, pharyngalised), which would see F_2 range from a near-maximum to a minimum (cf. Fant 1960:84). The trend apparent from Fig. 4.7 is in accord with an auditory impression of [ɨ] or [ɯ] superimposition rather than [ɑ], although the quite distinct auditory impressions of palatalised and velarised are not explained.

The qualities in the central cluster are ones, with the exception of uvularised voice, which do not involve a shift in the centre of gravity of the tongue from its neutral position. Uvularised voice appropriately (see Fant 1960:219, quoted above) has an F_2 between the high value for palatalised and the low value for pharyngalised, deviating little from neutral. Some differentiation of the five qualities in this cluster might be expected on the basis of F_3, since two of them involve adjustments of the lip opening, and F_3 in many vowels is known to be principally affiliated to the mouth cavity (Fant and Pauli 1974:125); neither F_1 nor F_2 differentiates effectively within the group. It may be remarked that impressionistically the five qualities differ less radically than many of the others.

Low F_2 settings will be mentioned in order of ascending F_1. With F_1 at 465 Hz, lowered larynx voice clearly reflects the effect of lengthening the pharyngeal cavity, by which the first formant is usually considerably determined – Fant (1960:121):

The frequency of the first formant F_1 is generally dependent more on the back cavity volume than on the volume of the other cavities.

The second formant is also low, although not as low as in the qualities which involve a constriction in the pharyngeal region. Close rounding (with labial protrusion) has an effect analogous to larynx lowering in that the vocal tract is being lengthened both actually and effectively (the frequency of resonances being lowered by lengthening, or reducing the orifice of, a tube (Lieberman 1977:44–5)). The variation from neutral is greater than that of open rounding, but in the same direction. Raised larynx voice would be predicted to occupy the bottom left of the plot, both on the *a priori* grounds that the vocal tract has deviated in the opposite direction from lowered larynx voice; and on the basis of Sundberg and Nordström's (1976) empirical findings, using both a vocal tract analogue and two human speakers, that the effects on formant frequencies of raising the larynx are (1976:39)

1) a substantial rise in the second formant frequency in high front vowels, 2) a rise in both the first and second formant frequency in open vowels, 3) a combined rise in several vowels of the third and fourth formant frequencies.

According to Table 4.2, however, raised larynx voice shares the same mean F_1 as neutral voice and has a considerably *lower* F_2 (1365, 1285 Hz respectively). Given such a lack of correspondence with predictions, it seems reasonable to delay detailed consideration of raised larynx voice until a wider data base is available (4.4.5). Both settings involving pharyngeal constriction cause a deviation of F_1 upwards, and F_2 downwards, from neutral, in accordance with what is known about [ɑ]-like vowels and from constrictions in that region in vocal tract analogues (e.g. Fant 1960:84).

The low F_2 of retroflex voice accords with the usual resonance pattern of retroflex continuants, for example Lehiste (1964:58):

The initial allophones of /r/ are characterised by low formant frequency positions for the first three formants.

The high F_1 is not in conflict with this, since Lehiste is concerned with formant frequencies during the maximum stricture of retroflex sounds whereas present measurements are largely of the most open phase in the syllable; the high F_1 seems likely to be the result of the relatively wide opening of the vocal tract which is necessary when retracting the tongue tip to the prepalatal region; Honikman (1964:79) notes an 'open setting of the jaws' in languages of the Indian subcontinent where retroflex consonants are frequent and suggests that this 'enables this tongue-setting to be made comfortably'. Furthermore it is conceivable that the tongue 'bunching' which is characteristic of the non-apical 'molar' *r*-sound is present at least to some extent also in articulatorily truly retroflex sounds – the visible part of the tongue at any rate clearly tends to be foreshortened and broadened. To the extent the articulations are similar it seems likely that a pharyngeal constriction is a component in the more usual production of retroflex quality, since Ladefoged (1979:11) shows a pharyngeal constriction accompanying a bunched tongue configuration on the basis of data from American English speakers producing such words as *heard*, and remarks that

these data, together with the observations of Uldall (1958) and Delattre and Freeman (1968) and our own experience in synthesising /r/ sounds from an articulatory model, all indicate that the shapes of the tongue which occur in these sounds cannot be produced without a constriction in the [lower (from the diagram)] pharynx.

Retroflexion, auditorily defined, may then involve a component of articulatory pharyngalisation, explaining the similar positions of the two settings on the formant plot. The feature 'Flat', under which retroflexion and pharyngalisation were subsumed in the Jakobsonian feature framework, may also in this case reflect an articulatory as well as an acoustic similarity.

Regarding the effect of the settings on F_3, plotted in the inset to Fig. 4.7, a convenient division may be made at 2.4 kHz. A low F_3 group comprises close rounding, retroflex, raised larynx, pharyngalised and open rounding (in order of ascending F_3). The F_3-lowering effect of lip rounding is well known (Fant 1968:239) as is that of retroflexion (Ladefoged 1975:204). In the case of lip rounding the effect on F_3 results from this formant being, at least for vowels of the [u], [o], [ɑ], and [i] types, chiefly dependent on the parts of the vocal tract in front of the tongue constriction (Fant 1960:121). The actual and effective lengthening of the vocal tract caused by lip protrusion and constriction may be expected to lower F_3. In retroflexion, the F_3-lowering effect presumably results from the expansion of the front mouth cavity when the tongue tip is raised and retracted; and, in addition, if the above suggestion that pharyngeal constriction is a characteristic articulatory component underlying auditory retroflexion is correct, this too might have an F_3-lowering effect, since vocal tract analogues predict a lowering of F_3 as the primary constriction of a vowel moves towards the pharyngeal region. According to Fant's synthetic predictions (1960:84), F_3 lowers from a peak around 7 cm from the glottis to a nadir between 4 and 1 cm (depending on the degree of constriction). The raised larynx setting again poses a problem, discussion of which will be deferred until 4.4.5.

Velarised voice has the highest F_3, followed by palato-alveolarised. This agrees with the prediction of the three-parameter vocal tract model with horn-shaped constriction used by Fant (1960:84) where F_3 peaks occur for constrictions located both in front of and behind the constriction yielding maximum F_2 – but the F_2 maximum itself (here achieved by palatalised voice) occurs with a slightly lower F_3. The fairly high F_3 of dentalised and alveolarised voice can be explained in terms of the general tendency for constrictions forward of the midpalatal region to raise F_3 in varying degrees (Fant 1960:84; 1973:11); that of uvularised voice by the next F_3 maximum – Fant (1960:89): 'The uvular point of articulation at 8 cm from the glottis coincides with the intermediate F_3 maximum'; and that of the lip-spread setting by the above-mentioned sensitivity of F_3 to labial configuration. Lowered larynx voice has a surprisingly high F_3, since (at least in open vowels) it might be expected to be a 5/4-wavelength resonance of the vocal tract (Fant 1975:7); it will be considered again in 4.4.3.4 (under number 6). The overall relation of modal to neutral – lower F_1, higher F_2 and F_3 – suggests that it was produced with a slight relative raising and fronting of the tongue, and acts as a reminder of the limitations of evidence based on a single performance by one speaker.

On the whole the preliminary analysis was deemed successful, as it showed that auditorily distinct articulatory settings could be differentiated on the basis of their first three formant frequencies measured at defined points, and that the trends of these formants were often, though not always, in accord with the predictions of previous work on the acoustics of speech production. In two respects the preliminary analysis is deficient: the number of measurement points is too small; and throughout there has been a tacit oversimplification residing in the lumping together of all vowels, rather than allowing that the settings may have differential effects on different vowels. A more extended analysis was therefore carried out on a subset of the qualities.

4.4.3 Main analysis

4.4.3.1 *Measurement points* A representative set of nine qualities was selected for the main analysis:

N neutral
L lowered larynx
R raised larynx
O labial setting with close rounding and protrusion of the lips
& retroflex
P pharyngalised
V velarised
J palatalised
D dentalised

Pole plots were then computed for the remainder of each reading, and measurement points defined as with the sentence first analysed. The whole of the passage is as follows:

When the sunlight strikes raindrops in the air they act like a prism and form a rainbow. The rainbow is a division of white light into many beautiful colours. These take the shape of a long, round arch, with its path high above, and its two ends apparently beyond the horizon. There is, according to legend, a boiling pot of gold at one end. People look, but no-one ever finds it. When a man looks for something beyond his reach, his friends say he is looking for the pot of gold at the end of the rainbow.

Then 51 additional measurement points were defined, as follows:

location	*definition*
17 sʌnlaɪt	highest F_1
18 sʌnlaɪt	first value after jump up in F_1 at end of lingual contact
19 sʌnlaɪt	highest F_1
20 straɪks	highest F_1
21 drɒp	highest F_1
22 ðɪɛə	highest F_2
23 ðɪɛə	lowest F_2
24 ðeɪækt	highest F_2
25 ðeɪækt	highest F_1
26 laɪk	highest F_1
27 prɪzm	highest F_2
28 əreɪnbəʊ	highest F_1
29 bəʊɪz	lowest F_3
30 ɪzədɪv	highest F_1
31 dɪvɪʒn	highest F_1
32 waɪt	highest F_1
33 laɪt	lowest F_1
34 laɪt	first value after jump up in F_1 at end of lingual contact
35 bju:tɪfl	middle value in voiced portion (of 'dark' /l/)
36 kʌləz	middle value between voice onset and F_1 jump down for /l/
37 kʌləz	middle value of low F_1 portion
38 kʌləz	highest F_1
39 ðɛərɪz	highest F_2
40 əkɔ:d	highest F_1
41 əkɔ:d	lowest F_2
42 təledʒ	lowest F_1
43 təledʒ	highest F_1
44 əbɔɪlɪŋ	first point in F_2 rise
45 əbɔɪlɪŋ	lowest F_1
46 gəʊld	mid-point between /g/ and /l/
47 gəʊld	lowest F_2
48 ətwʌn	highest F_1

	location	definition
49	pi:pl	highest F_1
50	pi:pl	lowest F_2 (in 'dark' /l/)
51	lʊk	highest F_1
52	bət	highest F_1
53	faɪndzɪt	highest F_1
54	faɪndzɪt	highest F_2
55	lʊks	highest F_1
56	fəsʌm	middle value in voiced portion between /f/ and /s/
57	bɪɒnd	highest F_2
58	hɪz	highest F_1
59	ri:tʃ	highest F_2
60	hɪzfrendz	middle value of voiced portion between [h] and [ʐf]
61	seɪ	highest F_1
62	hi:ɪz	highest F_2
63	hi:ɪzlʊk	highest F_1
64	pɒtəv	highest F_1
65	əvgəʊld	lowest F_2
66	ðɪend	highest F_2
67	reɪnbəʊ	highest F_1

The large number of measurement points which are defined by a peak in the first formant trajectory reflects the commonness of this feature; it corresponds to the point of least occlusion in the sequential opening and closing gestures of the vocal tract which constitute the succession of syllables. A consequence is that the majority of measurement points are maximally distinct from adjacent consonants, so that the effects of consonantal transitions will be minimised. It is necessary to bear in mind that part of the auditory impression of a voice quality such as dentalised or palatalised may result from shifts in consonantal targets, and so the present investigation cannot pretend to give an all-encompassing account of their relevant acoustic properties.

4.4.3.2 *Comparison with the preliminary analysis* Table 4.3 presents the results of the main analysis, and will be discussed section by section. Firstly the means for the preliminary measurement points (mp 1–16) are given for comparison with those of the new (mp 17–67); and the comparison is presented graphically in Fig. 4.8. From Fig. 4.8 it can be seen that there is a basic similarity in the disposition of the qualities: J, V and D have a higher F_2 than neutral; L, O, R, P and & a lower F_2 and wide spread in the F_1 dimension. It will be shown (4.4.3.4) that two of the ways in which the values

Table 4.3 Means of F_1, F_2, F_3 for long term qualities over the measurement points indicated – speaker JL

	N	L	R	O	&	P	V	J	D	
mp 1–16	2405	2450	2245	2195	2235	2265	2560	2480	2480	F_3
	1365	1390	1285	1300	1315	1265	1505	1515	1450	F_2
	545	465	545	515	575	565	515	530	535	F_1
mp 17–67	2410	2385	2290	2290	2225	2250	2565	2555	2460	
	1345	1280	1275	1270	1320	1265	1415	1525	1405	
	480	450	500	460	530	530	460	455	460	
mp 1–67	2415	2415	2275	2285	2210	2240	2565	2523	2475	
(laterals excluded)	1400	1320	1315	1310	1355	1305	1485	1565	1455	
	520	470	535	495	565	565	500	500	505	
HIGH FRONT	2510	2515	2375	2330	2345	2315	2640	2665	2600	
(21 mp)	1705	1605	1615	1615	1630	1585	1860	1945	1775	
	380	395	410	375	435	450	360	350	375	
LOW	2350	2395	2270	2270	2215	2200	2445	2435	2445	
(17 mp)	1205	1140	1160	1115	1205	1150	1295	1325	1255	
	760	580	745	680	775	755	730	765	725	
HIGH BACK	2210	2115	2070	2060	2065	2060	2555	2380	2240	
(10 mp)	1105	1070	1040	1035	1080	1045	1100	1195	1145	
	445	460	465	435	515	525	415	415	435	

for mp 17–67 depart from those for mp 1–16 (circled) – the less extreme L, and the lower F_1 of the cluster as a whole – can be accounted for by the different proportions of vowel types in the two groups, so that there is in reality an even closer agreement between the two in the $F_2 F_1$ plane than is at first evident.

The inset to Fig. 4.8 shows the equivalent comparison in the F_3 dimension. In the F_3 dimension, the qualities appear to form two clusters in each case: R, O, P, & with low F_3; and V, J, D, N, L with high F_3.

4.4.3.3 *Subcategorisation of measurement points* Now it is necessary to question the assumption that it should be possible to characterise supralaryngeal long term qualities by a single average value for each formant. Such an assumption is implicit in the synthesis work of Laver (1967, 1975) in which qualities were simulated by shifting up or down the range within which a particular formant could vary, and in some cases compressing the range; this however was probably a practical strategy rather than the reflection of a theoretical position. In fact there is every reason to expect that an adjustment made to the preferred configuration of the vocal

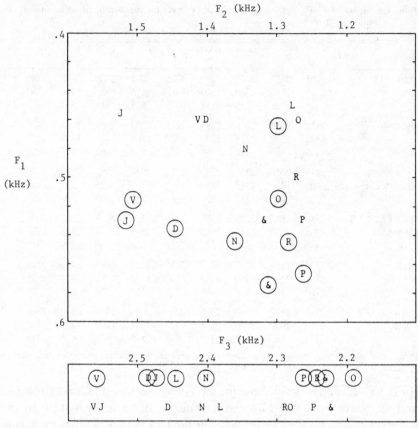

4.8 Means of formant frequencies for nine long term qualities: mp 17–67 and (circled) 1–16

tract will have differential effects according to the sound type being produced. Evidence comes, for example, from the work of Fant (1973) on male–female–child vowel normalisation which showed the non-uniformity of formant normalisation factors over different vowels; from that of Sundberg and Nordström (1976) who obtained both simulated and real data on larynx raising/lowering which had varied effects according to the vowel produced; and from vocal tract model predictions such as those of Fant (1960:82) where a change in lip aperture has varying effects on formants depending on the location of the main constriction in the vocal tract.

Subgroups of the measurement points were therefore separated out, their composition influenced by Fant (1973:84):

Actually the female to male relations are typically different in the three groups of (1) rounded back vowels (2) very open unrounded vowels, and (3) close front vowels.

A total of 10 points, comprising those located in realisations of the /u:/, /ʊ/, /ɔ:/ and /əʊ/ phonemes, were allocated to a class HIGH BACK; 17, located in /ɑ:/, /ʌ/, /ɒ/ and the first elements of /aɪ/, /aʊ/, to a class LOW; and 21, located in /i:/, /ɪ/, /e/ and /eɪ/, to a class HIGH FRONT. The labels are clearly of mnemonic rather than precise phonetic value. The measurement points grouped into each class were as follows:

HIGH FRONT   1,2,3,7,11,14,22,24,27,31,39,43,49,54,57,58,59,60,61,
             62,66
LOW   5,6,8,10,15,16,17,18,19,20,21,25,26,32,34,36,53
HIGH BACK   28,29,41,44,46,47,51,55,63,67

4.4.3.4 *Results of subcategorisation* Mean values for the first three formants of each of the nine qualities are shown for the subgroups in Table 4.3; they are plotted in Fig. 4.9, where the triangles each enclose the values of a subgroup, HIGH FRONT being at the top left, HIGH BACK at the top right, and LOW at the bottom. The central grouping is included for comparison, and is the mean of all measurement points excluding laterals.

From Fig. 4.9 it can be seen that the general $F_2 F_1$ pattern already observed – by which a high F_2 group comprising J, V and D is contrasted with a lower than N group L, O, R, P, & (internally differentiated primarily by F_1) – holds to a first approximation for each subgroup of vowels. The two minor exceptions are V in the HIGH BACK group, which has F_2 5 Hz lower than N; and & (retroflex) in the LOW group, which has F_2 the same as that of N.

Looking more closely, a number of differences between the groups emerge. Salient among these are the following:

1 F_1 of L is fractionally higher than that of N in the HIGH vowel groups, but strikingly lower than that of any other quality in the LOW vowels.
2 F_1 of O is only very slightly lower than that of N in the HIGH FRONT and HIGH BACK categories, but considerably lower in LOW.
3   Both & and P have much higher F_1 than N in the HIGH vowel categories, but this difference is nullified in LOW vowels.
Each of these will now be examined in turn.

1   The primary effect of lowering the larynx will be to lengthen and dilate the pharynx – Sundberg and Nordström (1976:35):

a lowered larynx will lengthen the pharynx. Moreover, assuming a pharynx wall volume, we can postulate an. . .expansion of the lower part of the pharynx when the larynx is. . .pressed downwards.

The change is thus in the same direction as the primary differentiator of a male vocal tract from a female vocal tract – Fant (1973:88):

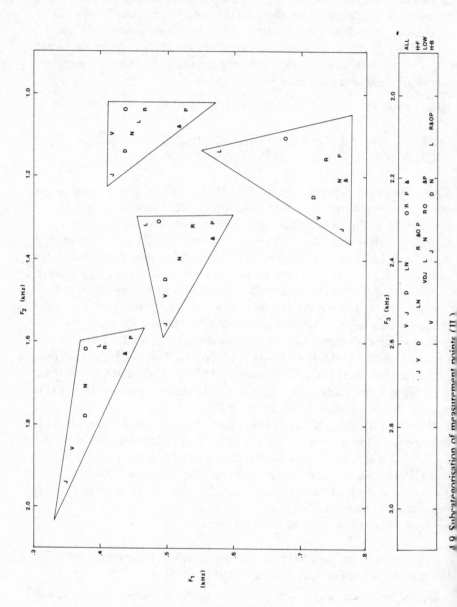

4.9 Subcategorisation of measurement points (II)

the relatively greater pharynx length and more pronounced laryngeal cavities of grown up males compared with females,

and so his findings on the non-uniform normalisation of vowel formants are relevant here. He summarises the deviations from an overall scaling factor valid across all vowels as follows:

a) the first and second formants of all rounded back vowels have relatively low scale factors;
b) this is also the case with the first formant scale factor of any close or highly rounded vowel, i.e. high front vowels;
c) very open front or back vowels display a first formant 'sex factor' which is substantially higher than the average.

These are in accord with the present findings on the relation of L to N. In (rounded) HIGH BACK vowels F_1 of L is 15 Hz higher (rather surprisingly) than F_1 of N, and F_2 35 Hz lower. In HIGH FRONT, F_1 of L is similarly 15 Hz higher than that of N, but F_2 of L is appreciably (100 Hz) lower. The most striking difference from N, however, is in the LOW vowels, where larynx lowering effects a 180 Hz reduction of F_1 from 760 (N) to 580 (L). Taking N as a 'female' and L as a 'male' vocal tract these values may be substituted in Fant's 'k' scaling factor equation (1973:85):

$$k_1 = \left[\frac{F_1 \text{ female}}{F_1 \text{ male}} - 1 \right] \times 100$$

$$= \left[\frac{760}{580} - 1 \right] \times 100$$

$$= 31\%$$

This 'scaling factor' of 31% is comparable to those obtained by Fant for Swedish [ɑ] (26%), [æ] (30%), and [ɛ] (24%), or American English [æ] (30%). Although one of the Swedish vowels, [ə], has a negative scaling factor, this is probably not related to the apparently systematically slightly higher F_1 of L in HIGH vowels; a possible explanation of the present finding might lie in some mechanical effect, bearing in mind the unaccustomed muscular effort required to keep the larynx low. It is possible that it is not easy to resist the indirect pull upwards on the hyoid bone and thyroid cartilage suspended from it when the tongue is raised; Hardcastle (1976:69–73, 97–106) indicates that the palatoglossus, styloglossus, stylohyoid, and (posterior belly of the) digastricus muscles may contribute both to the raising and backing of the tongue body, and to the raising of the hyoid bone.

Here it is appropriate to return to the two apparent discrepancies noted in

4.4.3.2 between the average formant positions for the preliminary analysis and those for the additional measurement points 17–67 (Fig. 4.8): namely the less extreme L, and the lower F_1 of the cluster as a whole, of mp 17–67 (not circled).

The F_1 value is 80 Hz lower for L than for N in mp 1–16, and only 30 Hz lower in mp 17–67. The explanation lies in the composition of the two data sets in terms of vowel category membership. As has been discussed above, larynx lowering causes a proportionately greater lowering of F_1 in LOW vowels than in those of either of the other two categories; thus if a given data set has a preponderance of LOW vowels its F_1 value for L will be proportionately low. This is the case with the preliminary data set, in which six out of the 16 measurement points (37.5%) are categorised as LOW, in contrast to only 11 out of the additional 51 points (21.6%).

This smaller ratio of LOW measurement points also accounts for the other discrepancy noted – the lower F_1 of the 17–67 cluster as a whole compared with that of the preliminary analysis. The means of all settings are 480 Hz (mp 17–67) and 530 Hz (mp 1–16). Since F_1 is inversely proportional to vowel height, the smaller ratio of LOW vowels will result generally in a lower F_1.

2   Close lip rounding (O) results in an F_1 only 5 or 10 Hz lower than that of N in the HIGH FRONT and HIGH BACK groups, but 80 Hz lower in LOW. This may be compared with the nomograms of Fant (1960:82, 83) in which the tongue constriction is held at a constant area, and lip aperture varied. It can be seen that both for the narrower (0.65 cm²) and wider (2.6 cm²) tongue constrictions, a narrowing of the lip aperture tends to inhibit the rise in F_1 which takes place as the tongue constriction moves back from the front of the mouth cavity to the pharynx. Since open vowels, to the extent that they can be considered to have a main point of constriction (doubtful in the case of front open vowels), have it located in the pharynx (cf. Fant 1960:113–14), it can be expected that lip rounding will inhibit their normally high F_1. This seems to be borne out by the present data, since (excluding L) O has clearly the lowest F_1 in LOW vowels, but only a value comparable to that of J, V, D and N in the HIGH vowel groups.

3   Pharyngalised (P) and retroflex (&) settings result in F_1 values higher than those of N by 70 Hz and 55 Hz respectively in the HIGH FRONT group, and 80 Hz and 70 Hz in the HIGH BACK vowels; but in LOW vowels F_1 of & is only 15 Hz higher than that of N, and F_1 of P is in fact 5 Hz lower than the equivalent N value. In the case of & it has been suggested (4.4.2) that the generally higher F_1 of the retroflex setting may result from the more open vocal tract which the retroflexion of the tongue tip necessitates. If this is the case here, it is however possible that this effect only takes place when the vowels are relatively high, and therefore no further lowering effect occurs on vowels which are already low. This would explain why the F_1-lowering effect of & is absent in LOW vowels.

The general lowering of F_2 and raising of F_1 brought about by pharyngalisation (P) are in accord with a shift of the tongue constriction in the direction of the pharyngeal region and a generally more open vocal tract. It appears that if the vocal tract already finds itself in an open configuration, as for the LOW vowels, it does not adopt a more open configuration, so that F_1 of P is very similar to that of N. It appears then that an asymmetry is revealed: 'close' settings such as palatalisation make close vowels closer, while the 'open' setting of pharyngalisation does not affect the openness of open vowels. The evidence is of course indirect, and might usefully be supplemented – as in the case of much of this discussion – by physiological measurements. If the asymmetry is genuine, however, it might be explained in terms of a maximum degree of opening of the vocal tract during a syllable, governed by the need to give the articulators adequate support during the adjacent consonantal syllable margins.

The general behaviour of the third formant in the light of the additional measurement points now remains to be considered. As noted at the end of 4.4.3.2 the F_3 dimension exhibits a primary split on the basis of both data sets (1–16 and 17–67) into 'low F_3' settings comprising R, O, P, &, and 'high F_3' settings comprising V, J, D, N, L. Fig. 4.9 (inset) shows firstly the result of lumping together all vowels in measurement points 1–67 (that is, excluding laterals but including neutral vowels). Here O, R, P and & group below 2.3 kHz, and the other settings above 2.4 kHz with N and L possibly forming a lower subgroup within the 'high F_3' group.

The reasons for the low F_3 in O, P and & have been discussed in 4.4.2 and will be summarised briefly here. Lip rounding generally has the effect of lowering the frequency of F3 which for most vowels is affiliated closely with the mouth cavity. O (close rounding of the lips with protrusion) will cause both an actual and an effective lengthening of this cavity. Pharyngalisation exploits the region extending from the glottis for about 4 cm where narrowing from a straight-sided tube will coincide with the first volume velocity maximum of the 5/4-wavelength resonance, thus lowering the third resonance. Retroflexion, it is suggested in 4.4.2, may be combining these two mechanisms by enlarging the mouth cavity and constricting the pharynx.

The settings with highest F_3 are the ones which exploit the area of maximum F_3 just behind and in front of the palatal region – the former in the case of V, and the latter in the case of J and D. Lowered larynx voice is problematical with respect to F_3, and will be discussed below. Three specific points arising from the breakdown by vowel category shown in the inset to Fig. 4.9 will be dealt with:

4 F_3 of V in the HIGH BACK category is high in relation to that of other settings.

5   The spread of F_3 values in LOW vowels is small compared with the other two categories.

6   L exhibits an F_3 relative to N which is lower in HIGH BACK vowels than in other vowel categories.

4   V in general terms exhibits the highest F_3 of all the settings, and an F_2 which is high, but less so than that of J – both of which are consonant with a shift in the 'centre of gravity' of articulation in a post-palatal direction. It is likely that the target position for HIGH BACK vowels facilitates the tongue in making a stricture in the region (around 7 cm from the glottis according to Fant (1960:84)) where optimal raising of F_3 results. In other categories of vowel, however, the vowel and long term quality targets are not in the same harmony, and the F_3-raising effect of V in relation to that of the other 'front of the vocal tract' settings is less clear cut.

5   The spread of F_3 values for the different settings is 350 Hz in the HIGH FRONT category, 495 Hz in the HIGH BACK category, but only 245 Hz in the LOW category. This is explicable in terms of the formant frequency predictions of Fant's vocal tract model (1960:84). It is clear from the nomogram that the degree to which F_3 is perturbed, by changing the distance of the constriction from the glottis, increases the smaller the area of the constriction becomes. Clearly, then, shifts in the 'centre of gravity' of the tongue and resultant effects on location of constrictions will perturb F_3 less when superimposed on open as opposed to close vowels.

6   Although the behaviour of F_3 of L appears to be exceptional in the HIGH BACK category, in that only in this category is it lower than F_3 of N, this exception in fact coincides with the norm as predicted by acoustic theory, assuming L to be a simple lengthening of the vocal tract – Sundberg and Nordström's model, for example, predicts lowered F_3 in all vowels. Their evidence from live speech, however, is less uniform. One of their speakers produces an F_3 in lowered larynx voice which is consistently lower than that of the same vowel in neutral voice, but the other speaker's F_3 is higher in the lowered larynx condition except for front non-low rounded and unrounded vowels. Although such results reflect the variability in the present data, the detail of the variation does not match, since in the present data it is high back, rather than front non-low, vowels which exhibit the predicted lowering of F_3. Sundberg and Nordström attempt to explain instances of higher F_3 values associated with larynx lowering by suggesting that (1976:38)

When the larynx is lowered this subject is likely to resort to his singing habits including not only a low larynx position but also a fronted position of the tongue tip. This last mentioned gesture effectively closes the cavity behind the lower incisors and raises the third formant frequency which in turn adds to the amplitude of the 'singing formant'.

This explanation does not seem convincing in that it fails to account for the fact that only in some of the vowels is F_3 higher when the larynx is lowered. Nor, of course, is it of help in the present data where there is no reason to suppose that the speaker has trained singing habits to which he is likely to revert when lowering the larynx.

4.4.4 *Cross-speaker comparison*

4.4.4.1 *Analysis* Hitherto, comparison of the effects of the settings has been internal to the output of a single speaker; the settings have been characterised by opposing their acoustic properties one to another, and in particular with reference to those of the neutral setting, and to the formant space defined by the group of settings. The questions arise: firstly whether a similar acoustic patterning of the long term qualities would be found in the output of other individuals, and secondly to what extent a speaker-independent acoustic characterisation of the supralaryngeal qualities would be possible. Now that a method has been established for the acoustic description of long term supralaryngeal qualities, the way is opened for their empirical exploration across speakers.

As a first step in this exploration, nine of the supralaryngeal voice quality recordings made by the author (FN) and described in 4.3.4 were used as data. Analysis followed exactly the same procedure as in the main analysis of the recordings by JL, with estimated pole frequencies being measured at each of 67 measurement points. The first 16 are listed in 4.4.2, and the remainder in 4.4.3.1.

4.4.4.2 *General comparison of results* Table 4.4 presents the results of the analysis for FN, and is directly comparable to Table 4.3 for JL. The patterning of the qualities is summarised in Fig. 4.10, which is comparable to Fig. 4.9 for JL, and in which the central cluster shows the results over all

Table 4.4 Means of F_1, F_2, F_3 for long term qualities over the measurement points indicated – speaker FN

	N	L	R	O	&	P	V	J	D	
mp 1–16	2465	2395	2255	2300	2270	2360	2580	2590	2573	F_3
	1420	1245	1265	1355	1345	1330	1470	1610	1555	F_2
	515	410	510	510	535	545	485	500	500	F_1
mp 17–67	2450	2395	2260	2235	2205	2430	2570	2515	2470	
	1385	1235	1205	1300	1330	1305	1365	1610	1520	
	490	400	500	475	535	535	475	470	490	
mp 1–67	2445	2385	2265	2240	2215	2390	2570	2535	2510	
(laterals excluded)	1445	1265	1255	1355	1370	1355	1440	1640	1570	
	510	415	515	495	550	555	490	495	510	
HIGH FRONT	2480	2385	2330	2295	2225	2430	2525	2650	2630	
(21 mp)	1850	1540	1470	1710	1690	1675	1825	1950	1900	
	400	360	435	410	450	465	405	390	415	
LOW	2535	2480	2285	2250	2360	2460	2665	2575	2590	
(17 mp)	1210	1090	1115	1135	1195	1170	1195	1430	1350	
	690	495	620	640	705	685	620	670	650	
HIGH BACK	2270	2290	2040	2120	2060	2310	2535	2315	2225	
(10 mp)	1055	1000	1075	1025	1010	1010	1090	1385	1250	
	485	405	505	480	515	530	480	485	500	

measurement points with the exclusion of the nine laterals, and the peripheral clusters show results for HIGH FRONT, HIGH BACK and LOW vowel categories, in order clockwise from top left.

Immediately striking is the less clear separation of the clusters in Fig. 4.10 (FN) than in Fig. 4.9 (JL), resulting from greater spread of the qualities within each vowel group. This must be interpreted as indicating that the settings employed by FN involved, in general, more extreme deviations from neutral.

In Fig. 4.9, JL's central cluster was found to exhibit J, V and D with a higher than neutral F_2, and L, O, R, P and & with a lower F_2 and a wide spread in the F_1 dimension (4.4.3.2). The same applies to Fig. 4.10 (FN), with the exception that V has an F_2 lower than neutral voice. Within the low F_2 group, it is again L and O which have lower than neutral F_1, and R, & and P which have a higher F_1.

As far as F3 is concerned, JL's qualities over all measurement points except laterals showed a high F_3 group (V, J, D, N, L) and a low F_3 group (O, R, P, &); for FN, the grouping is similar, except that P appears to have a higher F_3, since it is now marginally higher than L.

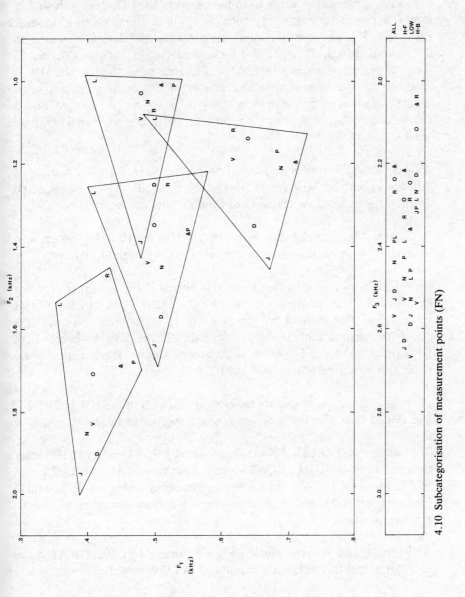

4.10 Subcategorisation of measurement points (FN)

179

In general, comparison of the four clusters in Fig. 4.10 with those in Fig. 4.9 shows qualities deviating from the centres of the clusters with similar signs (i.e. positive or negative) in the F_1 and F_2 dimensions, although in some cases (e.g. R in the central cluster) the proportion of deviation in the two dimensions differs. It might also be argued that in FN's production, N (neutral voice) provides a less stable reference point, and in the HIGH vowel groups is displaced from the centre of the cluster. This might reflect a greater freedom of articulation in this setting, so that the tongue moved freely to articulate vowels in the palatal, or velar, region even without an 'enabling' setting.

4.4.4.3 *Comparison of results of subcategorisation* In 4.4.3.4 a number of differences between vowel categories were examined. These are considered again here, to enable assessment of their validity across speakers.

1 F_1 of L is fractionally higher than that of N in the HIGH vowel groups, but strikingly lower than that of any other quality in the LOW vowels.

It is clear from Fig. 4.10 that F_1 of L is *always* lower than that of N for speaker FN. If the explanation given for the higher F_1 of L in JL's HIGH vowels (based on indirect 'tongue pull' raising the larynx) is correct, it is clearly not an irresistible tendency. Nevertheless, the pattern whereby F_1 of L is strikingly lower in LOW vowels, in accord with findings in male–female scaling, is very clearly repeated in FN.

2 F_1 of O is only very slightly lower than that of N in the HIGH FRONT and HIGH BACK categories, but considerably lower in LOW.

The pattern is repeated in FN's realisations, with F_1 of O in fact 10 Hz higher than that of N in HIGH FRONT vowels, 5 Hz lower in HIGH BACK, and 50 Hz lower in LOW vowels. The explanation, based on lip rounding inhibiting the otherwise high F_1 of open 'pharynx constriction' vowels, remains possible.

3 Both & and P have much higher F_1 than N in the HIGH vowel categories, but this difference is nullified in LOW vowels.

FN's pharyngalised voice (P) clearly confirms this pattern (its F_1 is 65 and 45 Hz higher than that of N in HIGH FRONT and HIGH BACK vowels, but 5 Hz lower in LOW vowels); and retroflex voice (&) does not contradict it (50, 30 and 15 Hz higher in the three vowel categories). As will be recalled, it was suggested in 4.4.3.4 that a putative greater openness of the vocal tract facilitating sublamino-prepalatal 'retroflex' articulations might not be necessary in vowels which are already open; and likewise that the open vocal tract specification of pharyngalisation might simply be congruent with that of (at least certain) low vowels.

4   F_3 of V in the HIGH BACK category is high in relation to that of other settings.

This pattern is very clearly manifested again in Fig. 4.10 (inset), where F_3 of V in HIGH BACK vowels is a clear 220 Hz higher than that of the next quality. Its likely explanation, as suggested above, is the cooperation of setting and vowel type to exploit the post-palatal region where optimal raising of F_3 results from increasing constriction.

5   The spread of F_3 values in LOW vowels is small compared with the other two categories.

Although in the case of FN the spread of F_3 in LOW vowels is 10 and 80 Hz lower than in HIGH FRONT and HIGH BACK vowels respectively, this can hardly be adduced as strong supporting evidence. Some less general explanation may be required for the more striking effect in JL.

6   L exhibits an F_3 relative to N which is lower in HIGH BACK vowels than in other vowel categories.

It will be recalled that F_3 of L has already proved problematical. Only one of Sundberg and Nordström's (1976) speakers conformed to model predictions in having a generally lowered F_3 with larynx lowering. The other one had a higher than neutral F_3 for all except non-low front vowels. Speaker JL has a higher than neutral F_3 in all except HIGH BACK vowels; and now it appears that speaker FN has a higher than neutral F_3 for L *only* in HIGH BACK vowels. This added confusion underlines the need for research on the consequences of changing the height of the larynx, which will further become apparent from the following section on raised larynx voice.

It seems reasonable to conclude from the discussion of the last two sections that whilst the results of the analysis of data from a second speaker do not correspond in every detail to those obtained from the first speaker's data, a sufficient number of details, as well as more general patternings, are common to the two analyses to permit optimism that the acoustic

181

characterisation is capturing at least in part the categories of the auditor descriptive system.

4.4.5 *Raised larynx voice*

It is appropriate, now that data from two speakers are available, to return to the problem of raised larynx voice (R), deferred from 4.4.2. F_1 of R appear generally to be higher than that of N; F_2, with the exception of FN's HIGH BACK vowels, is lower than F_2 of N; and F_3 (see insets to Figs. 4.9 and 4.10 is lower than that of N in all vowel groups for either speaker. The exception to the F_1 generalisation is provided by the LOW vowels, where F_1 of R i lower, for both speakers, than that of N. Apart from this, the trend observed in the original small scale analysis of JL's reading is confirmed, and the findings remain in conflict with the expectation of a general raising o formant frequencies with a shortening of the effective length of the voca tract, and with the specific model predictions and real-life findings in raised larynx voice of Sundberg and Nordström (1976:39; see p. 164 above). In contrast the present data show a sharp drop in F_2, most substantial in the case of HIGH FRONT vowels; a slight drop in F_2 (and also F_1) in LOW vowels; and a substantial drop in F_3.

In fact the patterning of R most closely resembles that of P (pharyngal ised), and this gives the clue to the explanation – namely that raised larynx voice in the production of these speakers involves considerable constriction of the pharynx. The acoustic evidence so far points to this conclusion, bu what other reasons are there to suppose a relation between larynx raising and pharyngalisation?

Firstly, radiographic stills were made of the author producing a mid central vowel [ə] with the superimposed voice qualities of neutral larynx extreme larynx raising, and extreme larynx lowering. These were made with the kind assistance of staff of the Radiography Department, New Addenbrooke's Hospital, Cambridge as an extension to a project organised by Geoff Bristow of Cambridge University Engineering Department and intended to provide data on vocal tract lengths. Tracings made by him of the radiographs are presented as Fig. 4.11.

A comparison of the neutral, raised and lowered qualities reveals a number of articulatory correlates. The height of the larynx varies in the expected way; and the higher the larynx, the greater the curvature of the larynx tube appears to be, as though it were 'folding' to accommodate the raising. Most significant for the present discussion, and resulting partly from this curvature, is the appreciable progressive narrowing of the larynx tube and lower pharynx as the larynx moves from its lower to higher positions

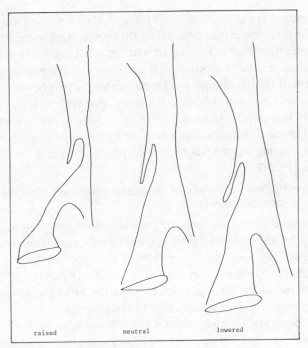

raised   neutral   lowered

4.11 Tracings for x-ray pictures of the larynx and pharynx in neutral, extreme raised larynx, and extreme lowered larynx settings

Secondly, the physiology of larynx raising suggests the likelihood of pharyngeal constriction occurring. On the one hand there is the point made by Sundberg and Nordström (1976:35) that

assuming a pharynx wall volume, we can postulate a narrowing. . .of the lower part of the pharynx when the larynx is pulled upwards;

and on the other hand some of the musculature active in raising the larynx may have the secondary effect of pharyngeal constriction. Laver (1980:26) suggests there are two possible strategies for raising the larynx, the first requiring the hyoid bone, from which the larynx is suspended, to be anchored 'by using mainly the *hyoglossus, geniohyoid, mylohyoid* and *middle pharyngeal constrictor* muscles', and the larynx to be pulled up towards it by contraction of the thyrohyoid muscle; the second involving an active raising of the hyoid bone – pulled upwards and forwards by contraction of the geniohyoid, genioglossus, mylohyoid, and (anterior belly of the) digastricus, and pulled upwards and backwards by contraction of the stylohyoid, (posterior belly of the) digastricus, palatopharyngeus, and middle pharyngeal constrictor – and then either an active raising of the larynx (thyrohyoid contraction), or a passive 'lifting' as the hyoid rises, by virtue of the thyrohyoid membrane. But the musculature of the body is such that discrete adjustments of one part without consequential adjustment of others through muscular interaction is unlikely, and the pharyngeal region provides a particularly complex example of this (in part because the hyoid bone is the only bone in the body not articulated with at least one other). Specifically the action of the middle pharyngeal constrictor muscle, mentioned above as active in anchoring the hyoid, or pulling it upwards and backwards, during larynx raising, may justify its name. According to Hardcastle (1976:126):

When the hyoid is fixed. . .[the middle pharyngeal constrictor] can act to narrow the pharynx by. . .sphincter activity.

This sphincteric narrowing may be supplemented by a tendency of this muscle to draw the body of the tongue backwards; retraction and lowering of the tongue may also be a by-product of the hyoid anchoring or raising function of the hyoglossus muscle (Hardcastle 1976:99). In short, the complex of muscles which interact to raise the larynx contain elements which are conducive to a constriction of the pharynx.

Thirdly, perceptual evidence from Laver's synthesis of R (1975:285–6) lends support to a link between larynx raising and pharyngeal constriction. The quality was successfully simulated by making the following changes in formant frequency range of the PAT synthesiser:

	neutral		raised larynx
F_3	1400–3400	→	1500–3000
F_2	500–2500	→	600–2100
F_1	100–1000	→	150–1050

From these values it is not clear what the effect of the changes would be on individual vowels, but the general effect seems to be a rise in F_1, and an effective reduction in F_2 (the lowering of the top of the range will be more relevant than the raising of the bottom limit, as F_2 values below 800 Hz are not usually found), which is in agreement with the present findings. To the extent that the F_3 adjustment represents a lowering of vowel third formants, which will normally occur in the range 2.0–2.5 kHz, this also agrees with the present data. The synthesis was apparently successful only if accompanied by a higher fundamental frequency – if the normal F_0 range was used (1975:286)

the effect was that of a tongue setting where the body of the tongue was lowered and retracted, giving the auditory impression of laryngo-pharyngalisation.

Laver further states that this quality is shared by his own attempts to produce raised larynx voice without a rise in F_0, and continues

It may be that what we are prepared to accept auditorily as corresponding to a constriction of the upper larynx and lower pharynx is the same resonatory distortion of the vocal tract that results from raising the larynx; and that the upward shift in the fundamental frequency in most raised larynx voices is the factor chiefly responsible for the differentiation of the two qualities.

Thus a number of pieces of acoustic evidence point clearly to the conclusion that the quality under discussion here and labelled 'raised larynx voice' is characterised primarily by a constriction of the pharynx, and that the effect of shortening the vocal tract is only of secondary importance; this conclusion is supported furthermore by physiological plausibility, and the evidence of radiographs of the articulation of a neutral vowel produced with and without an extreme variety of 'raised larynx voice'. It has not, of course, been demonstrated that this pharyngeal constriction is an inevitable concomitant of raising the larynx; its effects are not evident in the formant values obtained by Sundberg and Nordström from their subjects, and informally it can readily be demonstrated that a number of rather different voice qualities can be produced with the larynx raised from the neutral position.

A small scale experiment which was carried out to assess the effects of superimposing raised larynx voice on three peripheral vowels provided results which only partially supported the suggestion that the acoustic correlates observed for raised larynx voice are the consequence of a predominantly pharyngalised setting. The author recorded vowels of 2 second duration approximating to Cardinal Vowels 1 [i], 5 [ɑ], and 8 [u]. Initially each vowel was produced with a radical raising of the larynx, monitored by palpating the thyroid cartilage. Half way through the utterance of each vowel the larynx was lowered to a neutral position, while the vowel quality was as far as possible kept unchanged; whilst it is certainly not transparent how far the auditory abstraction of vowel quality from voice quality is possible under such circumstances, to the extent that it is, vowel quality seemed to remain fairly constant. Two tokens of each vowel were recorded. No attempt was made to counteract the rather high fundamental frequency which the high initial larynx position induced.

Expanded scale spectrograms (0–4 kHz) were made of each vowel, and sections taken before and after the obvious abrupt change in larynx height. To facilitate quantification of the effects the pole-finding routine described in 4.4.1 was used to analyse each vowel.

From the spectrograms the most dramatic effect of the larynx raising was a lowering of the third and fourth formants, with the result that all the first four formants were compressed below about 2.5 kHz. F4 in particular was lowered dramatically, to the extent that in [i] (where F_3 is relatively high) this resonance may well have 'crossed over' the 'genuine' F3 and taken over its role. On the spectrograms only a single broad band of energy is discernible, but the polegram shows clearly that two poles are juxtaposed, and more questionably that at the change in larynx height the trajectories of third and fourth poles cross.

Table 4.5 shows the frequencies of the poles corresponding to the first four formants before and after the raised larynx has returned to the neutral position. The values relate to single frames, selected so as to be representative of the steady states on either side of the change. To the left of the value for 'raised' a plus (+) or minus (−) indicates that the frequency value is higher or lower, respectively, than the equivalent in the neutral position. Differences of less than 20 Hz are indicated by a zero (0).

Although the raised larynx quality manifests in general a lowering of F_3 and F_2 as would be expected from a pharyngalised configuration, and most clearly does not manifest a general raising of formant frequencies as would follow from a simple shortening of the vocal tract, three problems are evident. Firstly, in the vowel [u], the second formant is in fact higher when the larynx is raised. It will, however, be recalled that in speaker FN, raised larynx voice does bring with it a higher than neutral F_2 in the HIGH BACK group. Secondly, in no case is there an appreciable raising of the first formant – on the contrary, the vowel [i] shows F_1 lowering when the larynx is raised. In Figs. 4.9 and 4.10 F_1 of R is lowered only in the LOW vowel group. Finally in Table 4.5 there is the problem of explaining the dramatic drop in F_4 which this kind of larynx raising brings about. Sundberg and Nordström's (1976) model predictions are for a rise in F_4 with larynx raising, and in

Table 4.5 Pole frequencies of vowels produced with a change in larynx height

	[i]		[ɑ]		[u]	
	raised→neutral		raised→neutral		raised→neutral	
	− 2570	3395	− 2280	3440	− 2480	3360
first	− 2405	2715	− 2090	2380	− 1835	2000
token	− 1905	2155	− 950	1070	+ 795	645
	− 320	380	0 600	605	0 325	325
	− 2480	3595	− 2360	3410	− 2330	3160
second	− 2415	2830	− 2155	2480	− 1595	2030
token	− 1835	2180	− 985	1105	+ 945	645
	− 315	360	0 600	600	0 330	320

general their subjects bear this out (exceptions are drops usually of the order of only 100 Hz or so).

Further work, firstly to ascertain the physiological mechanisms of larynx-height adjustment and their consequences for latitudinal as well as longitudinal vocal tract dimensions, and secondly to model the acoustic transformation of such adjustments, is clearly required before the various problems discovered with raised and lowered larynx voice can be resolved.

There may also be a theoretical question concerning the descriptive system at issue here. If it is established that larynx raising can be achieved without pharyngeal constriction, but that (in some definable sense, such as the number of muscle systems which need to be recruited) it is more natural to allow a concomitant pharyngeal constriction, should the componential voice quality feature 'raised larynx' be taken to include, or exclude, such pharyngalisation? The next stage of refinement in the descriptive framework may well be to capture the interactions between the analytically separate components, and work out implicational relations among them on the basis of what is 'mechanically natural' in the vocal tract; for example, lamino-dentalisation may 'naturally' bring with it a degree of palatalisation, as a supportive tongue body setting; and a similar possibility already discussed is that (sublamino-prepalatal) retroflexion might require an enabling open jaw setting.

4.4.6 *Identification of qualities across speakers*

Acoustic characterisations of nine supralaryngeal voice qualities, based on performances by two individuals, have been presented. Now, it is clear that the auditory–articulatory framework provides characterisations of a kind which are independent of the individual. Experience has shown (e.g. Esling 1978) that phoneticians who undergo rigorous auditory and productive training in the framework on the basis of a limited number of individuals, can then, as in the case of the Cardinal Vowel framework (see e.g. Ladefoged 1967:Ch. 2), generalise the framework to other speakers and achieve a consensus which makes possible verbal communication of perceived quality. The question arises as to what extent the acoustic description which has been achieved is speaker-independent in the way that the auditory framework is. This question is of great importance, of course, if instrumental analysis of voice quality is to be used as a method of classifying voices – especially if the classification resulting is to be readily mappable onto an auditory reality.

As a first step in answering this question, acoustic descriptors of voice qualities were compared across the two speakers involved in the present study. If, for example, the acoustic descriptor for JL's palatalised voice is compared to all nine of the descriptors for the other speaker, FN, it should ideally turn out to be nearest to that for FN's palatalised voice; and a particular ranking of the other qualities might also be predicted on the basis of their auditory similarity.

In attempts at speaker-independent characterisation of supralaryngeal qualities a number of descriptors were tested, both including and excluding the third formant. Better results were found when the third formant was excluded from consideration; this may suggest that the tuning of the third formant by, for example, lip position, is less carefully attended to by the speakers implementing the voice qualities than is the tuning of the first two formants. Only the use of the first two formants will be dealt with here.

The descriptor for each quality initially used consisted of its first two formant frequencies in each of the three vowel groups (HIGH FRONT, HIGH BACK and LOW). This six-value descriptor was compared with the descriptor for each of the other speaker's nine qualities, as though the second speaker's qualities were serving as a reference set for identification of the voice quality of samples from the first speaker. The distance between any pair of descriptors X and Y was computed using the Euclidean distance measure

$$d_{XY} = [\sum_{k=1}^{6} (x_k - y_k)^2]^{1/2}$$

The other speaker's qualities were rank ordered from nearest to furthest. The procedure was repeated for each of the first speaker's qualities; and then the roles were reversed so that now the first speaker's qualities were used as a reference set. For each quality and speaker, the ranking of the other speaker's qualities are presented in Table 4.6, in which the 'correct' quality in the ranking is enclosed in square brackets.

It is apparent from Table 4.6 that the use of this descriptor is impressively unsuccessful – the 'error score', which is simply the sum of the qualities incorrectly ranked as 'nearer', is 63 – which is little short of the value (72) that would be predicted on the basis of chance.

The lack of success is not after all surprising. The attempt to match qualities has been made here on the basis of the absolute values of the first two formants in the three vowel groups. Yet these absolute values must be expected to vary according to the size of a speaker's vocal tract, so that it is not meaningful to compare absolute formant values across speakers unless it has been established that the speakers have identical or very similar vocal tracts. A method is needed of scaling the absolute mean formant values, so

188

Table 4.6 Identification of voice qualities across speakers: six-value descriptor (F_1 and F_2 in each of three vowel groups)

Speaker JL:	N	L	R	O	&	P	V	J	D
Speaker FN	V	J	V	J	V	O	N	D	N
qualities	J	[L]	O	[O]	O	V	&	N	&
ranked by	[N]	R	J	V	J	J	D	P	V
distance	O	O	[R]	R	R	R	[V]	&	J
	&	V	N	L	N	N	J	V	[D]
	R	&	&	&	[&]	&	O	[J]	O
	L	N	L	N	L	L	P	O	P
	D	D	D	D	D	D	L	R	R
	P	P	P	P	P	[P]	P	L	L
Speaker FN:	N	L	R	O	&	P	V	J	D
Speaker JL	V	[L]	L	P	D	J	R	O	J
qualities	D	O	P	R	V	V	&	L	V
ranked by	[N]	R	O	&	N	D	P	R	[D]
distance	J	P	[R]	[O]	L	N	N	N	N
	&	N	&	L	O	&	O	P	&
	R	&	N	N	R	R	L	&	L
	O	D	D	D	[&]	L	D	D	R
	L	V	V	V	J	O	[V]	V	O
	P	J	J	J	P	[P]	J	[J]	P

Error score 63

that the information about voice quality conveyed by the relations between formants is no longer obscured in cross-speaker matching.

A different descriptor was therefore devised; this one consisted not of absolute formant frequencies, but of the *ratio* of F_2 to F_1 in each of the vowel groups (yielding a three-value descriptor). This descriptor involves a kind of formant scaling which assumes that within a vowel category the ratio of first to second formant remains relatively constant across speakers. This assumption may be tested using, for example, the vowel formant data from male, female and child speakers of American English in the classic study of Peterson and Barney (1952), and from male and female speakers of Swedish in Fant (1973:36). In Table 4.7 below, ratios of mean F_2 to F_1 of pairs of vowels are given for the three types of speaker (only two are represented in the Swedish data) the pairs representing approximately the HIGH FRONT, LOW, and HIGH BACK categories of the present study.

It can be seen that the ratios do remain relatively constant across speakers in this data, with the exception of women producing HIGH FRONT vowels. Although it is not justified to ascribe perceptual significance at this stage to these ratios, if it were the case that they played a part in perceptions of

Table 4.7 Mean F_2 and F_1, and the ratio between them, for pairs of vowels representing three vowel categories, according to speaker type (based on American English data from Peterson and Barney (1952) and Swedish data from ·Fant (1973))

	HIGH FRONT		LOW		HIGH BACK	
American	/i/,/ɪ/		/ɑ/,/ɔ/		/ʊ/,u/	
Men	2140:330	6.5	965:650	1.5	945:370	2.6
Women	2635:370	7.1	1070:720	1.5	1055:420	2.5
Children	2965:450	6.6	1215:855	1.4	1290:495	2.6
Swedish	/i/,/e/		/a/,/ɑ/		/o/,/u/	
Men	2058:295	7.0	1005:631	1.6	719:355	2.0
Women	2530:322	7.9	1135:771	1.5	753:387	2.0

'sameness' of vowels, the disparate male and female values in these vowels might have to be explained in terms of their functioning sociolinguistically as sex markers; however the recurrence of the pattern across languages suggests that the explanation more probably lies in the universal possibilities for and limitations on compensation for vocal tract size in different types of vowel (cf. Fant 1979:156).

Nevertheless, it is clear that overall the ratios give a characterisation of the vowel categories relatively independent of gross speaker type. Table 4.8 shows the equivalent ratios derived from the present data. The ratios, as is obvious from the two formant plots presented above, vary according to the

Table 4.8 Mean F_2: F_1 ratios for vowels of three categories, for nine voice qualities realised by two speakers

	N	L	R	O	&	P	V	J	D
JL HIGH FRONT	4.5	4.1	3.9	4.3	3.8	3.5	5.2	5.6	4.7
FN HIGH FRONT	4.6	4.3	3.4	4.2	3.8	3.6	4.5	5.0	4.6
JL LOW	1.6	2.0	1.6	1.6	1.6	1.5	1.8	1.7	1.7
FN LOW	1.8	2.2	1.8	1.8	1.7	1.7	1.9	2.1	2.1
JL HIGH BACK	2.5	2.3	2.2	2.4	2.1	2.0	2.7	2.9	2.6
FN HIGH BACK	2.2	2.5	2.1	2.1	2.0	1.9	2.3	2.9	2.5

Mean difference between speakers		Range for each speaker	
HIGH FRONT	0.3	JL	2.1
		FN	1.6
LOW	0.2	JL	0.5
		FN	0.4
HIGH BACK	0.2	JL	0.9
		FN	1.0

voice quality employed by the two speakers. Within a vowel type, the ratios follow recognisably similar trends in the two speakers according to voice quality, and in turn have absolute values which are comparable across the speakers.

Table 4.8 also reveals that, for a given vowel category, the mean difference in ratio between the two speakers is considerably less than the range of variation in that ratio over the voice qualities for either speaker. This offers hope that the use of a three-term vector composed of $F_2:F_1$ formant ratios for each vowel category might prove a more useful descriptor in attempts to characterise voice qualities across speakers.

It can be seen from Table 4.9 that the new descriptor yields matching results which are considerably more successful. The error score is reduced from 63 to 17, and in 13 (out of 18) decisions the correct match is ranked either first or second. It is interesting to note that 7/17 of the error score is accounted for by velarised voice. This raises the question of whether there may have been some difference in interpretation on the part of the two speakers of this term in the framework. In turn, a fundamental problem is highlighted: the matching tests involve two unknowns – the appropriateness

Table 4.9 Identification of voice qualities across speakers: three-value descriptor (ratio $F_2: F_1$ in each three vowel groups)

Speaker JL:	N	L	R	O	&	P	V	J	D
Speaker FN	V	O	&	V	[&]	[P]	J	[J]	V
qualities	[N]	[L]	O	[O]	P	R	D	D	[D]
ranked by	D	V	P	N	R	&	N	N	N
distance	O	&	[R]	D	O	O	[V]	V	J
	L	D	V	L	V	V	L	L	L
	J	N	N	&	N	N	O	O	O
	&	P	L	P	L	L	&	&	&
	P	R	D	R	D	D	P	P	P
	R	J	J	J	J	J	R	R	R
Speaker FN:	N	L	R	O	&	P	V	J	D
Speaker JL	[N]	[L]	P	L	[&]	[P]	N	V	[D]
qualities	O	O	&	[O]	R	&	O	D	N
ranked by	D	N	[R]	R	P	R	D	[J]	L
distance	L	D	L	&	L	L	L	N	V
	V	R	O	N	O	O	[V]	O	O
	R	V	N	D	N	N	R	L	R
	&	&	D	P	D	D	&	R	&
	P	P	V	V	V	V	P	&	J
	J	J	J	J	J	J	J	P	P

Error score 17

of the acoustic descriptor, and the between-speaker reliability in respect of the descriptive framework. It is hard to imagine, however, how a completely objective control on the latter could be achieved. A parallel situation was faced by Ladefoged (1967:Ch. 2) in his acoustic investigation of the Cardinal Vowel framework; and the strategy he adopted, though of course on a more viable scale, is similar to the control applied here – namely to seek approval by the originator of the framework (Daniel Jones in the case of the Cardinal Vowels) of the realisations used in the experiments. A larger scale experiment along the present lines would need to emulate the scale of Ladefoged's experiment more closely, and have a number of phoneticians trained in the voice quality framework producing a number of tokens of each type, from which the originator might select the most accurate examples.

Nevertheless, the considerably better-than-chance agreement across speakers in the present matching experiment can reasonably be taken to support both the consistency of the realisations of the qualities, and the ability of the three-term formant ratio descriptor to capture the similarity between realisations of a voice quality perceived to be alike. This ability is reflected not only in the generally high ranking of the other speaker's equivalent quality, but also the presence near the top of the ranking in Table 4.9 of qualities which would generally be perceived as similar, such as O (close rounding) in the case of L (lowered larynx voice), and vice versa.

It remains to be explored whether the relatively crude scaling technique employed here will be adequate to yield a speaker-independent characterisation of the supralaryngeal long term qualities not only across adult males, but across all types of speakers including women and children, whose inclusion will greatly extend the range of vocal tract dimensions to be coped with. A more sophisticated scaling technique may be required, perhaps utilising information from higher formants.

4.5 **Long term properties: conclusions**

4.5.1 *Characterisation of voice qualities*

The work presented in this chapter has been directed towards the discovery of objective acoustic characterisations of long term or 'voice' qualities, in the sense of quasi-permanent properties of speech. 4.3 explored the usefulness of long term spectra, already used in speaker recognition experiments, to discover their relation to long term qualities. The conclusion reached was that the long term spectrum is considerably sensitive to changes in laryngeal voice quality (long term phonation type), but relatively insensitive to fairly gross changes in supralaryngeal vocal tract setting. In particular, a spectral slope measure or a measure of the amplitude ratio between upper and lower parts of the long term spectrum will distinguish subgroups of phonation type, but fail to differentiate many supralaryngeal settings.

Whilst it is probable that finer discrimination of phonation type would be achieved with reference to detail in individual cycles of the glottal volume velocity or area waveform, the inaccessibility of accurate information about such source characteristics in investigations using normal recordings leaves the long term spectrum as the most practically measurable correlate of laryngeal voice quality.

The lack of clearly definable correlates in the long term spectrum of changes in supralaryngeal voice quality, however, led to the exploration of an alternative technique for their characterisation. The technique explicitly recognises that long term qualities result from articulatory tendencies manifested over a large number of segments, and it averages formant frequencies measured at a selection of measurement points defined in a sample of speech. Initially, over a small sample, this technique was shown effectively to differentiate between most supralaryngeal qualities; and the results were confirmed for a subset of these qualities over a larger sample of speech, and for another such sample from a second speaker. Even using the simplest of normalisation techniques, the characterisations were shown to be relatively speaker independent.

Again it must be stressed that the technique has not been optimised; not all supralaryngeal voice qualities have, as judged from their auditory impression at any rate, their primary effect on the same kind of elements in the speech stream, and since the majority of measurement points used exploited syllable-central information it may be that perceptually prominent transitional and consonantal information in qualities such as retroflexion and dentalisation have been discarded at a cost.

The approach has been successful, however, in as much as it has enabled distinct acoustic correlates to be identified for a number of auditorily categorised long term qualities, and it thus provides (probably for the first time) a detailed acoustic hypothesis about each of these qualities. Since these hypotheses are about auditorily categorised qualities, they will be appropriately tested by auditory judgments on speech synthesised using parameters whose values are derived from the three-formant characterisations presented here. The present results indicate that attempts to synthesise these qualities are likely to have to recognise differential acoustic effects of the settings on (at least) three major classes of vowel.

To the extent that such synthesis fails to replicate the auditory qualities aimed for, further analysis will be indicated in two directions: firstly, the further refinement of the present kind of analysis, possibly with attention to higher formants; and secondly, as hinted at above, its extension in particular to syllable-marginal characteristics including the acoustic effects of consonantal articulator placement and dynamics.

Other methods of acoustic characterisation, particularly ones susceptible to automatic implementation, need to be explored. One currently under investigation in the course of a project on 'The Acoustic Analyses of Voice Features' (Linguistics Department, University of Edinburgh; MRC research grant G820/7136N), and developed by Robert Hanson and Steve Hiller, derives a long term averaged area-function and associated smoothed spectrum via autocorrelation of the speech waveform, followed by a pressure and volume velocity transformation. Each stretch of voiced speech is analysed as a single event, and the results from each event contribute equally to the long term average. Such a method might be made more sensitive in discriminating supralaryngeal long term qualities if phonetically similar events (like the vowels of the three major classes used here) were averaged, rather than undifferentiated voiced stretches, to yield more than one long term area function and spectrum. Automatic classification of events is clearly the main problem to be overcome in the operation of such a scheme, but it might be achieved by the use of spectral 'templates', comparable to those used by e.g. Stevens and Blumstein (1981) to identify place of articulation from consonant transitions.

At the same time future research will profitably proceed from the physiological basis of voice qualities. Throughout the preceding discussion attempts have been made to relate the acoustic characteristics discovered for a quality to the putative mechanism underlying it. A sufficiently flexible articulatory synthesis model should enable the effects of the settings, such as the raising of the larynx with or without pharyngeal narrowing, or the displacement of the centre of activity of the tongue in a particular direction, to be evaluated quantitatively. This should lead to advances in the study of voice qualities, but may also lead to a reassessment of the degrees of configurational freedom which an articulatory model should incorporate, dependencies between voice quality effects perhaps being relatable to interactions between muscle systems.

4.5.2 *Long term quality and speaker recognition*

Long term quality has been presented as an analytic abstraction over relatively long stretches of speech, enabling a unified statement to be made on pervasive and recurrent properties of that speech; an abstraction which corresponds furthermore to a perceptual reality. In a model of speech production the speaker is here considered as having control over certain aspects of long term quality – the extrinsic aspects – while others (intrinsic) are beyond his volitional control. In theory, then, speaker recognition may hope to find values characteristic of speakers or groups of speakers along voice quality dimensions – most usefully those which they are unable to control, and which do not otherwise alter from occasion to occasion; or those where the speaker volitionally aims to achieve a target, but one which is not subject to variation under the constraints of communicative intent.

From the practical point of view, some long term parameters have the attraction that they are susceptible of automatic extraction, by virtue of not requiring segmentation for their identification. This is particularly true of the long term reflexes of the suprasegmental strand, as, for example, in work on the long term statistics of fundamental frequency (4.2). Long term spectra (4.3), already explored for use in speaker recognition schemes, tap laryngeal voice quality, and to a lesser extent supralaryngeal voice quality. Automatic extraction of supralaryngeal voice quality, the long term reflex of the segmental strand, is less practicable.

It will be stressed in Chapter 5 that absolute speaker recognition is not theoretically possible, but that a more realistic goal is voice classification. An advantage of a technical speaker recognition system which classified voices in terms of voice quality parameters is that it might correspond sufficiently to perceptual realities to allow impressionistic descriptions of voices (via translation into terms in a phonetic descriptive framework) to be compared with objective analyses.

If Chapter 4 demonstrates one thing above all, it is the limitation which any system attempting to recognise individuals on the basis of their voices must operate under. The plasticity of the human vocal tract, the mutability of its acoustic output, have been amply demonstrated. A single individual, in identical circumstances, and in quick succession, was characterised by a long term spectral slope of –8 or 0 dB/octave; by average formant frequencies of 415, 1265, and 2385 Hz, or 510, 1445, and 2445 Hz. Of course it may be objected that the range of settings adopted for the purposes of the recordings used in this experiment constitutes a totally abnormal use of the vocal apparatus, which would never occur in 'real-life' communication.

Nevertheless onus of proof rests on those who claim as their goal the recognition of an individual. Even if we set aside changes in intrinsic voice quality components – those which might occur due to pathologies of the vocal organs such as laryngitis, or due to the emotional state of the speaker, and over which he has no control – and consider only the extrinsic components, it is clear that the potential for alteration of a speaker's long term vocal product is very great. The present experiment has demonstrated many of the directions in which that variation may take place, but it has not by any means even defined the upper bounds on such variation, since the settings involved did not represent physiologically possible extremes. Before speech can ever be used positively to identify an individual as opposed to classifying a voice sample, evidence will need to be adduced to show that the parameters on which the identification is founded are immune to the effects of voice quality choices made by the speaker in mapping communicative intent. So little is known yet about the relation between, for example, sociolinguistic or affective communicative intent and voice quality, that the evidence will be unavailable for some time to come.

And there will still remain the special case of (extrinsic) voice quality alteration – voice disguise. Voice disguise at one level involves precisely the violation of the communicative rules governing choice of voice quality. It is not adequate to assert that it is obvious when a voice is being disguised, and that therefore such samples can be disregarded. A person who normally speaks with a neutral larynx position will, when he lowers his larynx for disguise purposes, not necessarily offer cues to the fact that he does not belong to the set of speakers who habitually lower their larynx. To take a more complex view, a speaker of social class X who knows that it is affectively appropriate for him to adopt creaky voice when communicating sentiment Q may instead violate this rule complex and adopt breathy voice – which may act as a marker in this context for a speaker of social class Y. However, it is in this very complexity of the rules governing spoken communication that some hope may reside for detecting disguise. It may be that in disguising his voice a speaker, rather as when dialect change is attempted, will attend successfully only to subparts of the spoken event, resulting in a whole which manifests inconsistencies and incongruities. Knowledge of the linguistic system of the language in question might enable the use of these inconsistencies as diagnostics of disguise. It seems – however surprisingly, considering the confidence with which those who advocate the use of voiceprints in legal cases suggest that the examiner will leave out of consideration speech samples where the speaker was disguising his voice (e.g. Tosi 1979:49) – that thorough research even into the feasibility of detecting disguise, let alone neutralising its effect, lies in the future rather than the past (see 5.2.2 below).

5

Conclusions

5.1 Summary

It was the stated intention of this book (p. 1) to 'explore in detail the relationship between the individual and his "voice" ', and thus to help to fill the theoretical vacuum in which practical work in speaker recognition has proceeded. In fulfilling this intention, it was suggested, 'an emerging discipline of speaker recognition should develop as an integral element of phonetics, which itself. . .must constitute part of a broadly delimited linguistics'. The reason for this symbiosis is twofold: firstly, particularly at the level of phonetics, the principal data of speaker recognition – between-speaker variation – should have an increasingly important role to play in understanding the production and perceptual processing of speech; but secondly, and more importantly in the present context, if experimental research in speaker recognition is to allow valid extrapolation to the real world, its premises must stem from as accurate and complete a model of speech communication as the linguistic sciences can currently provide.

The aim of Chapter 2 was to present such a model of speech communication, which, drawing together insights from a number of the branches of linguistic science, would provide a more complete and reliable theoretical account of between-speaker and within-speaker variation than has hitherto been available in work on speaker recognition. This model is, of necessity, complex; it hinges on the interaction between a multi-faceted communicative intent and a mechanism of linguistic expression comprising several strands. In section 5.2.3, in particular, current practices in speaker identification will be critically examined in the light of this model.

In Chapter 3, the experiments reported assessed the relative merits of two English sounds, and their coarticulation with neighbouring sounds, for speaker recognition – for a synopsis of the practical conclusions see 3.5.1. Clearly, the previous use of both 'segments' and 'coarticulation' in speaker recognition evidences a reliance on phonetic theory (a theory which postulates at some underlying and unobservable level discrete segments, the boundaries of which are obscured in the physical manifestations of speech);

197

3.5.2.2, on the other hand, explored the implications of between-speaker differences in coarticulatory behaviour for a theoretical account of the phenomenon. That distinct acoustic effects can be heard as the 'same sound' (e.g. the 'same vowel' spoken by a man and a woman) has long been a challenge to perceptual phonetics, which has tried to model the normalisation which the auditory system is capable of performing; at this level it is clear that speaker recognition and speech recognition are complementary parts of the same problem. On the production side, there is now increasing interest in the varying implementational strategies which different speakers arrive at to produce the same 'primary' auditory effects (see 2.3.7), while perhaps betraying the strategies through 'secondary' effects – 2.3.8. The data point towards the conceptualisation of speech production adopted here, where a 'phonetic representation' is not seen as in many approaches (e.g. some versions of Generative Phonology) as a set of instructions to the articulators as to how to perform, but rather as a set of properties commonly agreed by the speakers yet to be implemented by each speaker in whatever way he has found satisfactory, given his vocal apparatus. 'Implementation' is an area which should provide fertile common ground for research on speaker identity, on the one hand, and developments in the phonetic theory of speech production, on the other.

Chapter 4 explored the acoustic correlates of long term qualities ('voice qualities'). The area of long term quality is one where only recently has phonetics come to grips with the task of providing a descriptive framework comparable to that which has long been available for other aspects of vocal performance – segmental quality in particular – and it is clearly one which is of great importance to speaker recognition. In particular Laver's (1980) categories of voice quality draw attention to the variety and extent of long term settings which can be achieved by a single vocal tract, and provide a systematic framework within which to investigate the acoustic consequences of such variation. The experiments cannot claim to have established the outer limits of the long term changes which a speaker can induce in the speech signal, but they nevertheless amply demonstrate the potential problems for speaker recognition which originate from the plasticity of the vocal apparatus.

5.2 Criticism of principle and practice in speaker recognition

The following sections offer criticisms of some of the views and methodology current among proponents of the legal application of speaker recognition, which at present still consists mainly in the practice of visual examination of spectrograms (leaving aside opinions offered by phoneticians on the basis of purely auditory examination and analysis of recordings). The position under review here is one which, though more moderate than some in its claims, clearly supports the forensic application of speaker identification, and which is set out in detail by Tosi (1979).

5.2.1 *Plasticity of the vocal apparatus*

The plasticity of the vocal apparatus, the fact that only limitations to variation, not absolute values, are intrinsic to a speaker, has been repeatedly emphasised above (2.2; 2.4; Ch. 4). This clearly invalidates any belief in the existence of immutable cues to speaker identity in the speech signal. It would also, given the discussion in 2.3.10 of the variety of ways in which communicative intent can exploit the variability of the vocal apparatus, place the onus of proof firmly on those who advocate the use of speaker identification – proof that, for example, a paralinguistic use of creaky voice by one speaker in a specific context will not cause him to be misidentified with a speaker who habitually uses creaky voice. Far too little attention has been paid to within-speaker variability which is not random, but controlled by the speaker.

It is hard to be reassured, with respect to this plasticity, by confident assertions that (Tosi 1979:143)

When intratalker variations. . .become so great, a trained examiner will render either a no-opinion decision or, at worst, a false elimination,

and (Bolt *et al.* 1979:77)

Dissimilarities found in both sets of voicegrams can be attributed to either intraspeaker or interspeaker variation. The experience and subjective judgment of an examiner are used to determine whether the differences are due to intraspeaker or interspeaker variability, thus lending credibility toward identification or elimination respectively.

A priori the examiner does not have as data within- and between-speaker variation – he just has variation; and it has not been established that variation in one speaker cannot make him more like another speaker. Nor is confidence restored by an astonishing suggestion for aural examination (Tosi 1979:115):

In many cases a difference in pitch is observed between the unknown voice and the known voice. . .a good practice is to alter the pitches from either recording, using the 'Varimax' tape recorder, for instance, to bring them to equality. This procedure eliminates one variable that is not a comparable feature while not interfering too much with those variables that are to be compared (within some limits of course).

The fundamental frequencies are to be manipulated until they match; and if the other features, spectral and durational (equally susceptible to variations in recording and playback speed), are similar, the samples will be identified. Bolt *et al.* (1979:77) mention similar manipulation 'if the examiner believes that the difference is due to the incriminating recording's being at the wrong speed', but at least admit concerning this practice (ideal, it would seem, for convicting fast talking children of the crimes of slow spoken men, and vice versa), with understatement, that: 'Justifying this speed change is likely to be difficult'.

5.2.2 *Disguise*

Disguise constitutes exploitation of the plasticity of the vocal tract for a very specific communicative effect. According to Tosi (1979:50–1) disguise is not a problem as examiners are trained to disregard 'distorted' samples, and as disguise does not make one person's voice more similar to another's.

On the first point, it has not been adequately demonstrated that 'distortions' of a kind likely to be found in the speech of a speaker wishing to disguise his voice, but nevertheless still to be perceived as speaking naturally, can always be detected.

Reich (1981), following up experiments demonstrating a deterioration in speaker identification by spectrogram (Reich *et al.* 1976) and by listening (Reich and Duke 1979) where tests included disguised as well as undisguised voice samples, investigated the accuracy of 18 naive listeners and 18 speech scientists at making a 'disguised–undisguised' decision on voice samples. Results for both groups were similar, at around 90% response accuracy; of the errors, just over 70% were of the 'false detection' type, the listener deciding that a sample was disguised when it was in fact natural, and the remainder being the cases where disguise was missed.

Superficially this seems to support the view that most distortions can be detected; but as Reich himself admits this experiment is relevant only to those forensic situations where a speaker wishes to disguise his identity, but is not concerned about this disguise being obvious, since (1981:1460)

the instructions given to the speakers in the present study allowed any vocal disguise, regardless of whether the voice sounded natural or realistic.

The kinds of vocal devices used by the speakers might well, by their extreme nature, have clearly signalled the disguise attempt.

Underlying the training of voiceprint examiners to disregard 'distorted' samples is the assumption that disguise necessarily involves 'distortion', presumably implying that the resultant speech is outside the range of that produced by the normal human population. Given the wide range of long term qualities dealt with in Chapter 4, all of which are likely to be found in greater or smaller degree as intrinsic (organically determined) or extrinsic voice quality features among a population of speakers, this is a questionable assumption. There are a large variety of ways open to a speaker to alter his voice without either consciously imitating another speaker, or exceeding the limits of the 'normal' range of the population.

An experiment which had any chance of supporting the hypothesis that listeners can always detect *disguise* (as opposed to distortion) would have to meet at least the following two requirements: the 'disguised' voice samples used would have to fall within the normal range of voices encountered in the population; and the undisguised voice samples would have to cover a wide range of voice types. The reason for this latter stipulation stems from the danger of a contrast effect – if all the undisguised voice samples were near the mean values for the population on the voice quality parameters, samples which strayed from these values would be easily detectable as disguised; whereas the listener's 'baseline' would be much less secure if the undisguised samples included for example an extremely breathy voice, and a strongly denasalised voice. In practice a voice examiner has no 'baseline', since he must be prepared to encounter the total range in the population – extreme denasalised voice may be a disguise, but equally well a natural intrinsic voice quality feature (caused, for example, by adenoids). In such an experiment, the 'disguised' samples should include utterances by phoneticians consciously adopting slight or moderate degrees of voice quality settings such as larynx-lowering/-raising, (de)nasalisation, and different phonation types. There are no *a priori* grounds for supposing that listeners would be able to judge reliably whether a sample was spoken in the manner habitual to the speaker or not; while all these modifications may be expected to hamper speaker identification in some degree.

On the question of whether disguise makes one person's voice more like that of another, it is hard to see how a speaker who naturally uses as a default a 'neutral' value for nasality (audible nasality only where necessary for linguistic purposes (Laver 1980:(14)), for instance, but to disguise his voice adopts a denasalised setting, can fail at least in this dimension to become 'more like' a speaker with intrinsic denasality (or, of course, default (habitual) extrinsic denasality); and the same argument applies to all the voice quality dimensions. Aside from the question of disguise, another aspect of the problem of whether one speaker can become more like another is dealt with in the next section.

Tate (1979) investigated the detectability of an assumed accent; specifically, linguistically naive listeners from Florida in the south-eastern USA were asked to decide whether samples of speech were from native 'southerners' or from speakers imitating southerners – the imitations being obtained from a group of untrained impostors, and a group of actors. These two groups attained on average 30.0% and 37.5% 'southern' judgments – perhaps higher than might be expected, given the complexity of the phonological rules which define the complete sound system of any particular accent. However in this case it is unlikely that the imitators were doing more than exploiting what Labov terms *stereotypes* (see 2.3.10.3 above), and detailed phonetic analysis would probably reveal the imitators without difficulty. The fact that native listeners were so tolerant of the imitations perhaps stems from the broadness of the category 'southern' – the generality of the term causing them to rely not on detailed knowledge of their own speech patterns, but on the stereotypes equally available to the imitators. In general an attempt at disguise through adopting a different accent or dialect is likely to be betrayed, under detailed linguistic analysis, by numerous inconsistencies. Changes in voice quality features remain the more serious problem for the detection of disguise.

5.2.3 Context

Bolt *et al.* (1979:74) suggest that

Ideally in recording known voices the investigator should attempt to duplicate the physical circumstances associated with the unknown call,

using the same recording device, and, if relevant, the telephone system. But as is apparent from 2.3.10 there are aspects of the context in which a person is speaking which actually affect his choice of speaking style – so a concern for properties of the transmission line is not sufficient. For instance it will be recalled from 2.3.10.3 that the values of certain variables, *markers*, change with the speaker's perception of the formality of the context in which he is speaking. A speaker's interpretation of the context, in a broad sense, depends on factors such as the physical location, who the other interactants are, and the power and status relationships he perceives to exist between himself and the others. It is therefore highly unlikely that a suspect will interpret the context of giving samples of his speech in police custody as equal in formality to, for example, conferring over the telephone with a fellow criminal. It is a dangerous oversimplification to believe that duplicating the 'physical circumstances' of the original recording will elicit speech samples comparable to the originals – except at the lowest 'signal processing' level.

It might be tempting to dismiss stylistic changes of this sort as unfortunate, but merely liable to increase the number of 'false elimination' decisions, were it not for the demonstration by Labov and others (2.3.10.3) that the dimensions along which stylistic variation occurs are also among those of social stratification, which can have precisely the effect of bringing the speech of different speakers closer together – Labov (1972:240):

it may therefore be difficult to interpret any signal by itself – to distinguish, for example, a casual salesman from a careful pipefitter

– which raises the possibility of errors of 'false identification'.

Also dealt with in 2.3.10.3 is *convergence*, the phenomenon whereby a speaker makes his speech more like that of another participant in the interaction. In view of this possible effect of context, it seems particularly surprising that a standard practice among voice examiners to control for 'manner of utterance' (Tosi 1979:48) in obtaining samples from suspects is to require the suspect to *repeat* a sentence *spoken by the examiner or a police officer*:

The officer in charge utters one single sentence from [the criminal] text and requests the defendant to repeat the words after him.

Without experimental evidence there is no reason to believe that the gain in contextual similarity between the recordings through avoiding the formal context of reading the criminal text will outweigh the problems of convergence, and possibly imitation (conscious or subconscious) which may be inherent in the repetition exercise. The strategy becomes particularly questionable if the speaker uttering the phrase to be repeated has been exposed to the criminal utterance, as a chain of convergence or imitation might then occur and result in spurious similarities between the speech of the suspect and that in the criminal recording.

5.2.4 *Communicative intent*

The comments above on the plasticity of the vocal apparatus, disguise, and context, can be subsumed under the general observation that the output of the vocal tract can be greatly varied according to communicative intent, and that, hitherto, work in speaker identification has taken too narrow a view of communicative intent. In addition it will be recalled from 2.3.10 that the speech of an individual will be influenced also by the attitude he wishes to convey (affective), by the image he is trying to present (self-presentational), and by the organisation he tries to impose on an interaction (interaction management). It may prove to be the case that the mapping of none of these aspects of communicative intent in practice has an effect on the reliability, or even the efficiency, of speaker-identification methods; but it lies with the proponents of such methods to demonstrate this, rather than as at present simply omitting from consideration many of the implications of the complexity of spoken communication.

5.2.5 *Relation of speaker recognition to the linguistic sciences*

The present separation of linguistic phonetics from speaker recognition increases the danger, ever-real between different disciplines, that an onlooker from one side may misinterpret the meaning of someone on the other – either by lacking shared presuppositions, or by misexpanding shorthand expressions.

Thus the linguist who encounters the following passage from Bolt *et al.* (1979:102) may find it problematical:

> Virtually all voicegram experiments have used adult male speakers of General American English with no noticeable speech defects. In the forensic situations, suspects (known voices) are generally also adult males, but in a significant number of cases, some form of dialect or accent is involved. No attempt has been made to determine if visual identification performance is sensitive to the sometimes stylized speech patterns of speakers with dialects. Populations of speakers may be sufficiently homogeneous to affect visual identification performance.

Taking this at its face value the linguist will be surprised and puzzled by at least three points. Firstly, the passage seems to assume that General American English is not itself a dialect or accent, but has some unique ontological status; whereas for the linguist any variety of language or pronunciation constitutes a dialect, or accent, respectively – whatever special social status it may have attained (as a 'standard' or 'prestige' variety) through non-linguistic factors. Secondly, it suggests that accents (by contrast to General American English pronunciation) may exhibit 'stylized speech patterns'. This, the linguist has to presume, must be a technical term the definition of which is well known to workers in speaker identification; it does not figure in the vocabulary of linguistics and, given the point made above that in the linguistic view *all* speakers must be regarded as using an accent, it is unclear why it should apply to speakers of only some varieties. Thirdly, and most alarmingly, the passage implies that voiceprint examiners are at present likely to give 'positive identification' decisions as long as known and unknown samples are spoken by any one or more speakers from a homogeneous accent community – hardly a recipe for justice. The linguist would have expected ability to cope with homogeneity of accent an absolute prerequisite of any speaker-identification technique – not a luxury to be afforded at some unspecified later date.

Likewise a phonetician may be perplexed when, for instance, he examines the spectrograms presented by Tosi (1979:117) of a 'known' and an 'unknown' sample of the word *mad*. Certainly the feature which Tosi draws attention to in the two spectrograms as an idiosyncrasy of the same individual is remarkable; it is a transient spike occurring in the *middle* of a vowel *between* first and second formant. To understand how such a transient could appear in a dip in the vocal tract transfer function in the middle of a vowel articulation, the phonetician at least requires some comment from Tosi in terms of an acoustic theory of speech production. Since this is not provided, there is a danger that the phonetician will begin to consider the possibility that the spike is some sort of artefact.

The main cause for alarm is not that questions such as these, and the ones raised in the previous sections, should come to mind among those taking a broader view of spoken communication – they may in any case as suggested above be founded on misunderstandings – but rather that certain of those involved in legal speaker identification should seek to deny broader based scientists a platform for their views (cf. Hollien 1974a:211, quoted above at the end of 1.1.8). Thus Tosi (1979:117, 145):

A general speech scientist, with no special training in voice identification by use of spectrograms, can hardly give an opinion on this subject no matter how excellent are his credentials in the speech sciences.

to offer a well-founded opinion on the validity of the method it is essential to have practical experience in dealing with it.

By the same token alchemy, and phrenology, would be immune from criticism by chemists, and psychologists/neurologists. Tosi further asks, concerning a 1977 decision by Michigan Supreme Court that voiceprints could in future only be used with the agreement of 'disinterested scientists' (1979:145–6),

how a 'disinterested scientist' could ever express a valid opinion on a subject that does not appeal to his interest. Maybe this is only a matter of semantics.

Unfortunately for Tosi it is not merely a matter of semantics, though his discussion would be clearer for an appreciation of the distinction between *uninterested* (= finding boring) and *disinterested* (= not having a vested interest in, impartial). Rather the question is whether those who earn their living in total or in part by 'voiceprint' identification, those who are 'selling a product' (Hollien 1977:14), can be as impartial in judging the validity of the technique as those who have nothing to gain or lose whether the technique is accepted or not.

The same problem arises on a smaller scale in the case of auditory identification by phoneticians (1.1.7), though it must be emphasised that the positions here are much less polarised, since none of those who give auditory evidence regard themselves as specifically trained in the auditory analysis of *speaker* characteristics, and none have livelihoods dependent on the results they produce. Nevertheless the phonetician who wishes to oppose the use in a court of auditory identification evidence may find himself in a quandary: if he gives identification evidence for the opposing side he inevitably implies acceptance of the validity of the technique (though questioning the accuracy of its application by his opponent expert witness); if his testimony is to the effect that the technique, which he himself does not practise, is unproven, then it is left to the court to make a decision on admissibility of evidence which properly could only be made after extensive empirical work – and in making that decision it might quite possibly be influenced by the (spurious) argument (cf. Tosi above) that the person who practises a technique must necessarily be in a better position to judge it than a person who does not.

The crux of the problem is that the reliability of speaker identification in the field does not, in general, constitute an empirical question. Although correlations may be quoted between 'positive identifications' and convictions, these correlations (even where the speaker-identification decision has not been used to influence the proceedings) cannot be taken as empirical evidence, since 'guilty' verdicts themselves are no more than hypotheses. Volunteered confessions possibly provide more acceptable evidence, though even here it is clear that the factors motivating a confession do not necessarily include guilt in every instance.

A more moderate stance than that of Tosi (1979) is adopted by Bolt *et al.* (1979:43):

The committee believes that consensus in the scientific community is obtainable and should be sought in establishing the expected level of accuracy in the use of voicegram evidence.

This position is realistic with regard to speaker identification by spectrograms or any other 'technical' method which may be applied; and is unobjectionable provided that the scientific community within which the consensus is obtained is sufficiently broad; it must include, for instance, those whose specialist knowledge concerns the way in which speech changes according to social context, or the variation it undergoes in accordance with the effective communicative intent of a speaker. This brings the discussion back again to the theme of this book (1.1; 5.1) that speaker recognition as a discipline can develop successfully only as an integral element of linguistic phonetics.

5.3 Directions for speaker recognition

The preceding sections give a rather negative picture of present theory and practice in speaker recognition, particularly in its identification sub-branch.

The comments, however, should not be taken to imply that research in this field is without value, or that no degree of recognition of individuals from their voices is feasible – the latter is controverted by everyday evidence, as well as the comparative success of speaker verification devices. Instead, the implications are that the research should be based on a more comprehensive model of spoken communication than at present; that any component of such a model must be assumed capable of confounding speaker recognition until it is demonstrated not to be; and, given that absolute recognition is scarcely a likelihood, that research should be directed towards establishing the degree of accuracy that may be relied on in particular circumstances.

In relation to this last point, Bolt *et al.* write (1979:7):

In principle, two different persons could have voices that are not distinguishable from each other within the limits of measurement precision available. Acoustical analysis. . .gives direct information about a voice, but only indirect, inferential information about the identity of the person talking. The probability of correct identification of a speaker depends both on the probability of a match between a specified voice and the voicegram it produces, and upon the probability of a match between that voice and the person to whom it is attributed.

In consequence, Bolt *et al.* opt for the term *voice* identification rather than *speaker* identification. This terminological change is not especially helpful, since it is clear that in practical applications the interest is in identifying speakers (speakers rather than voices are accused of crimes, convicted, etc.); but the point is correct, and in keeping with the demonstration above (Chapter 4) that one speaker has the potential to produce a very wide range of 'voices'. Research needs to be directed towards discovering the ways in which speakers exploit this potential for communicative purposes – in addition, of course, to delineating the ways in which voices change spontaneously as a result of changes in the current physical and psychological state of the speaker.

Mead (1974:3) writes that any statistical method of speaker identification

cannot provide unique identification of a talker from a large population unless it is discovered that every talker gives significantly different statistics from those of all other talkers.

(In the light of the potential for variation in the voice of a speaker, a more precise formulation might be '. . .unless it is discovered that every point in the voice quality range of any talker gives significantly different statistics from any point in the voice quality ranges of all other talkers'.) Mead goes on to suggest that

in view of the extreme improbability of such a result the subject of this report should, perhaps, be called voice classification rather than identification. There is a hope, however, that the degree of classification will be sufficient for the process to assist in

207

Conclusions

unique identification when the population of possible talkers is known to be fairly small,

and this emphasis on classification is echoed by Bolt *et al.* (1979:60):

if an effective method of classifying voices were to be developed, it would assist greatly in identifying voices.

Chapter 4 began the work of specifying the acoustic correlates of an auditory phonetic framework for classifying voice qualities. It will be worth developing and improving this work since, from the point of view of speaker identification, it provides an approach to the problem of classifying voices alternative, and complementary, to the more usual one of picking readily measurable acoustic features and investigating, in a relatively unguided way, how these features vary among a population of speakers.

Furthermore, if the acoustic correlates of the auditory framework lead to a useable objective classification of voice samples, then this classification is more likely than one emanating from purely acoustic research to correspond to the ways in which human beings auditorily classify voices. This would enable the gap between machine based, and human, capabilities for speaker recognition to be bridged – which might be of practical value, in forensics for instance, in the following way. A witness might have heard a voice, and be able to describe it in casual impressionistic terms, or even be able to imitate it. This primary description would then be translated into the formal auditory terminology of the components of the voice quality framework, and thence (assuming, remember, advances in knowledge of the appropriate mapping) into acoustic terms. Subsequently, perhaps, a large number of suspects for whom acoustic voice analysis and classification were available could be reduced rapidly and automatically to a subset with voices best corresponding to the witness's impressionistic description.

Given a good knowledge of the mapping between auditory voice quality components and their acoustic correlates, the possibility is opened up of driving a (sufficiently flexible) speech synthesiser. As suggested at the end of 4.5.1, synthesis will undoubtedly play a heuristic role in the discovery of this mapping. If the glottal waveform, or formant frequency, characteristics believed to underlie the perception of particular voice quality components are in fact correct, then when programmed with these values the synthesiser should evoke the appropriate voice quality percept. But once the mapping is established, the possibility opens up for the forensic field of 'analysis-by-synthesis' on the basis of a witness's description of a voice. This would be parallel to the use for facial description of 'identikit' or 'photofit' pictures, where a replica of a face is built up from component parts. The witness's primary impressionistic description would, as above, be formalised in terms of the voice quality framework, and the acoustic mapping of this description used to control the synthesiser. Further modifications would then be made until the witness was satisfied that the synthetic voice sample was a good replica of the voice remembered. This stage achieved, the current acoustic parameters of the synthesiser constitute a classification of the voice, to be checked against known voices; and the synthetic sample itself might have a role in investigation similar to that of the identikit picture. Clearly this schematic account glosses over the very considerable, and (it may turn out) insurmountable, problems entailed in such a technique; but the concept provides a well-defined research goal, of which even partial attainment should greatly increase knowledge of voice classification.

Exciting as such projects are, especially in the challenges they pose for phonetics, it is clear that their practical application must be approached with the same cautious and sceptical attitude as has been shown to be necessary towards present speaker recognition methods.

References

A number of frequently cited journals and periodicals are abbreviated, as follows:

IEEE Trans. Ac., Sp. & Sig. Proc.
Institute of Electrical and Electronics Engineers: Transactions on Acoustics, Speech and Signal Processing.

IEEE Trans. Aud. & Electroac.
Institute of Electrical and Electronics Engineers: Transactions on Audio and Electroacoustics.

JASA
Journal of the Acoustical Society of America.

JSHR
Journal of Speech and Hearing Research.

STL-QPSR
Quarterly Progress and Status Report, Speech Transmission Laboratory, Royal Institute of Technology (Stockholm).

Abberton, E. R. M. 1976. A laryngographic study of voice quality. PhD Thesis, University College London.
Abercrombie, D. 1967. *Elements of General Phonetics*. Edinburgh: Edinburgh University Press.
Al-Bamerni, A. 1975. An instrumental study of the allophonic variation of /l/ in RP. MA dissertation, University College of North Wales, Bangor.
Amerman, J. D. and R. G. Daniloff 1977. Aspects of lingual coarticulation. *Journal of Phonetics* 5, 107–13.
Argyle, M. 1967. *The Psychology of Interpersonal Behaviour*. Harmondsworth: Penguin.
Atal, B. S. 1972. Automatic speaker recognition based on pitch contours. *JASA* 52, 1687–97.
1974. Effectiveness of linear prediction characteristics of the speech wave for automatic speaker identification and verification. *JASA* 55, 1304–12.
1976. Automatic recognition of speakers from their voices. *Proceedings of the IEEE* Vol. 64, No. 4, 460–75.
Atkinson, J. E. 1976. Inter- and intraspeaker variability in fundamental voice frequency. *JASA* 60, 440–5.
Baldwin, J. 1977. The forensic application of phonetics. *Police Review* (18th November), 1609.
Beek, B., E. P. Neuberg and D. C. Hodge 1977. An assessment of the technology of automatic speech recognition for military applications. *IEEE Trans. Ac., Sp. & Sig. Proc.* ASSP-25, 310–22.
Bell-Berti, F. 1975. Control of pharyngeal cavity size for English voiced and voiceless stops. *JASA* 57, 456–61.
Bell-Berti, F., L. J. Raphael, D. B. Pisoni and J. R. Sawusch 1978. Some relationships between articulation and perception. *Status Report on Speech Research* SR-55/56, 21–32. New Haven, Conn: Haskins Laboratories.

van den Berg, J. 1968. Mechanism of the larynx and the laryngeal vibrations. In: B. Malmberg (ed.), *Manual of Phonetics*. Amsterdam: North Holland.

Bernstein, A. L. 1965. *A Handbook of Statistical Solutions for the Behavioural Sciences*. New York: Holt, Rinehart and Winston.

Black, J. W., W. Lashbrook, E. Nash, H. J. Oyer, G. Pedrey, O. I. Tosi and H. Truby 1973. Reply to 'Speaker identification by speech spectrograms: some further observations'. *JASA* 54, 535–7.

Bladon, R. A. W. and A. Al-Bamerni 1976. Coarticulation resistance in English /l/. *Journal of Phonetics* 4, 137–50.

Bladon, R. A. W. and B. Lindblom 1981. Modeling the judgment of vowel quality differences. *JASA* 69, 1414–22.

Bladon, R. A. W. and F. Nolan 1977. A video-fluorographic investigation of tip and blade alveolars in English. *Journal of Phonetics* 5, 187–93.

Bolt, R. H., F. S. Cooper, E. E. David, P. B. Denes, J. M. Picket and K. N. Stevens 1970. Speaker identification by speech spectrograms: a scientists' view of its reliability for legal purposes. *JASA* 47, 597–612.

1973. Speaker identification by speech spectrograms: some further observations. *JASA* 54, 531–4.

Bolt, R. H., F. S. Cooper, D. M. Green, S. L. Hamlet, J. G. McKnight, J. M. Pickett, O. I. Tosi and B. D. Underwood 1979. *On the Theory and Practice of Voice Identification*. Washington: National Academy of Sciences.

Bricker, P. D. and S. Pruzansky 1966. Effects of stimulus content and duration on talker identification. *JASA* 40, 1441–9.

1976. Speaker recognition. In: N. J. Lass (ed.), *Contemporary Issues in Experimental Phonetics*.

Bricker, P. D., G. Gnanadesikan, M. V. Mathews, S. Pruzansky, P. A. Tukey, K. W. Wachter and J. L. Warner 1971. Statistical techniques for talker identification. *Bell System Technical Journal* 50, 1427–54.

Broderick, P. K., J. E. Paul and R. J. Rennick 1975. Semi-automatic speaker identification system. *Proceedings of the 1975 Carnahan Conference on Crime Countermeasures* 29–37. Lexington: University of Kentucky.

Brown, P. and S. Levinson 1979. Social structure, groups and interaction. In: K. R. Scherer and H. Giles (eds.), *Social Markers in Speech*. Cambridge: Cambridge University Press.

Brown, R. 1982. What is speaker recognition? *Journal of the International Phonetic Association* 12, 13–24.

Carlson, R., G. Fant and B. Granström 1975. Two-formant models, pitch and vowel perception. In: G. Fant and M. A. A. Tatham (eds.), *Auditory Analysis and Perception of Speech*. London: Academic Press.

Catford, J. C. 1977. *Fundamental Problems in Phonetics*. Edinburgh: Edinburgh University Press.

Chiba, T. and M. Kajiyama 1958. *The Vowel: Its Nature and Structure*. Tokyo: Phonetic Society of Japan.

Chomsky, N. 1965. *Aspects of the Theory of Syntax*. Cambridge, Mass: MIT Press.

Chomsky, N. and M. Halle 1968. *The Sound Pattern of English*. New York: Harper and Row.

Coleman, R. O. 1971. Male and female voice quality and its relationship to vowel formant frequencies. *JSHR* 14, 565–77.

1976. A comparison of the contributions of two voice quality characteristics to the perception of maleness and femaleness in the voice. *JSHR* 19, 168–80.

Crompton, A. 1981. Phonetic representation. Unpublished paper, University of Nottingham.

References

Crystal, D. 1969. *Prosodic Systems and Intonation in English.* London: Cambridge University Press.

1975. *The English Tone of Voice.* London: Edward Arnold.

Daniloff, R. G. and R. E. Hammarberg 1973. On defining coarticulation. *Journal of Phonetics* 1, 239–48.

Das, S. K. and W. S. Mohn 1971. A scheme for speech processing in automatic speaker verification. *IEEE Trans. Aud. & Electroac.* AU-19, 32–43.

Delattre, P. 1967. Acoustic or articulatory invariance? *Glossa* 1, 3–25.

Doddington, G. R. 1971. A method of speaker verification. *JASA* 49, 139(A).

Doherty, E. T. and H. Hollien 1978. Multiple-factor speaker identification of normal and distorted speech. *Journal of Phonetics* 6, 1–8.

Douglas-Cowie, E. 1978. Linguistic code-switching in a Northern Irish village. In: P. Trudgill (ed.), *Sociolinguistic Patterns in British English.*

Duncan, S. 1973. Toward a grammar for dyadic conversation. *Semiotica* 9, 29–46.

Endres, W., W. Bambach and G. Flösser 1971. Voice spectrograms as a function of age, voice disguise and voice imitation. *JASA* 49, 1842–8.

Esling, J. H. 1978. Voice quality in Edinburgh: a sociolinguistic and phonetic study. PhD Dissertation, University of Edinburgh.

Fant, G. 1960. *Acoustic Theory of Speech Production.* The Hague: Mouton.

1968. Analysis and synthesis of speech processes. In: B. Malmberg (ed.), *Manual of Phonetics.* Amsterdam: North Holland.

1971. Distinctive features and phonetic dimensions. In: G. E. Perren and J. L. M. Trim (eds.), *Applications of Linguistics.* Cambridge: Cambridge University Press.

1973. A note on vocal tract size factors and nonuniform F-pattern scalings. *Speech Sounds and Features.* Cambridge, Mass: MIT Press.

1975. Non-uniform vowel normalisation. *STL-QPSR* 2–3/1975, 1–19.

1979. The relations between area functions and the acoustic signal. *Proceedings of the 9th International Congress of Phonetic Sciences,* Vol. 1, 155–60. Copenhagen: Institute of Phonetics.

Fant, G. and S. Pauli 1974. Spatial characteristics of vocal tract resonance modes. In: G. Fant (ed.), *Speech Communication* Vol. 2. Stockholm: Almqvist and Wiksell.

Fant, G., K. Ishizaka, J. Lindqvist and J. Sundberg 1972. Subglottal formants. *STL-QPSR* 1/1972, 1–12.

Fischer-Jørgensen, E. 1975. *Trends in Phonological Theory.* Copenhagen: Akademisk.

Flanagan, J. L. 1965. *Speech Analysis, Synthesis and Perception.* Berlin: Springer.

Flanagan, J. L., K. Ishizaka and K. Shipley 1975. Synthesis of speech from a dynamic model of the vocal cords and vocal tract. *Bell System Technical Journal* 54, 485–506.

Fourcin, A. J. and E. Abberton 1976. The laryngograph and the voiscope in speech therapy. *Proceedings of the 16th International Congress of Logopedics and Phoniatrics, 1974.* Basel: Karger.

Fowler, C. A. 1980. Coarticulation and theories of extrinsic timing. *Journal of Phonetics* 8, 113–33.

Frøkjaer-Jensen, B. and S. Prytz 1976. Registration of voice quality. *Bruel and Kjær Technical Review* No. 3, 3–17.

Fry, D. B. 1947. The frequency of occurrence of speech sounds in Southern English. *Archives Néerlandaises de Phonétique Expérimentale* 10.

1979. *The Physics of Speech.* Cambridge: Cambridge University Press.

Fujimura, O. and J. B. Lovins 1978. Syllables as concatenative phonetic units. In: A. Bell and J. B. Hooper (eds.), *Syllables and Segments.* Amsterdam: North Holland.

Furui, S. 1981. Cepstral analysis technique for automatic speaker verification. *IEEE Trans. Ac., Sp. & Sig. Proc.* ASSP-29, 254–72.

Furui, S., F. Itakura and S. Saito 1972. Talker recognition by longtime averaged speech spectrum. *Electronics and Communications in Japan* Vol. 55-A No. 10, 54–61.

Garvin, P. L. and P. Ladefoged 1963. Speaker identification and message identification in speech recognition. *Phonetica* 9, 193–9.

Giles, H., K. R. Scherer and D. M. Taylor 1979. Speech markers in social interaction. In: K. R. Scherer and H. Giles (eds.), *Social Markers in Speech*.

Gimson, A. C. 1980. *An Introduction to the Pronunciation of English* (3rd edition). London: Edward Arnold.

Glenn, J. W. and N. Kleiner 1968. Speaker identification based on nasal phonation. *JASA* 43, 368–72.

Goldsmith, J. 1976. An overview of autosegmental phonology. *Linguistic Analysis* 2, 23–68.

Green, N. 1972. Automatic speaker recognition using pitch measurements in conversational speech. JSRU Report No. 1000. Joint Speech Research Unit, Ruislip, Middlesex.

Gubrynowicz, R. 1973. Application of a statistical spectrum analysis to automatic voice identification. In: W. Jassem (ed.), *Speech Analysis and Synthesis*, Vol. 3. Warsaw: Polish Academy of Sciences.

Hall, M. and O. Tosi 1975. Spectrographic and aural examination of professionally mimicked voices. *JASA* 58, S-107 (A).

Hammarberg, R. 1976. The metaphysics of coarticulation. *Journal of Phonetics* 4, 353–63.

Hardcastle, W. J. 1976. *Physiology of Speech Production*. London: Academic Press.

Harshman, R., P. Ladefoged and L. Goldstein 1977. Factor analysis of tongue shapes. *JASA* 62, 693–707.

Hazen, B. 1973. Effects of differing phonetic contexts on spectrographic speaker identification. *JASA* 54, 650–9.

Hecker, M. H. L. 1971. Speaker recognition: basic considerations and methodology. *JASA* 49, 138(A).

Höfker, U. 1977. Phoneme-ordering for speaker recognition. *Contributed Papers to the 9th International Congress on Acoustics, Madrid 1977*. Madrid: Spanish Acoustical Society.

Hollien, H. 1974a. Peculiar case of 'Voiceprints'. *JASA* 56, 210–13.

1974b. On vocal registers. *Journal of Phonetics* 2, 125–43.

1977. Status report of 'voiceprint' identification in the United States. *Proceedings of the 1977 International Conference on Crime Countermeasures* 9–20. Lexington: University of Kentucky.

1981. Review of *Voice Identification: Theory and Legal Applications* by O. Tosi. *JASA* 70, 263–5.

Hollien, H. and R. E. McGlone 1976. An evaluation of the 'voiceprint' technique of speaker identification. *Proceedings of the 1976 Carnahan Conference on Crime Countermeasures*. Lexington: University of Kentucky.

Hollien, H. and M. Majewski 1977. Speaker identification by long-term spectra under normal and distorted speech conditions. *JASA* 62, 975–80.

Honikman, B. 1964. Articulatory settings. In: D. Abercrombie *et al.* (eds.), *In Honour of Daniel Jones*. London: Longman.

Horii, Y. 1972. Some statistical characteristics of voice fundamental frequency. *JASA* 52, 146(A).

Jakobson, R., G. Fant and M. Halle 1952. *Preliminaries to Speech Analysis*. Cambridge, Mass: MIT Press.

Jaschul, J. 1982. Speaker adaptation by a linear transformation with optimised parameters. *Proceedings of the IEEE International Conference on Acoustics, Speech and Signal Processing, Paris 1982*, 1657–60. New York: IEEE.

Jassem, W. 1971. Pitch and compass of the speaking voice. *Journal of the International Phonetic Association* 1, 59–68.

213

References

Jones, D. 1972. *An Outline of English Phonetics*. Cambridge: Heffer.

1975. *English Pronouncing Dictionary* (13th edition). London: Dent.

Kent, R. D. and F. D. Minifie 1977. Coarticulation in recent speech production models. *Journal of Phonetics* 5, 115–33.

Kersta, L. G. 1962a. Voiceprint identification. *Nature* 196, 1253–7.

1962b. Voiceprint identification infallibility. *JASA* 34(A), 1978.

1971. Progress report on automated speaker-recognition systems. *JASA* 49, 139(A).

Kerswill, P. 1980. Socially sensitive phonological variables: evidence from a variable in Cambridge English. MPhil essay, Department of Linguistics, Cambridge University.

Knowles, G. 1978. The nature of phonological variables in Scouse. In: P. Trudgill (ed.), *Sociolinguistic Patterns in British English*.

Kosiel, U. 1973. Statistical analysis of speaker-dependent differences in the long-term average spectrum of Polish speech. In: W. Jassem (ed.), *Speech Analysis and Synthesis*, Vol. 3. Warsaw: Polish Academy of Sciences.

Kozhevnikov, V. A. and L. A. Chistovich 1965. *Speech: Articulation and Perception*. Translation: Joint Publications Research Service, 30–543. US Department of Commerce.

Kratochvil, P. 1973. Tone in Chinese. In: E. Fudge (ed.), *Phonology*. Harmondsworth: Penguin.

Labov, W. 1966. *Social Stratification of English in New York City*. Washington DC: Center for Applied Linguistics.

1972. *Sociolinguistic Patterns*. Philadelphia: University of Pennsylvania Press.

Ladd, D. R. 1980. *The Structure of Intonational Meaning*. Bloomington: Indiana University Press.

Ladefoged, P. 1967. *Three Areas of Experimental Phonetics*. Oxford: Oxford University Press.

1971. *Preliminaries to Linguistic Phonetics*. Chicago: University of Chicago Press.

1975. *A Course in Phonetics*. New York: Harcourt Brace Jovanovich.

1979. What are linguistic sounds made of? *Working Papers in Phonetics* 45, 1–24. UCLA.

Ladefoged, P. and R. Vanderslice 1967. The 'voiceprint' mystique. *Working Papers in Phonetics* 7, 126–42. Los Angeles: UCLA.

Lass, N. J. (ed.) 1976. *Contemporary Issues in Experimental Phonetics*. New York: Academic Press.

Lass, N. J., A. S. Beverly, D. K. Nicosia and L. A. Simpson 1978. An investigation of speaker height and weight identification by means of direct estimation. *Journal of Phonetics* 6, 69–76.

Laufer, A. and I. D. Condax 1979. The epiglottis as an articulator. *Working Papers in Phonetics* 45, 60–83. Los Angeles: UCLA.

Laver, J. 1967. Synthesis of components in voice quality. *Proceedings of the 6th International Congress of Phonetic Sciences*, 523–5. Prague (1970): Czechoslovak Academy of Sciences.

1975. Individual features in voice quality. PhD Thesis, University of Edinburgh.

1976. The semiotic nature of phonetic data. *York Papers in Linguistics* 6, 55–62.

1979. *Voice Quality: A Classified Bibliography*. Amsterdam: John Benjamins.

1980. *The Phonetic Description of Voice Quality*. Cambridge: Cambridge University Press.

Laver, J. and R. Hanson 1981. Describing the normal voice. In: J. Darby (ed.), *Evaluation of Speech in Psychiatry*. New York: Grune and Stratton.

Laver, J. and S. Hutcheson (eds.) 1972. *Communication in Face to Face Interaction*. Harmondsworth: Penguin.

Laver, J., S. Hiller and R. Hanson 1982. Comparative performance of pitch detection algorithms on dysphonic voices. *Proceedings of the IEEE International Conference on Acoustics, Speech and Signal Processing, Paris 1982*, 192–5. New York: IEEE.

Laver, J., S. Wirz, J. Mackenzie and S. Hiller 1981. A perceptual protocol for the analysis of vocal profiles. *Work in Progress* 14, 139–55. University of Edinburgh, Department of Linguistics.

Lehiste, I. 1964. Acoustical characteristics of selected English consonants. *International Journal of American Linguistics* 30, No. 3.
1970. *Suprasegmentals*. Cambridge, Mass: MIT Press.
1973. Vowel and speaker identification in natural and synthetic speech. *Language and Speech* 16, 356–64.
1975. The phonetic structure of paragraphs. In: A. Cohen and S. G. Nooteboom (eds.), *Structure and Process in Speech Perception*. Berlin: Springer.
1977. Isochrony reconsidered. *Journal of Phonetics* 5, 253–63.
1979. Perception of sentence and paragraph boundaries. In: B. Lindblom and S. G. Öhman (eds.), *Frontiers of Speech Communication Research*.
Li, K-P. and G. W. Hughes 1974. Talker differences as they appear in correlation matrices of continuous speech spectra. *JASA* 55, 833–7.
Liberman, M. Y. 1978. *The Intonational System of English*. Bloomington: Indiana University Linguistics Club.
Lieberman, P. 1967. *Intonation, Perception and Language*. Cambridge, Mass: MIT Press.
1977. *Speech Physiology and Acoustic Phonetics*. New York: Macmillan.
Lindblom, B. 1972. Phonetics and the description of language. *Proceedings of the 7th International Congress of Phonetic Sciences*, 63–97. The Hague: Mouton.
Lindblom, B. and S. Öhman (eds.) 1979. *Frontiers of Speech Communication Research*. London: Academic Press.
Lindblom, B. and J. Sundberg 1971. Acoustical consequences of lip, tongue, jaw and larynx movement. *JASA* 50, 1166–79.
Lindblom, B., J. Lubker and T. Gay 1979. Formant frequencies of some fixed mandible vowels and a model of speech motor programming by predictive simulation. *Journal of Phonetics* 7, 147–61.
Lummis, R. C. 1973. Speaker verification by computer using intensity for temporal registration. *IEEE Trans. Aud. & Electroac.* AU-21, 80–9.
Lyons, J. 1977. *Semantics*. Cambridge: Cambridge University Press.
McGonegal, C. A., A. E. Rosenberg and L. R. Rabiner 1979. The effects of several transmission systems on an automatic speaker verification system. *Bell System Technical Journal* 58, 2071–87.
MacNeilage, P. F. 1979. Status report on speech production. *Proceedings of the 9th International Congress of Phonetic Sciences*, Vol. 1, 9–39. Copenhagen: Institute of Phonetics.
Majewski, W. and H. Hollien 1975. Euclidean distances between long term speech spectra as a criterion for speaker identification. In: G. Fant (ed.), *Speech Communication*, Vol. 3. Stockholm: Almqvist and Wiksell.
Markel, J. D. and S. B. Davis 1979. Text-independent speaker recognition from a large linguistically unconstrained time-spaced data base. *IEEE Trans. Ac., Sp. & Sig. Proc.* ASSP-27, 74–82.
Markel, J. D., B. T. Oshika and A. H. Gray 1977. Long term feature averaging for speaker recognition. *IEEE Trans. Ac., Sp. & Sig. Proc.* ASSP-25, 330–7.
Matsumoto, H., S. Hiki, T. Sone and T. Nimura 1973. Multidimensional representation of personal quality of vowels and its acoustical correlates. *IEEE Trans. Aud. & Electroac.* AU-21, 428–36.
Mead, K. O. 1974. Identification of speakers from fundamental-frequency contours in conversational speech. JSRU Report No. 1002. Joint Speech Research Unit, Ruislip, Middlesex.
Miller, R. J. 1968. Pitch determination by measurement of harmonics. *JASA* 44, 390(A).
1970. Pitch determination by measurement of harmonics II – the Hipex system. *JASA* 47, 84(A).

215

References

Miller, R. L. 1959. Nature of the vocal cord wave. *JASA* 31, 667–77.

Ní Chasaide, A. 1977. The laterals of Donegal Irish and Hiberno-English: an acoustic study. MA Dissertation, University College of North Wales, Bangor.

Nie, N. H., C. H. Hull, J. G. Jenkins, K. Steinbrenner and D. H. Bent 1975. *Statistical Package for the Social Sciences* (2nd edition). New York: McGraw-Hill.

Nolan, F. J. 1978. The 'coarticulation resistance' model of articulatory control: solid evidence from English liquids? *Nottingham Linguistics Circular* 7, 28–51.

——— 1980. Dips in long term spectra. Unpublished paper.

——— 1982a. The nature of phonetic representations. *Cambridge Papers in Phonetics and Experimental Linguistics* 1, Cambridge University Linguistics Department.

——— 1982b. Review of *The Phonetic Description of Voice Quality* by J. Laver. *Journal of Linguistics* 18(2).

——— 1982c. The role of 'action theory' in models of speech production. *Linguistics* 20, 287–308.

O'Connor, J. D. 1973. *Phonetics*. Harmondsworth: Penguin.

O'Connor, J. D. and G. F. Arnold 1973. *Intonation of Colloquial English* (2nd edition). London: Longman.

O'Connor, J. D., L. J. Gerstman, A. M. Liberman, P. Delattre, and F. S. Cooper 1957. Acoustic cues for the perception of initial /w,j,r,l/ in English. *Word* 13, 24–43.

Papçun, G. and P. Ladefoged 1974. Two 'voiceprint' cases. *JASA* 55, 463.

Paul, J. E., A. S. Rabinowicz, J. P. Riganati and J. M. Richardson 1975. Development of analytical methods for a semi-automatic speaker identification system. *Proceedings of the 1975 Carnahan Conference on Crime Countermeasures* 52–64. Lexington: University of Kentucky.

Pellowe, J. and V. Jones 1978. On intonational variability in Tyneside speech. In: P. Trudgill (ed.), *Sociolinguistic Patterns in British English*.

Perkell, J. S. 1979. On the nature of distinctive features: implications of a preliminary vowel production study. In: B. Lindblom and S. Öhman (eds.), *Frontiers of Speech Communication Research*.

Peterson, G. E. and H. E. Barney 1952. Control methods used in a study of the vowels. *JASA* 24, 175–84.

Pollack, I., J. M. Pickett and W. H. Sumby 1954. On the identification of speakers by voice. *JASA* 26, 403–6.

Pruzansky, S. 1963. Pattern matching procedure for automatic talker recognition. *JASA* 35, 354–8.

Pruzansky, S. and M. V. Mathews 1964. Talker-recognition procedure based on analysis of variance. *JASA* 36, 2041–7.

Rabiner, L. R. and R. W. Schafer 1978. *Digital Processing of Speech Signals*. Englewood Cliffs, N.J.: Prentice-Hall.

Rabiner, L. R., M. J. Cheng, A. E. Rosenberg and C. McGonegal 1976. A comparative performance study of several pitch detection algorithms. *IEEE Trans. Ac., Sp. & Sig. Proc.* ASSP-24, 399–418.

Reich, A. 1981. Detecting the presence of disguise in the male voice. *JASA* 69, 1458–61.

Reich, A. and J. Duke 1979. Effects of selected vocal disguises upon speaker identification by listening. *JASA* 66, 1023–8.

Reich, A., K. Moll and J. Curtis 1976. Effects of selected vocal disguises upon spectrographic speaker identification. *JASA* 60, 919–25.

Riordan, C. J. 1977. Control of vocal tract length in speech. *JASA* 62, 998–1002.

Roach, P. 1982. On the distinction between 'stress-timed' and 'syllable-timed' languages. In: D. Crystal (ed.), *Linguistic Controversies*. London: Edward Arnold.

Rosenberg, A. E. 1973. Listener performance in speaker verification tasks. *IEEE Trans. Aud. & Electroac.* AU-21, 221–5.

1976. Automatic speaker verification: a review. *Proceedings of the IEEE* 64, No. 4, 475–86.

Sambur, M. R. 1973. Speaker recognition and verification using linear prediction analysis. *JASA* 53, 354(A).

1975. Selection of acoustic features for speaker identification. *IEEE Trans. Ac., Sp. & Sig. Proc.* ASSP-23, 176–82.

1976. Speaker recognition using orthogonal linear prediction. *IEEE Trans. Ac., Sp. & Sig. Proc.* ASSP-24, 283–9.

Sawashima, M., H. Hirose and H. Yoshioka 1978. Abductor (PCA) and adductor (INT) muscles in the larynx in voiceless sound production. *Annual Bulletin of the Research Institute of Logopedics and Phoniatrics* 12, 53–60. Tokyo.

Scherer, K. R. 1979. Personality markers in speech. In: K. R. Scherer and H. Giles (eds.), *Social Markers in Speech*.

Scherer, K. R. and H. Giles (eds.) 1979. *Social Markers in Speech*. Cambridge and Paris: Cambridge University Press and Editions de la Maison des Sciences de l'Homme.

Shearme, J. N. and J. N. Holmes 1959. An experiment concerning the recognition of voices. *Language and Speech* 2, 123–31.

Snow, T. B. and G. W. Hughes 1969. Fundamental frequency estimation by harmonic identification. *JASA* 45, 316(A).

Steffen-Batóg, M., W. Jassem and H. Gruszka-Koscielak 1970. Statistical distributions of short term F_0 values as a personal voice characteristic. In: W. Jassem (ed.), *Speech Analysis and Synthesis*, Vol. 2. Warsaw: Polish Academy of Sciences.

Stevens, K. N. and S. E. Blumstein 1981. The search for invariant acoustic correlates of phonetic features. In: P. D. Eimas and J. L. Miller (eds.), *Perspectives on the Study of Speech*. Hillsdale, N.J.: Erlbaum.

Stevens, K. N., C. E. Williams, J. R. Carbonell and B. Woods 1968. Speaker authentication and identification: a comparison of spectrographic and auditory presentation of speech material. *JASA* 44, 1596–1607.

Su, L-S., K-P. Li and K. S. Fu 1974. Identification of speakers by use of nasal coarticulation. *JASA* 56, 1876–82.

Sundberg, J. 1974. Articulatory interpretation of the 'singing formant'. *JASA* 55, 838–44.

Sundberg, J. and P-E. Nordström 1976. Raised and lowered larynx – the effect on vowel formant frequencies. *STL-QPSR* 2–3/1976, 35–9.

Tarnóczy, T. W. 1962. Über das individuelle Sprachspektrum. *Proceedings of the 4th International Congress of Phonetic Sciences*, 259–64. The Hague: Mouton.

Tate, D. A. 1979. Preliminary data on dialect in speech disguise. In: H. Hollien and P. Hollien (eds.), *Current Issues in the Phonetic Sciences*. Amsterdam: John Benjamins.

Tatham, M. A. A. 1969. Classifying allophones. *Occasional Papers* 3, 14–22. Language Centre, University of Essex.

Terepin, S. 1980. A vocal tract model for speech synthesis. PhD Dissertation, Department of Engineering, Cambridge University.

Thomas, K. R. 1975. Voiceprint–myth or miracle? In: J. G. Cederbaums and S. Arnold (eds.), *Scientific and Expert Evidence in Criminal Advocacy*. New York: Practising Law Institute.

Tosi, O. I. 1975. The problem of speaker identification and elimination. In: S. Singh (ed.), *Measurement Procedures in Speech, Hearing and Language*. Baltimore: University Park Press.

1979. *Voice Identification: Theory and Legal Applications*. Baltimore: University Park Press.

Tosi, O. I., H. Oyer, W. Lashbrook, C. Pedrey, L. Nicol and E. Nash 1972. Experiment on voice identification. *JASA* 51, 2030–43.

Trim, J. L. M. 1959. Major and minor tone units in English. *Le maître phonétique* 112, 26–9.

Trubetzkoy, N. S. 1969. *Principles of Phonology*. Translation: C. A. M. Baltaxe. Berkeley and Los Angeles: University of California.

217

References

Trudgill, P. 1974a. *The Social Differentiation of English in Norwich*. London: Cambridge University Press.

1974b. *Sociolinguistics*. Harmondsworth: Penguin.

(ed.) 1978. *Sociolinguistic Patterns in British English*. London: Edward Arnold.

Umeda, N. 1977. Consonant duration in American English. *JASA* 61, 846–58.

Vanderslice, R. 1969. The 'Voiceprint' myth. Educational Resources Information Center, Document ED 028 442. Washington D.C.

Verbrugge, R. R., W. Strange, D. P. Shankweiler and T. R. Edman 1976. What information enables a listener to map a talker's vowel space? *JASA* 60, 198–212.

Wakita, H. 1976. Instrumentation for the study of speech acoustics. In: N. J. Lass (ed.), *Contemporary Issues in Experimental Phonetics*.

Wakita, H. and G. Fant 1978. Toward a better vocal tract model. *STL-QPSR* 1/1978, 9–29.

Wang, W. S-Y. and C. J. Fillmore 1961. Intrinsic cues and consonant perception. *JSHR* 4, 130–6.

Wells, J. C. 1970. Local accents in England and Wales. *Journal of Linguistics* 6, 231–52.

1982. *Accents of English: an Introduction*, 3 vols. Cambridge: Cambridge University Press.

Wendahl, R. W. 1972. Acoustic correlates of vocal roughness: a resume and an extension. *Proceedings of the 7th International Congress of Phonetic Sciences*, 427–30. The Hague: Mouton.

Wolf, J. J. 1972. Efficient acoustic parameters for speaker recognition. *JASA* 51, 2044–56.

Young, M. A. and R. A. Campbell 1967. Effects of context on talker identification. *JASA* 42, 1250–4.

Zalewski, J., W. Majewski and H. Hollien 1975. Cross-correlation of long term speech spectra as a speaker-identification technique. *Acustica* 34, 20–4.

Index

accent, 68–9, 84, 106, 204
action theory, 58
allophones, 38, 42–4, 51, 79

between-speaker differences, 26–73, 197
  relation to within-speaker variability, 27,
    71–2, 199
  types of: incidental, 41–2, 49–50; long
    term, 45–6, 51; phonotactic, 41, 49;
    realisational, 44–5, 50–1; systemic,
    40–1, 49

cardinal vowels, 142, 187, 192
coarticulation, 42–4, 58, 77, 78–9, 80–1, 91,
    93–100, 108–20, 134–5, 159, 197–8
coarticulation resistance, 117–20, 134–5
communicative intent, 30–1, 35–7, 61–73
  effects on recognition, 61, 62, 63, 67–8,
    71, 72–3, 203–4
  mapping of, 35–7, 61–71, 72–3
  types of, 35–7; affective, 62; cognitive,
    61–2; interaction management, 71;
    self-presentational, 69–71; social, 63–8
compensatory articulation, 3, 55–6, 80, 139
context of speaking, 63–8, 73, 134, 202–3
convergence, 67, 134, 203

data used in speaker recognition
  distortion in recordings, 13–14, 23, 25,
    81–2, 122, 133, 199–200
  equipment used, 13, 23, 122, 132
  sample size required, 13, 107–8, 114,
    115, 123, 125, 130–1, 143
  time elapsed between recordings, 25,
    101, 105–8, 113–14, 115, 125, 130–1
dialect, 63, 204
disguise, 8–9, 10, 11, 12–13, 82, 125–6, 130,
    131–2, 135, 156, 196, 200–2
  detection of, 196, 200–2
divergence, 67

F ratio, 12, 101–2
formants
  in long term spectra, see long term
    spectra

measurement and definition of, 86–9,
    155–9
  relation to vocal tract shape, 162–3

health, 12, 60, 133, 195

imitation, see mimicry
implementation rules, 28, 33, 58–9, 106,
    118–20, 198
indicators (sociolinguistic), 65–6
integration rules, 33, 51–2

lexicon, 39, 46, 49–50
linear prediction, 14, 103, 156, 159
long term quality, 4, 33–5, 45–6, 51, 56,
    121-96
  acoustic correlates of, 121, 142–96
  configurational and dynamic constraints
    on, 60–1
  default and determined values in, 56, 62,
    134
  extrinsic and intrinsic features of, 33–4,
    122, 133, 195
  framework for description of, 46, 122,
    128, 135–42, 187, 191–2, 198
  interaction with short term targets, 34,
    130, 134, 169–81, 194
  null and non-null values in, 56–8, 133
  supralaryngeal v. laryngeal, 136
  suprasegmental v. segmental, 34
  susceptibility of segments to, 134
  synthesis of, 155–6, 169, 193–4, 208–9
long term spectra, 12, 13, 121, 192–3,
    130–5, 143–55
  dips in, 155
  formants in, 147

markers (sociolinguistic), 65–6, 67–8
meaning, see communicative intent
mimicry, 8–9, 10, 11, 12, 82, 125–6, 201–2

normalisation
  acoustic, 5, 170, 171–3, 187–92, 193, 198
  perceptual, 3, 5, 16, 53–4, 187, 198
  of time-base by computer, see
    time-warping

219

parameters for speaker recognition
  coarticulatory, *see* coarticulation
  criteria for evaluation of, 11–14
  segmental: short term, 74–120; long
    term, 130–96
  suprasegmental: short term, 74–5; long
    term, 122–30
personal voice quality, 1, 26–73, 197
personality in speech, 69–71
phonation type, 33–4, 62, 127, 140–1, 147,
  151–5
phonemes, 13, 30, 31, 37–8, 40–2, 43, 74,
  77, 81, 105
phonetic representation, 33, 39–40, 52–8,
  118–20, 198
  default and determined values in, 56, 62,
    66, 72–3
  null and non-null values in, 56–8
phonetics, relation to speaker recognition,
  2–3, 115–16, 197, 204–6
physical constraints in vocal apparatus,
  27–8, 59–61, 70, 72, 121, 133
plasticity of vocal apparatus, 4, 27, 59, 72,
  121, 195, 198, 199–200
pole, 156–9

rate of speech, 14, 124, 129
realisation rules, 38, 42–5, 48–9, 50–1
recordings, *see* data used in speaker
  recognition
rhythm, 42, 127–9

sample size, *see* data used in speaker
  recognition
secondary articulations, 134, 138
segmental strand, 31–3, 37–46, 74–120,
  130–96
segmentation of speech, 14, 37–8, 58, 74,
  103–4, 195, 197
settings, 34, 136–42, 194, 198
  acoustic correlates of, *see* long term
    quality
  incompatability of, 139, 140
  interaction between, 138–9, 151, 173,
    182–7, 194
  laryngeal (phonation type), 140–1
  of overall tension, 141–2
  supralaryngeal, 136–40
sociolinguistic variation, 63–9
  significance for speaker recognition, 65,
    67–8, 196
speaker classification, *see* voice
  classification
speaker identification, *see under* speaker
  recognition

speaker recognition
  across languages, 130–1
  auditory, by non-phoneticians, 1, 6–7,
    200, 207
  auditory, by phoneticians, 7, 15–18,
    205–6
  definition of, 5–6
  forensic application of, 1, 6–10, 13–25,
    198–209
  motivation for research in, 14–15
  naive, 7
  parameters for, *see* parameters for
    speaker recognition
  relation to the linguistic sciences, *see*
    phonetics
  speaker classification in, *see* voice
    classification
  speaker identification v. verification in:
    different problems for, 8–10, 13, 14;
    distinction between, 8–10; relation to
    applications, 8–9
  types of task in, 6–10
  types of test in, 9
  by 'voiceprint', *see* spectrograms
speaker verification, *see under* speaker
  recognition
spectrograms
  comparison with fingerprints, 18,
    22
  forensic examiners of, 22, 24–5, 196,
    199–200, 204–6
  forensic use and reliability of, 6–7, 15,
    18–25, 204–9
  use in research, 82, 85–8, 157, 159
  visual examination of, v. listening, 23–4,
    200
speech recognition, 5, 74, 75, 198
stereotypes (sociolinguistic), 66, 202
stress (emotional), 12, 60, 131–2,
  133
stress (linguistic), 42, 48, 128
stress-timing, 128
style of speech, *see* context of speaking
suprasegmental strand, 31–3, 46–51, 74–5,
  122–30
syllable-timing, 128
synthesis of long term quality, *see* long
  term quality

time-warping, 14

voice, an individual's, *see* personal voice
  quality
voice classification, 63, 156, 187, 195, 196,
  207–9

voice quality, *see* long term quality;
  personal voice quality
  v. phonation type, 33–4
voiceprints, *see* spectrograms

within-speaker variability, 27, 28–73, 156,
  197
  relation to between-speaker differences,
  27, 71–2, 199